Methods for Analyzing Social Media

Social media is becoming increasingly attractive for users. It is a fast way to communicate ideas and a key source of information. It is therefore one of the most influential mediums of communication of our time and an important area for audience research. The growth of social media invites many new questions such as: How can we analyze social media? Can we use traditional audience research methods and apply them to online content? Which new research strategies have been developed? Which ethical research issues and controversies do we have to pay attention to? This book focuses on research strategies and methods for analyzing social media and will be of interest to researchers and practitioners using social media, as well as those wanting to keep up to date with the subject.

This book was originally published as a special issue of the *Journal of Technology in Human Services.*

Klaus Bredl, Dr. phil., is Professor at the Department of Media and Educational Technology at the University of Augsburg, Germany. His research interests include activity streams, immersion and methodological approaches to studies of new technologies in communication and education. He has worked and published in the fields of technology enhanced learning, social media, knowledge communication and competence development. He is Vice-Task-Force-Leader on the topic within the European COST Action "Transforming Audiences, Transforming Societies."

Julia Hünniger, MA, is Research Assistant at the Department of Media and Educational Technology at the University of Augsburg, Germany. From 2009 to 2010 she was a consultant for e-learning at the Georg Simon Ohm University of Applied Sciences, Nuremberg, Germany. Her research interests include computer-mediated communication and the psychology of the internet and how it affects mental health. She is YECREA representative for the Audience and Reception Studies Section.

Jakob Linaa Jensen, PhD, is Associate Professor at the Department of Aesthetics and Communication, Media Studies and the Center for Internet Studies at the University of Aarhus, Denmark. His research interests include democratic participation online, social media use and online methodologies. He is leading a European taskforce on methodological approaches to studies of social media.

Methods for Analyzing Social Media

Edited by
Klaus Bredl, Julia Hünniger and
Jakob Linaa Jensen

Routledge
Taylor & Francis Group
LONDON AND NEW YORK

cost
EUROPEAN COOPERATION
IN SCIENCE AND TECHNOLOGY

First published 2014
by Routledge
2 Park Square, Milton Park, Abingdon, Oxon, OX14 4RN

Simultaneously published in the USA and Canada
by Routledge
711 Third Avenue, New York, NY 10017

Routledge is an imprint of the Taylor & Francis Group, an informa business

British Library Cataloguing in Publication Data
A catalogue record for this book is available from the British Library

ISBN13: 978-0-415-81832-2

Typeset in Garamond
by Taylor & Francis Books

Publisher's Note
The publisher accepts responsibility for any inconsistencies that may have arisen during the conversion of this book from journal articles to book chapters, namely the possible inclusion of journal terminology.

Disclaimer
Every effort has been made to contact copyright holders for their permission to reprint material in this book. The publishers would be grateful to hear from any copyright holder who is not here acknowledged and will undertake to rectify any errors or omissions in future editions of this book.

Contents

Citation Information

The chapters in this book were originally published in the *Journal of Technology in Human Services*, volume 30, issue 3–4 (2012). When citing this material, please use the original page numbering for each article, as follows:

Chapter 1
Methods for Analyzing Social Media: Introduction to the Special Issue
Klaus Bredl, Julia Hünniger, and Jakob Linaa Jensen
Journal of Technology in Human Services, volume 30, issue 3–4 (2012) pp. 141–144

Chapter 2
The Open Laboratory: Limits and Possibilities of Using Facebook, Twitter, and YouTube as a Research Data Source
Fabio Giglietto, Luca Rossi, and Davide Bennato
Journal of Technology in Human Services, volume 30, issue 3–4 (2012) pp. 145–159

Chapter 3
Quantitative Approaches to Comparing Communication Patterns on Twitter
Axel Bruns and Stefan Stieglitz
Journal of Technology in Human Services, volume 30, issue 3–4 (2012) pp. 160–185

Chapter 4
Communities of Communication: Making Sense of the "Social" in Social Media
Pascal Jürgens
Journal of Technology in Human Services, volume 30, issue 3–4 (2012) pp. 186–203

Chapter 5
Talking of Many Things: Using Topical Networks to Study Discussions in Social Media
Tim Highfield
Journal of Technology in Human Services, volume 30, issue 3–4 (2012) pp. 204–218

Chapter 6
Researching Communicative Practice: Web Archiving in Qualitative Social Media Research
Stine Lomborg
Journal of Technology in Human Services, volume 30, issue 3–4 (2012) pp. 219–231

Chapter 7
Social Navigation on the Internet: A Framework for the Analysis of Communication Processes
Marco Lünich, Patrick Rössler, and Lena Hautzer
Journal of Technology in Human Services, volume 30, issue 3–4 (2012) pp. 232–249

Chapter 8
Employing Creative Research Methods with Tweens in Estonia and Sweden: Reflections on a Case Study of Identity Construction on Social Networking Sites
Andra Siibak, Michael Forsman, and Patrik Hernwall
Journal of Technology in Human Services, volume 30, issue 3–4 (2012) pp. 250–261

Chapter 9
Social Media Use in the Bronx: New Research and Innovations in the Study of YouTube's Digital Neighborhood
Matthew Crick
Journal of Technology in Human Services, volume 30, issue 3–4 (2012) pp. 262–298

Chapter 10
Digital Media Stories Through Multimodal Analysis: A Case Study of Erahoneybee's Song About a Child Welfare Agency
Tara La Rose
Journal of Technology in Human Services, volume 30, issue 3–4 (2012) pp. 299–311

Chapter 11
Mark My Words: The Design of an Innovative Methodology to Detect and Analyze Interpersonal Health Conversations in Web and Social Media
Martine P. A. Bouman, Constance H. C. Drossaert, and Marcel E. Pieterse
Journal of Technology in Human Services, volume 30, issue 3–4 (2012) pp. 312–326

Notes on Contributors

Davide Bennato is Assistant Professor of Sociology of Digital Media at the University of Catania, Italy, and his research interests are focused on technological cultures, digital media consumption and digital media socialization. He is author of *Sociologia dei Media Digitali* (Sociology of Digital Media [2011]) and co-author of *Dizionario di informatica, dell'ICT e dei media digitali* (2012). He writes about the social impact of the internet in his blog Tecnoetica (www.tecnoetica.it/).

Martine P. A. Bouman is Scientific Director of the Center for Media & Health and Associate Professor at the University of Twente, The Netherlands. Her research interests are communication for social change and popular media. She is the first woman and European to win the Everett M. Rogers Award for Achievement in Entertainment-Education (2010). She is principal investigator and initiator of the Mark My Words research project.

Klaus Bredl, Dr. phil., is Professor at the Department of Media and Educational Technology at the University of Augsburg, Germany. His research interests include activity streams, immersion and methodological approaches to studies of new technologies in communication and education. He has worked and published in the fields of technology enhanced learning, social media, knowledge communication and competence development. He is Vice-Task-Force-Leader on the topic within the European COST Action "Transforming Audiences, Transforming Societies."

Axel Bruns is Associate Professor in the Creative Industries Faculty at Queensland University of Technology in Brisbane, Australia, and a Chief Investigator in the ARC Centre of Excellence for Creative Industries and Innovation (http://cci.edu.au/). He is the author of *Blogs, Wikipedia, Second Life and Beyond: From Production to Produsage* (2008) and *Gatewatching: Collaborative Online News Production* (2005), and a co-editor of *A Companion to New Media Dynamics* (2012, with John Hartley and Jean Burgess) and *Uses of Blogs* (2006, with Joanne Jacobs). Bruns is an expert on the impact of user-led content creation, or produsage, and his current work focuses especially on the study of user participation in social media spaces such as *Twitter*, especially in the context of acute events. His research blog is at http://snurb.info/, and he tweets at @snurb_dot_info. See http://mappingonlinepublics.net/ for more details on his current social media research.

Matthew Crick, PhD, is Assistant Professor of Media Production at William Paterson University in Wayne, New Jersey, USA. His current research interests focus on social media, storytelling and power and surveillance in online environments. He has directed and produced a feature-length documentary, and directed, edited, produced and shot a documentary short, and he is currently editing a second feature-length documentary that he co-wrote, directed and produced.

Constance H. C. Drossaert is Associate Professor in the Department of Psychology, Health & Technology at the University of Twente, The Netherlands. Her research interests involve the role of new technologies to improve health and "patient empowerment." Drossaert has contributed to the conception and design of the Mark My Words research project and has provided critical comments during the revision comments of the article.

Michael Forsman is Senior Lecturer in Media and Communication at Södertörn University, Sweden. His previous research has been on youth and media, television studies, public service and media history. He has published four monographs, five anthologies and many articles. Currently he is involved in research about identities online, media literacy, liberal arts and e-waste.

Fabio Giglietto, PhD, is Assistant Professor in the Department of Communication and Human Studies at the University of Urbino "Carlo Bo", Italy. His main research interests are theory of information, communication and social systems with a specific focus on the relationship between social systems and new technologies. He is currently working on developing metrics to understand the relationship between social media practices and "real world" phenomena. Since 2010 he has been a board member of RC51 on Sociocybernetics, a research committee of the International Sociological Association and member of editorial board of the *Journal of Sociocybernetics*. A full and up-to-date list of publications and CV is available at www.mendeley.com/profiles/fabio-giglietto.

Lena Hautzer completed her BA in Communication Studies and Economics at the University of Erfurt, Germany in 2011. She is currently studying Media Management as an MA at the HMTM in Hannover, Germany. Her research interests include online media, media effects and empirical research methods.

Patrik Hernwall is Associate Professor in Educology and in Media Technology. His main research interest is the condition of children in a media-saturated society, with special attention to issues such as gender and power structures, digital literacy and social networking. He is the head of the research project "Construction and normalisation of gender online among young people in Estonia and Sweden" (the.GTO. project).

Tim Highfield is Research Fellow with the ARC Centre of Excellence in Creative Industries and Innovation (CCI), Queensland University of Technology, Australia, and a sessional academic with Curtin University, Australia. He was awarded his PhD from Queensland University of Technology in 2011. His doctoral research investigated political blogging in Australia and France. Currently his research focuses on social media use around politics, sport and popular culture.

Julia Hünniger, MA, is Research Assistant at the Department of Media and Educational Technology at the University of Augsburg, Germany. From 2009 to 2010 she was a consultant for e-learning at the Georg Simon Ohm University of Applied

Sciences, Nuremberg, Germany. Her research interests include computer-mediated communication and the psychology of the internet and how it affects mental health. She is YECREA representative for the Audience and Reception Studies Section.

Pascal Jürgens, MA, is a doctoral candidate at the Department of Communication at the University of Mainz, Germany. He has published research on (among others) digital research methods, election campaigns on Twitter and online participation. Current research interests include the mutual influence of ITCs and cognitive strategies, processes of information diffusion and determinants of issue emergence in networked communication.

Jakob Linaa Jensen, PhD, is Associate Professor at the Department of Aesthetics and Communication, Media Studies and the Center for Internet Studies at the University of Aarhus, Denmark. He has a background in political science and his main research interests include democratic participation online, social media use and online methodologies. He is leading a European taskforce on methodological approaches to studies of social media.

Stine Lomborg, PhD in Media Studies, is Assistant Professor in the Department of Media, Cognition and Communication at the University of Copenhagen, Denmark. Her research on social media has been published in a number of international journals, including *New Media & Society, First Monday* and *Philosophy & Technology*. She is the author of *Social Media – Social Genres. Making Sense of the Ordinary* (Routledge, forthcoming).

Marco Lünich has a BA in Communication Studies with a minor in Law from the University of Erfurt, Germany. He is now studying in the Research Master Programme at the Graduate School of Communication in Amsterdam, The Netherlands. His research interests include media effects, political communication and empirical research methods.

Marcel E. Pieterse is Associate Professor in the Department of Psychology, Health & Technology at the University of Twente, The Netherlands. His research interests are addiction treatment and prevention, effectiveness and implementation of health promotion interventions, and cost-effectiveness methodology. Pieterse has contributed to the conception and design of the study and provided critical comments during the revision of the article.

Tara La Rose, MSW, RSW, is a PhD candidate in the Adult Education and Community Development Program in the collaborative programs in Work Place Learning and Social Change and Women and Gender Studies at the Ontario Institute for Studies in Education, University of Toronto, Canada. She also serves as a Sessional Lecturer with the School of Social Work, York University, Toronto, Canada. Her research focuses on social workers' use of digital media storytelling as a tool for critiquing the field and is informed by close to 20 years of experience working in the social service sector in areas ranging from community development and union activism, to child welfare and anti-violence services, to mental health crisis services and work–life research.

Luca Rossi is Fellowship Researcher in the Department of Communication Studies at the University of Urbino "Carlo Bo", Italy. His research interests are focused on

Internet studies particularly in the fields of Internet culture, games studies and social networks studies. He is currently working on Social Network Analysis methods applied to online propagation of information and cultural phenomena. Among his most recent publications: "Toward a Bridge between Sociocybernetics and Internet Studies," *Journal of Sociocybernetics* (2009), "Media & Generation: How User Generated Content Reshape Generational Identity in the Mass Media System," *Sociologia della Comunicazione* (2010) and Information Propagation in Social Network Sites in *Advances in Social Networks Analysis and Mining, 2010 International Conference on IEEE.*

Patrick Rössler, Dr. rer. soc., is Chair for Communication Studies (Empirical Research/Methods) at the Faculty of Philosophy and currently Vice President for Research at the University of Erfurt, Germany. He graduated in Communication Studies, Political Science and Law from the University of Mainz, Germany, worked as Research Assistant at the University of Stuttgart-Hohenheim, Germany, and started as an Assistant Professor at the University of Munich, Germany. His research interests focus on media effects, political communication, new media technologies and the history of visual communication.

Andra Siibak is Senior Research Fellow of Media Studies in the Institute of Journalism and Communication at the University of Tartu, Estonia. Her research interests include generations and intergenerational relations on new media, and young people's social media use.

Stefan Stieglitz is Assistant Professor of Communication and Collaboration Management in the Department of Information Systems at the University of Münster, Germany. He studied business economics and received his doctorate degree from the University of Potsdam, Germany. He is founder and academic director of the Competence Center Smarter Work at the European Research Center for Information Systems (ERCIS). Of particular interest in his work is the investigation of the usage of social media in enterprises and political contexts. His research focuses on economic, social and technological aspects of collaboration software. He published several articles in reputable international journals such as *Journal of Management Information Systems*, *MIS Quarterly Executive* and *International Journal of Social Research Methodology.*

Methods for Analyzing Social Media: Introduction

KLAUS BREDL and JULIA HÜNNIGER
Institute for Media and Educational Technologies at Augsburg University, Augsburg, Germany

JAKOB LINAA JENSEN
Center for Internet Research, University of Aarhus, Aarhus, Denmark

INTRODUCTION

Social media are becoming increasingly attractive for users. It is a fast way to communicate ideas and can be a key source of information about how people interact. Today it is among the most influencial communication channels. For this reason, social media are important for audience research as well as for technologies that can be used in human services. Social media can be generally understood as web-based services "that build on the ideological and technological foundations of Web 2.0, and that allow the creation and exchange of User Generated Content" (Kaplan and Haenlein, 2010, p. 61).

Researchers are confronted with the following questions:

How can we analyze social media? Which methods and strategies can we use? Can we just use traditional audience research methods and apply them to online content? Which new research strategies have been developed? What about research ethics – which issues and controversies do we have to pay attention to? How can we develop technical tools for analyzing social media? Which existing tools can we use?

This special issue focuses on research strategies and methods for analyzing social media. It contains research articles that report on the latest social science results and advances in this area.

The articles of this special issue include innovative research methods within the field of social media analysis. Topics are:

- innovative research methods that shed light upon patterns of social media use
- qualitative observation techniques to examine the use of social media

- triangulation of qualitative and quantitative methods
- case studies and evaluations of social media platforms such as (micro-) blogs, social networks, and video platforms

The issue starts with the article of Fabio Giglietto, Luca Rossi and Davide Bennato who give an overview of different approaches for studying social media. Given the growing number of diverse studies from different disciplines with a differing focus, the need exists for identifying the various methodologies used. The focus of the article is a categorization between ethnographical, statistical and computational perspectives. The analysis is clarified by the use of studies about Facebook, YouTube and Twitter.

Twitter is also the focus of the second article, authored by Axel Bruns and Stefan Stieglitz. They present a comparative study to demonstrate quantitative approaches that compare communication patterns in microblogging platforms. As a result, distinct types of discussion were identified. A range of metrics regarding the communications in Twitter is presented, and the influencing factors of subjects and context in relation to different communication channels are demonstrated. Also in the area of major topics and events, they found stable patterns of usage from the analysis.

In the following article, Pascal Jürgens concentrates on the "social" in social media and analyzes the aspect of communities. Using the example of Twitter, he shows the integration occuring in the range of digital methods used. The analytic framework starts with the digital traces each user leaves on the net. This formerly hidden aspect of social interaction is now accessible for researchers. Especially, it is possible to observe the interaction patterns in networks. These new approaches evoke special challenges, which can be overcome by the application of innovative methodologies. The detection of communities stays at the center of the discussed methods. The discovery of "proximity in groups" is the basis for further network analysis.

The article by Tim Highfield describes topical network analysis as a method for studying online activity. Topical networks are units of analysis within large datasets. By using qualitative and quantitative methods, the approach can supplement the analysis of large datasets to provide further detail into what is being tracked. It enables researchers to determine why and when connections were made. The article shows an important method for improving our understanding of the structure of online communication.

Stine Lomborg's article also touches upon the analyses of large bodies of data. She discusses the method of web archiving in qualitative social media research. She highlights that social media archives (i.e. complete recordings of posts and comments on given social media) are highly useful data corpuses for studying the social media users' communicative practices. She presents a theoretical examination of web archiving and engages in an example-based discussion of the methodological, technical and ethical challenges of harvesting social media archives.

The article by Lünich, Rössler and Hautzer focuses on the study of media use patterns, more precisely the impact of relationship-related information. By studying what they call social navigation on the Internet, i.e., media use patterns that are driven by the previous media activities of others, the authors shed light on the dynamics of relationships within online media content. By using mainly online news media, they discuss how to investigate rating, forwarding, and even the production of media items.

Siibak, Forsman and Hernwall take a more qualitative, anthropologically inspired approach and discuss creative research methods as a tool for investigating young people's identity construction on social network sites. Methodologically, they address physical focus groups combined with online interaction as a way to observe the construction and use of gender codes and norms. They argue that such creative research methods are useful for engaging young people in participatory, creative activities, thereby facilitating reflections and interactions not attainable through alternative methods.

Matthew Crick's article presents his point of departure in YouTube which he claims is the least scholarly researched form of social media, particularly when it comes to so-called under-represented and under-researched populations. He builds up a formalized approach based on systematic measurement to study how YouTube is used for information seeking and learning among young people, a topic often neglected in similar studies. Thus, he claims, such an approach should provide valuable information about use, which is normally neglected in the dominant research on social media.

Tara La Rose presents a case study of a digital media story on YouTube that gives a glimpse into a student intern's experience of human service work. By using multi-modal analysis, La Rose provides a complex understanding of the potential role that social media processes may play in human services. The article shows the complexity of personal stories and the need for additional research into the possibilities of digital media stories.

The last article also deals with new technologies in human services and the health sector and seeks methods to analyze these new formats. Bouman, Drossaert and Pieterse propose a new methodology to measure the potential impact of new digital health communication formats. It is called "Mark My Words (MMW)" and is based on the concept of "markers" and on data analysis via text mining techniques. MMW is being used to evaluate the impact of a web-based Entertainment-Education series on teens and young adults in the Netherlands. MMW is applied in an innovative web-based Entertainment-Education series. The article outlines the research design and shows the methodological advantages and challenges.

The content of this issue addresses scientists who are dealing with the use and effect of Social Media in communication processes. The focus is on different methods of analyzing social interaction in online communication. These innovative research methods target the interest of media and communication researchers, sociologists, social science researcher and media psychologists as well as all practitioners working with methods in applied research on social media.

REFERENCE

Kaplan, A. M., & Haenlein, M. (2010). Users of the world, unite! The challenges and opportunities of social media. *Business Horizons, 53*(1).

The Open Laboratory: Limits and Possibilities of Using Facebook, Twitter, and YouTube as a Research Data Source

FABIO GIGLIETTO and LUCA ROSSI
University of Urbino Carlo Bo, Urbino, Italy
DAVIDE BENNATO
University of Catania, Catania, Italy

A growing amount of content is published worldwide every day by millions of social media users. Most of this content is public, permanent, and searchable. At the same time, the number of studies proposing different techniques and methodologies to exploit this content as data for researchers in different disciplines is also growing. This article presents an up-to-date literature review that frames available studies using Facebook, Twitter, and YouTube as data sources, in the perspective of traditional approaches for social scientists: ethnographical, statistical, and computational. The aim is to offer an overview of strengths and weaknesses of different approaches in the context of the possibilities offered by the different platforms.

INTRODUCTION

With the expression "social media," we describe a varied category of Internet services inspired by Web 2.0 (O'Reilly, 2007) principles and enabling the users of the site to create and share digital contents (Kaplan & Haenlein,

2010). Social network sites based on visible, interconnected, and navigable profiles (boyd & Ellison, 2008) belong to this category, as well as the sites focused on content sharing. Despite the large variety of possibilities—from the short 140 characters of Twitter to the video sharing of YouTube—it is clear that the focus of a social media is on both the users' activities and the users' relationships and social networks.

The social media success that we have been observing for a decade has undoubtedly boosted the online diffusion of already existing creative practices (Burgess, 2006) and has formed the background for a growing interest of academic research on these platforms and on the phenomena that they are able to host.

This new digital scenario challenges, in a very radical way, the standard research practices within the social sciences, bringing an unprecedented rate of innovation (the Internet changes at an extraordinarily fast pace) and an exceptional data availability (Karpf, 2012). To meet these challenges, there is a new wave of studies coming from very different backgrounds—from computer sciences to behavioral sciences.

While social media are undoubtedly a broad research field, it can be surely claimed that the contemporary scenario is composed of a small group of very big actors—in terms of users and daily usage—and a large number of minor services that are often addressed to specific communities. This article presents a structured, up-to-date literature review of the studies focusing on three of the largest and most famous social media sites: Facebook, YouTube, and Twitter.

The reasons we deliberately focused on these three platforms is mainly related to their huge popularity among both users and researchers. YouTube, Facebook, and Twitter have, as a matter of fact, been studied from many different perspectives by many different researchers coming from various disciplines. The result of this success as new field of research is a wide spectrum of literature—albeit often confusing—coming from different scientific backgrounds that often ignore their reciprocal existence. The aim of this article is therefore to attempt a first categorization of a large part of the existing literature according to a methodological perspective rooted in the sociological tradition.

METHODOLOGICAL FRAMEWORK

Using social media as a data source is a relatively new phenomenon. The deeply interdisciplinary nature of these studies makes it difficult to retrieve a complete and up-to-date literature of papers employing this approach. At the same time, we felt the need to frame collected papers within a more solid and well-known analytical framework. In fact, even if social media data comprise a new phenomenon, social data—with their own large heterogeneity—have been used by sociologists for a long time. Therefore, we rooted the classification of the collected papers within the traditional distinction of sociological methodological approaches that have been summarized by Ricolfi (1997) in three major groups or research methods: ethnographical approaches, statistical approaches, and computational approaches. These categories follow the traditional distinction between quantitative/statistical methods and qualitative/ethnographic methods with the addition of the new computational methods that offer specific characteristics in terms of quantity and the nature of the data. The computational approach is different from the statistical one because data are not organized in a matrix of variables and cases. Data are instead organized in a structure that recalls more a relational database than a spreadsheet. This is the reason why computational approaches do not necessarily need the use of statistics, even if univariate or bivariate data representations are useful to visualize some results.

It is interesting to point out that even if this triple distinction dates back to the sociological tradition, it has recently been used—in a simpler form—to summarize the sociological research at large according to a scale defined by the depth of the analysis (high for ethnography and low for statistical approaches) and by the replicability of the scientific observations through time (high for statistical approaches and low for ethnography; Aharony, 2011). Therefore, due to the flexibility of this schema, we opted to use it as a common framework to describe the most relevant studies for every platform.

PLATFORMS, USERS' EXPERIENCE, AND DATA ACCESS POLICIES

Since the three platforms under examination expose data in a very different way, thus offering different user experiences and possibilities to researchers, it is necessary, before digging into the literature review, to provide an introduction on the characteristics that differentiate YouTube, Twitter, and Facebook under this perspective. This is of utmost importance because platforms matter both on the side of the social practices that are able to host and on the side of the research opportunities that offer to the researchers. Speaking of social media research *sui generis* with no connection to real-world platform makes, nowadays, very little sense.

YouTube is the most important video-sharing platform with 800 million users monthly, 4 billion videos viewed daily, and 60 hours of video uploaded every minute (YouTube, 2012). These numbers make YouTube the third website in the world based on traffic (Alexa, 2012). The user experience consists mainly in viewing videos. The videos can be found using the internal platform search engine, subscribing to a specific channel, or following links shared in other social networks (Facebook, Twitter). Users' interaction can range from video production to passive video viewing to video commenting or sharing (Burgess & Green, 2009). Therefore, the final user experience is different if the user is a content producer or a passive viewer (Cormode, Krishnamurthy, & Willinger, 2010). However, on a general level, it is possible to distinguish three different forms of interaction: audience interactions, social interactions, and platform interactions. Audience interactions can be measured by using metrics such as exposures—how many times a video or a channel is viewed. Different metrics are used to measure social interactions: number and type of comments posted by registered users, *likes* received by the video, or channel subscriptions. Platform interactions are measured by different kinds of information that are possible to enter when a video is uploaded (metadata): title, date, ID, tags, uploading account, description, category, copyright license, and so on. These pieces of information are used in different ways. One way they are used is in selecting which videos to analyze (e.g., the number of visualizations for choosing the most viewed videos). Another way is as contextual information for building social behavior patterns (e.g., strategies used in tagging). For these reasons, starting from the same data, every study that is using YouTube as its main data source can plan a brand new research strategy combining different metrics.

While YouTube was pushing the web into the online video era, Twitter introduced a text-only service that faced, since its early days, a worldwide success: microblogging. Born in 2006, Twitter reached the number of 340 million Tweets per day in 2012 (Twitter, 2012) and is now ranked as the eighth most visited website worldwide (Alexa, 2012). This result, in terms of number of users, rapidly produced a large volume of scientific research. This indisputable success of the Twitter platform among the research community, as well as its diffusion among third-party developers, can largely be explained by its data availability and structure. These data have always been freely available, public by default, mainly textual, and easily understandable. Additionally, free and public Application Programming Interface (API)-based access to the data has been available to developers and to skilled researchers since the launch of the platform, and, more recently, commercial services started selling specific portion or subset of Twitter data. Information available through Twitter API is of a very simple nature: It can be about the tweets or it can be about the users. Information about the tweets are the textual content of the tweet itself, time and location of its production, and the relational nature of the messages (whether there are replies to other messages or retweets of a previously produced message). Besides message-related information, user specific information is available: user name, user self-declared[1] location, the list of the users followed by the user, and the list of the users following the user. Despite its apparent simplicity, these sets of information can be combined in order to provide useful data on many aspects of Twitter usage—from posting topics and strategies to the establishment and the evolution of Twitter communities.

This data availability produced a large amount of research that can be sorted using the methodological schema we are adopting in this paper: ethnographic, statistical and computational. It is interesting to point out that these research approaches were not concurrent but followed a clear pattern representing the various scientific backgrounds currently involved in Twitter research. This led to an order of research approaches that is most likely different from those we are describing for the other platforms. While in many research fields related to online social activities, ethnographic approaches have predated statistical and, especially, computational approaches; in the "Twitter field," computational approaches appeared first, as can be observed by the venues or by the authors of the very first academic research on the topic (Huberman, Romero, & Wu, 2008; Java, Song, Finin, & Tseng, 2007).

With more than 900 million monthly active users worldwide and more than 500 million daily active users at the end of March 2012 (Facebook, 2012), Facebook is the most popular social medium in the world. One of the reasons for this worldwide success is the sense of protection, mainly developed during the early stages when the platform was open to selected colleges only (Joinson, 2008), experienced by users sharing their content with their bound community of "Friends" (boyd & Ellison, 2008). For this reason, Facebook managers devoted a growing amount of attention to developing a set of privacy settings and, more recently, to making these settings more usable (boyd & Hargittai, 2010). Despite that, recent research on Facebook privacy settings discovered that there is still a large gap between users' expected level of privacy and actual levels of access to their contents (Liu et al., 2011). Discussing the social implications or effectiveness of the Facebook strategy is beyond the scope of this article. However, the complexity of Facebook privacy settings deeply affects the extent and the type of data actually accessible to researchers. While most of the information is private by default in personal profiles, on pages—special profiles intended for organizations, public figures, and brands—information is publicly available. More recently, this simple distinction was blurred by new platform developments that allow the user to choose, on a post-to-post basis, the intended audience (some or all Friends or Public).

ETHNOGRAPHICAL APPROACHES

On a wide perspective, the ethnographical approach focuses on social meanings inferred by the researcher from the content intended as a unit of analysis. As an instance, YouTube videos usually define particular communities (e.g., the v-loggers in Griffith & Papacharissi, 2010) producing specific contents for the members of a community.

Studies following the ethnographical approach share common recognizable features. The group of units analyzed is usually small, with employment of different qualitative techniques, and usually a research design based on multiple methods or triangulation techniques.

There are different researchers—though not a great number of them—using ethnographic approaches, showing the potential of media ethnography when applied to YouTube (Lange, 2007; Rotman, Golbeck, & Preece, 2009). One of them is focused on a single video from the account Geriatric1927 whose title is "Teenagers and Drugs" (Harley & Fitzpatrick, 2009). By using a specific interpretive framework (multimodal interactional analysis: Norris, 2004) and different research techniques (conversation analysis audio transcription, transcription of nonlinguistic aspects of dialogues), applied also to the video responses it generates, the authors suggest that YouTube is mainly a social broadcast medium.

More recently than the attempts to describe the topological aspects of Twitter network, many researchers started to focus on the communicative practices of the platform, aiming at describing what kinds of social interactions were made possible by the exchange of simple 140-character-long text messages. These studies have been based both on quantitative-computational approaches (Huberman, Romero, & Wu, 2008) and on qualitative and often ethnographic approaches (Marwick & boyd, 2010). They have also provided precious insights, not only about the distribution of contacts and tweets but also on the tweeting and retweeting strategies of users, as well as their perception of their "invisible" audiences (boyd, 2008). Twitter research, even when it was mainly designed as an ethnographic investigation, has often been based on a computer-assisted data collection supported also through many freely available online tools that allowed one to retrieve and download Twitter messages.

The attempts of employing ethnographical approaches to data retrieved from Facebook tend to focus on small samples of "Friends" or public contents. The already-mentioned distinction between profiles and pages is important to understanding why this approach is not common among researchers. On the one hand, studies based on "Friends" profiles (boyd, 2008) tend to be biased and to produce results difficult to generalize. On the other hand, dealing with public contents (pages and groups) quickly increases the amount of data to analyze therefore discourages approaches based on in-depth observations. Nevertheless, the range of possibilities opened up by the analysis of content shared by users and organizations is as varied as the kinds of studies enabled. For instance, it is possible to analyze posted links pointing to online news articles in order to understand how a grass-roots agenda of topics can develop among a community of friends (Baresch, Knight, Harp & Yaschur, 2011).

STATISTICAL APPROACHES

Within the statistical approach, the reference model is the variable by cases data matrix, in which a single content (or a user) is the unit of analysis, and it is part of a sample extracted from the population of contents (or users).

Speaking about YouTube, the video is considered a trace of a social behavior, a way for accessing meanings of a community. For this reason, the video is not important per se, but in relation to the information it provides on the community it belongs to. Features of these studies are the use of sampling techniques and the use of content analysis (coded by humans or sometimes automatically by the computer). There are numbers of researchers using this approach, for example, the study by Bal, Campbell, Payne, and Pitt (2010) on mapping conversations around political spoof videos. In this study, researchers used a text analysis software (Leximancer) applied to the comments posted on three different political spoof videos, defining topics and words used by the commenting viewers in order to measure the sentiment of the audience.

Many researchers on Twitter used what can be defined as a *computational supported statistical approach* to sample the users' messages by acquiring—through the use of the public API—a Twitter-provided sample of the messages published on the public timeline (Honeycutt & Herring, 2009). While researchers moved into the Twitter world, the wide diffusion of Twitter as a social platform led to the emergence of unexpected social phenomena that found on this social network site a perfect sociotechnical environment able to host them. In just a few years, Twitter became a digital space where public issues could be discussed, critical information could be shared during natural disasters, and TV shows could be commented on by and with their fans. This user-led evolution of the platform produced a wave of studies focused on these phenomena with a closer perspective (Bruns, 2011; Rossi, Magnani, & Iadarola, 2011; Wohn & Na, 2011). These studies constitute the starting point for a more comprehensive understanding of the Twitter dynamics and of the wide range of social interactions that emerged from the platform, providing as well some interesting categorizations of these phenomena and of their Twitter-based characteristics. Thanks to the growing number of ad hoc studies and case studies, we now know that *crisis events* have communication patterns quite different from *media events* and that different actors are involved (Bruns, 2011). The study of Twitter usage during natural disasters has been particularly interesting and dates back to the early work of Earle (2010), which describes how the Twitter-based report of an earthquake experience provides a powerful tool to supplement instrument-based techniques in a quake's location and magnitude evaluation. Another important part of Twitter-based research—usually carried out with mixed *computational supported ethnographic or statistical methods*—is related to its political use. Following a series of political elections in 2009 and 2011, studies focused on describing how the politics were changed by the conversations taking place on the microblogging service (Bruns & Burgess, 2011) or whether Twitter itself could be used as a viable predictive tool to forecast the electoral outcomes (Jungherr, Jurgens, & Schoen, 2011; Lassen & Brown,

2010; Tumasjan, Sprenger, Sandner, & Welpe, 2010). These new approaches took a step forward toward the study of Twitter as a widely adopted social media and part of a larger media ecology. This is well beyond the studies aiming at describing Twitter as a network, and it places Twitter as a normal part of the contemporary media scene. When Lassen and Brown (2010) tried to use Twitter to predict electoral results, the basic underlying assumption was that Twitter was diffused enough within the politically active part of the society that a large-scale analysis of Twitter political communication could have represented a sample of the whole society. This should make clear the shift from a research approach focused on the whole Twitter network to an ad hoc social phenomenon-driven approach.

As opposed to Twitter, a stream analysis of public contents shared on Facebook is almost worthless since the great majority of users tend to share contents with their "Friends" only.

Most of the distinctions between profiles and pages also apply when dealing with statistical approaches to contents (posts, photos, videos, links, and activities) shared on Facebook by users or organizations. Retrieving and analyzing pages and group contents enables studies focused on specific organizations such as nonprofits (Waters, Burnett, Lamm, & Lucas, 2009) or political groups (Woolley, Limperos & Oliver, 2010). These studies often employ a statistical approach based on content analysis and are a reasonable follow-up of studies based on the analysis of pages and groups meta-information.

Profile meta-information is all the data available in the profiles' "about" and "favorites" sections. These sections contain information such as the user's list of "Friends," birthday, relationship status, family relationships, work, and education, as well as liked pages, music, books, movies, and so on. While in personal profiles these data are shared, by default, to "Friends" only, on pages and graph-enabled websites (e.g., webpages exposing the "like" button), this information (e.g., the number of users who liked a page or page description) is public. This crucial dissimilarity made Facebook pages and graph-enabled websites a viable target for studies on news dissemination (Lifshits & Clara, 2010) and brand engagement performances or popularity (Caren & Gaby, 2011; Lovari & Giglietto, 2012). Accessing most of the meta-information on personal profiles requires one to be a "Friend" of the subject. Once accepted as a "Friend," it is possible to study disclosure strategies (Kolek & Saunders, 2008) and user preferences and ego networks (Hogan, 2008).

COMPUTATIONAL APPROACHES

The computational approach is typical of the computer sciences, but when it is applied to social media, it provides interesting information for social scientists (Manovich, 2008). Within this approach, any software object expresses something about the users of the platform or the platform itself, and also helps to understand some properties that otherwise would not be directly observable. Studies based on computational approaches share common features: big or enormous data collection, a web services-based approach (e.g., Tubekit, Tubemogul: Shah, 2010), an Application Programming Interface (API) manipulation approach, the attempt to model the results (e.g., according to a power law model, or by the analysis of the graph structure). The studies based on a computational approach could be further classified: Those employing a web services approach often belong to the community of social scientists, due to the simpler use of these platforms in data collection and analysis, whereas those studies using the API manipulation approach belong to the computer scientist community because of the skills of computer programming that are needed for interacting with the platform through the API. The API manipulation is important because in this way it is possible to collect a great amount of data and to build a database with much information and metadata about the focus of the research. Although a growing number of social scientists are now using this approach thanks to the growing success of the so-called digital methods (Rogers, 2009), so far computer scientists have provided the major contributions from a pure computational perspective. An example of this approach is the study of Wallsten (2010) on the "Yes we can" viral video produced by Will.I.Am of the hip hop group The Black Eyed Peas. This study argues that bloggers and other Obama campaign supporters played a crucial role in convincing people to watch the video and attract the interest of the media mainstream. This research used Tubemogul web service to collect the data of total exposures and to create a viral model of the video. Another study on the popularity of YouTube videos (Chatzopoulou, Sheng, & Faloutsos, 2010) used YouTube's API to build a crawler for collecting different data in a database of 37 million videos to create a model of popularity of most viewed videos. An interesting result of this research is the "magic number" 400: A video receives one comment, one rating, and is added to someone's favorite list once for every 400 times it is viewed.

As previously stated, the disposal of public API makes Twitter data available to a large and growing number of researchers with some basic programming skills. In fact, many of the first studies on the topic are characterized by a computer science background and focused on the analysis of the network structure and on its topological characteristics studying the Twitter network as a whole. Within this perspective in their opening work, Java, Song, Finin, and Tseng (2007)—starting from a sample of 76,177 users—described Twitter's network structure, geographical distribution, and interaction between users. These studies were made possible by the relatively small size of the Twitter network at that time and have subsequently become less frequent, mainly due to both the growing size of the Twitter network—now 140 million daily users (Twitter, 2012)—and the consequent limits to data acquisition. Although we can still find recent studies regarding the global structure of the Twitter network (Wu, Hofman, Watts, & Mason, 2010), it has become apparent that these studies should be integrated with specific analyses of local phenomena that are not always visible at a *whole network* level of observation but still constitute the essence of the Twitter communication experience from the point of view of the users.

For the very same reason, the studies on Facebook whole-network structures are rare and always based on a data set provided by Facebook itself. Analyzing a large networks structure is often computationally challenging, and the results of these studies provide an abstract overview of users' behavior both in bonded communities (Lewis, Kaufman, Gonzales, Christakis, & Tastes, 2008) or entire countries (Traud & Mucha, 2011). Also, concerning stream analysis of public contents, the most interesting studies are made in partnership with Facebook itself (see the recent agreement between the Politico website and Facebook, which focused on the sentiment analysis of posts mentioning the candidates of the 2012 U.S. Republican primary elections). Although stream-based studies could be carried on with traditional manual-coded content analysis, the amount of data collected suggests instead the use of computational techniques.

Gaining access to meta-information for non-"Friends" requires the development of ad hoc Facebook applications such as the one described by Rauber and Almeida in their essay on users' privacy awareness (2011). An explicit informed consent of the subject is enforced by the platform and required by the standard norm of research ethics.

DISCUSSION AND CONCLUSIONS

Due to the complexity and heterogeneity of the described approaches, it is often challenging to classify a study within one of the categories of the methodological frames we have adopted. A classical distinction between ethnographic and statistical approaches, even if complemented by computational methods, is hardly able to describe all the ways in which social media data can be used to understand online users' behaviors.

The digital nature of the data, along with the amount of information available, makes the computational approach the most suitable way to collect it. Nevertheless, once data have been gathered, they can be analyzed with either a quantitative or a qualitative approach, depending on the research questions and strategies. Content analysis based on manual coding of "big data" is particularly hard because the amount of data makes the process extremely time-consuming. At the same time, sampling this data is also challenging because in most of the cases the distributions are extremely skewed (e.g., few extremely active users and a long tail of far less productive users). Under this perspective, although not yet perfect, the advances in the field of automatic semantic analysis appear to be promising, especially when used as a screening technique aimed to support manual coding.

Within this scenario, mixed methods approaches are often the most promising but the least frequently used. Although the amount of work required by these approaches may be an issue, a more pressing issue is the necessary collaboration among scholars coming from different backgrounds required by mixed methods approaches.

On the one hand, social scientists embracing social media as a data source for their studies need to gain a general understanding of the platforms from both the technical and the cultural point of view. This basic knowledge about the platform could be acquired by being part of the communities hosted by the platforms. This very first step is required not only for ethnographical approaches, where knowledge about the setting is somehow mandatory, but also for statistical and computational ones.

On the other hand, a researcher's background still matters when it comes to data interpretation. Even when research areas are similar, the perspective of analysis can be very different. When computer scientists look for online communities in social media, they usually adopt a graph mining approach to detect communities, which is, de facto, a direct evolution of graph clustering techniques (Leskovec et al., 2008) but is this a proper formalization of the sociological concept of community? Alternatively, many of the recent studies on online communities (Baym, 2007) coming from social scientist scholars still lack the level of formalization necessary to make the concepts suitable to be used in computational approaches to "big data" (boyd & Crawford, 2012; Wellman et al., 2002).

The literature review proposed in this article clearly points out a need to develop studies carefully designed to take advantage of a mixed methods approach including ethnographic, statistical and computational methods. However, the methodological skills required often exceed the traditional curriculum of social scientists. There is therefore a strong need for collaboration among scientists coming from different backgrounds in order to support studies that combine broad perspectives with in-depth and effective interpretations.

NOTE

1. The location field can be used both to communicate the user's real geographical coordinates using global positioning system (GPS)-enabled devices and to state more generic information (like the name of the country) or even to convey sarcastic or political messages, as noted by some recent studies (Takhteyev, Gruzd, & Wellman, 2011).

REFERENCES

Aharony, N. (2011). *Social fMRI: Measuring, understanding, and designing social mechanisms in the real world.* Cambridge, MA: Massachusetts Institute of Technology.

Alexa. (2012). *YouTube site info.* Retrieved from http://www.alexa.com/siteinfo/youtube.com

Bal, A. S., Campbell, C. L., Payne, N. J., & Pitt, L. (2010). Political ad portraits: a visual analysis of viewer reaction to online political spoof advertisements. *Journal of Public Affairs, 10*(4), 313–328. Wiley Online Library.

Baresch, B., Knight, L., Harp, D., & Yaschur, C. (2011). Friends who choose your news: An analysis of content links on Facebook. *ISOJ: The Official Research Journal of International Symposium on Online Journalism, 1*. Retrieved from http://online.journalism.utexas.edu/2011/papers/Baresch2011.pdf

Baym, N. K. (2007). The new shape of online community: The example of Swedish independent music fandom. *First Monday, 12*(8). Retrieved from http://firstmonday.org/htbin/cgiwrap/bin/ojs/index.php/fm/article/view/1978/1853

boyd, d. (2008). *Taken out of context: American teen sociality in networked publics*. University of California, Berkeley. Retrieved from http://www.danah.org/papers/TakenOutofContext.pdf

boyd, d., & Crawford, K. (2012). Critical questions for big data: Provocations for a cultural, technological, and scholarly phenomenon. *Information, Communication, & Society, 15*(5), 662–679.

boyd, d., & Ellison, N. B. (2008). Social network sites: Definition, history, and scholarship. *Journal of Computer-Mediated Communication, 13*(1), 210–230. doi:10.1111/j.1083-6101.2007.00393.x

boyd, d., & Hargittai, E. (2010). Facebook privacy settings: Who cares? *First Monday, 15*(8). Retrieved from http://www.uic.edu/htbin/cgiwrap/bin/ojs/index.php/fm/article/view/3086

Bruns, A. (2011). How long is a tweet? Mapping dynamic conversation networks on Twitter Using Gawk and Gephi. *Information, Communication & Society, 15*(9), 1–29. doi:10.1080/1369118X.2011.635214

Bruns, A., & Burgess, J. (2011). #Ausvotes: How twitter covered the 2010 Australian federal election. *Communication, Politics & Culture, 44*(2), 37–56.

Bruns, A., & Liang, Y. E. (2012). Tools and methods for capturing Twitter data during natural disasters. *First Monday, 17*(4-2). Retrieved from http://firstmonday.org/htbin/cgiwrap/bin/ojs/index.php/fm/article/view/3937/3193

Burgess, J. (2006). Hearing ordinary voices: Cultural studies, vernacular creativity and digital storytelling. *Continuum: Journal of Media & Cultural Studies, 20*(2), 201–214.

Burgess, J., & Green, J. (2009). *YouTube: Online video and participatory culture*. Cambridge, England: Polity Press.

Caren, N., & Gaby, S. (2011). Occupy online: Facebook and the spread of Occupy Wall Street. *SSRN Electronic Journal*. Retrieved from http://papers.ssrn.com/sol3/papers.cfm?abstract_id=1943168. doi:10.2139/ssrn.1943168

Chatzopoulou, G., Sheng, C., & Faloutsos, M. (2010, March). A first step towards understanding popularity in YouTube. In *INFOCOM IEEE Conference on Computer Communications Workshops, 2010* (pp. 1–6). IEEE.

Cormode, G., Krishnamurthy, B., & Willinger, W. (2010). A manifesto for modeling and measurement in social media. *First Monday, 15*(9-6). Retrieved from http://firstmonday.org/htbin/cgiwrap/bin/ojs/index.php/fm/article/view/3072

Earle, P. (2010). Earthquake Twitter. *Nature Geoscience, 3*(4), 221–222. doi:10.1038/ngeo832

Facebook. (2012). *Key facts*. Retrieved from http://newsroom.fb.com/content/default.aspx?NewsAreaId=22

Griffith, M., & Papacharissi, Z. (2009). Looking for you: An analysis of video blogs. *First Monday, 15*(1). Retrieved from http://firstmonday.org/htbin/cgiwrap/bin/ojs/index.php/fm/article/view/2769/2430

Harley, D., & Fitzpatrick, G. (2009). Creating a conversational context through video blogging: A case study of Geriatric1927. *Computers in Human Behavior, 25*(3), 679–689.

Hogan, B. (2008). Analyzing social networks via the Internet. In *The Sage handbook of online research methods* (pp. 141–160). London: Sage.

Honeycutt, C., & Herring, S. C. (2009). *Beyond microblogging: Conversation and collaboration via Twitter* (Vol. 0, pp. 1–10). Los Alamitos, CA, USA: IEEE Computer Society. doi:http://doi.ieeecomputersociety.org/10.1109/HICSS.2009.602

Huberman, B. A., Romero, D. M., & Wu, F. (2009). Social networks that matter: Twitter under the microscope. *First Monday, 14*(1). Retrieved from http://firstmonday.org/htbin/cgiwrap/bin/ojs/index.php/fm/article/view/2317/2063

Java, A., Song, X., Finin, T., & Tseng, B. (2007). Why we Twitter: Understanding microblogging. *Network, 1*, 56–65. doi:10.1145/1348549.1348556

Joinson, A. N. (2008). Looking at, looking up or keeping up with people? *Proceeding of the twenty-sixth annual CHI conference on human factors in computing systems—CHI '08* (p. 1027). New York, NY: ACM Press. doi:10.1145/1357054.1357213.

Jungherr, A., Jurgens, P., & Schoen, H. (2011). Why the Pirate Party won the German election of 2009, or The trouble with predictions: A response to Tumasjan, A., Sprenger, T. O., Sander, P. G., & Welpe, I. M., Predicting Elections With Twitter: What 140 Characters Reveal About Political Sentiment. *Social Science Computer Review, 1*(6). doi:10.1177/0894439311404119

Kaplan, A. M., & Haenlein, M. (2010). Users of the world, unite! The challenges and opportunities of Social Media. *Business Horizons, 53*(1), 59–68. Elsevier.

Karpf, D. (2012). Social science research methods in Internet time. *Information, Communication & Society, 15*(5), 639–661.

Kolek, E. A., & Saunders, D. (2008). Online disclosure: An empirical examination of undergraduate Facebook profiles. *Journal of Student Affairs Research and Practice, 45*(1), 1–25. doi:10.2202/1949-6605.1905

Lange, P. G. (2007). Publicly private and privately public: Social networking on YouTube. *Journal of Computer-Mediated Communication, 13*, 361–380. doi: 10.1111/j.1083-6101.2007.00400.x

Lassen, D. S., & Brown, A. R. (2010). Twitter: The electoral connection? *Social Science Computer Review, 29*(4), 419–436. doi:10.1177/0894439310382749

Leskovec, J., Lang, K. J., Dasgupta, A., & Mahoney, M. W. (2008, April). Statistical properties of community structure in large social and information networks. *Proceeding of the 17th International Conference on World Wide Web* (pp. 695–704). New York, NY: ACM.

Lewis, K., Kaufman, J., Gonzales, M., Wimmer, A., & Christakis, N. (2008). Tastes, ties, and time: A new social network dataset using Facebook.com. *Social Networks, 30*(4), 330–342. Retrieved from http://www.sciencedirect.com/science/article/pii/S0378873308000385

Lifshits, Y. (2010). *Ediscope: Social analytics for online news.* Yahoo—Yahoo Labs. Retrieved from http://www.research.yahoo.net/files/YL-2010-008.pdf

Liu, Y., Gummadi, K. P., Krishnamurthy, B., & Mislove, A. (2011, November). Analyzing Facebook privacy settings: User expectations vs. reality. *Proceedings of the 2011*

ACM SIGCOMM Conference on Internet Measurement Conference (pp. 61–70). New York, NY: ACM.

Lovari, A., & Giglietto, F. (2012). Social media and Italian universities: An empirical study on the adoption and use of Facebook, Twitter and Youtube. *SSRN eLibrary*. Retrieved from http://papers.ssrn.com/so13/papers.cfm?abstract_id=1978393. doi:10.2139/ssrn.1978393

Manovich, L. (2008). *Software takes command*. Unpublished. Retrieved from http://lab.softwarestudies.com/2008/11/softbook.html

Marwick, A. E., & boyd, d. (2010). I tweet honestly, I tweet passionately: Twitter users, context collapse, and the imagined audience. *New Media & Society, 13*(1), 114–133. doi:10.1177/1461444810365313

Norris, S. (2004). *Analyzing multimodal interaction: A methodological framework*. London, UK: Psychology Press.

O'Reilly, T. (2007). *What is Web 2.0. Design patterns and business models for the next generation of software*. Retrieved from http://oreilly.com/lpt/a/6228

Rauber, G., & Almeida, V. A. F. (2011). Privacy albeit late. *Networks, 13*, 26. Retrieved from http://precog.iiitd.edu.in/Publications_files/GR_VA_PK_SMW_2011.pdf

Ricolfi, L. (2001). *La ricerca qualitativa*. Rome, Italy: Carocci.

Rogers, R. (2009). *The end of the virtual: Digital methods*. Amsterdam, The Netherlands: Amsterdam University Press.

Rossi, L., Magnani, M., & Iadarola, B. (2011). #rescatemineros: Global media events in the microblogging age. *Selected papers of Internet research*, 0(12.0). Retrieved from http://spir.aoir.org/index.php/spir/article/view/30

Rotman, D., Golbeck, J., & Preece, J. (2009). The community is where the rapport is—On sense and structure in the youtube community. *Proceedings of the Fourth International Conference on Communities and Technologies* (pp. 41–50). New York, NY: ACM.

Shah, C. (2010). Supporting research data collection from YouTube with TubeKit. *Journal of Information Technology & Politics, 7*(2–3), 226–240.

Takhteyev, Y., Gruzd, A., & Wellman, B. (2011). Geography of Twitter networks. *Social Networks, 34*(1), 73–81.

Traud, A., & Mucha, P. (2011). Social structure of Facebook networks. *Physica A, 391*, 4165–4180. Retrieved from http://www.sciencedirect.com/science/article/pii/S0378437111009186

Tumasjan, A., Sprenger, T. O., Sandner, P. G., & Welpe, I. M. (2010). Election forecasts with Twitter: How 140 characters reflect the political landscape. *Social Science Computer Review, 29*(4), 402–418. doi:10.1177/0894439310386557

Twitter, Inc. (2012). Twitter turns six. *Twitter Blog*. Retrieved from http://blog.twitter.com/2012/03/twitter-turns-six.html

Wallsten, K. (2010). "Yes we can": How online viewership, blog discussion, campaign statements, and mainstream media coverage produced a viral video phenomenon. *Journal of Information Technology & Politics, 7*(2–3), 163–181.

Waters, R. D., Burnett, E., Lamm, A., & Lucas, J. (2009). Engaging stakeholders through social networking: How nonprofit organizations are using Facebook. *Public Relations Review, 35*(2), 102–106. doi:10.1016/j.pubrev.2009.01.006.

Wellman, B., Boase, J., & Chen, W. (2012). The networked nature of community: Online and offline. *IT & Society, 1*(1), 151–165.

Wohn, D. Y., & Na, E. K. (2011). Tweeting about TV: Sharing television viewing experiences via social media message streams. *First Monday, 3*(16). Retrieved from http://firstmonday.org/htbin/cgiwrap/bin/ojs/index.php/fm/article/view/3368/2779

Woolley, J. K., Limperos, A. M., & Oliver, M. B. (2010). The 2008 Presidential election, 2.0: A content analysis of user-generated political Facebook groups. *Mass Communication and Society, 13*(5), 631–652. doi:10.1080/15205436.2010.516864.

Wu, S., Hofman, J. M., Watts, D. J., & Mason, W. A. (2010, March). Who says what to whom on Twitter. In *Proceedings of the 20th international conference on world wide web* (pp. 705–714). New York, NY: ACM.

YouTube. (2012). *Statistic: Traffic*. Retrieved from http://www.youtube.com/t/press_statistics

Quantitative Approaches to Comparing Communication Patterns on Twitter

AXEL BRUNS
Queensland University of Technology, Brisbane, Australia
STEFAN STIEGLITZ
University of Münster, Münster, Germany

To date, the available literature mainly discusses Twitter activity patterns in the context of individual case studies, while comparative research on a large number of communicative events and their dynamics and patterns is missing. By conducting a comparative study of more than 40 different cases (covering topics such as elections, natural disasters, corporate crises, and televised events) we identify a number of distinct types of discussion that can be observed on Twitter. Drawing on a range of communicative metrics, we show that thematic and contextual factors influence the usage of different communicative tools available to Twitter users, such as original tweets, @replies, retweets, and URLs. Based on this first analysis of the overall metrics of Twitter discussions, we also demonstrate stable patterns in the use of Twitter in the context of major topics and events.

INTRODUCTION

Since 2006, microblogging has become an increasingly widely used tool for communication on the Internet. Twitter, as one of the first and most popular microblogging providers, has some 140 million users, with some 340 million tweets posted each day (Twitter, 2012). In contrast to social networking sites (SNS) such as Facebook, the reach of posts on Twitter is not necessarily limited to a specific group (such as subscribed "friends" or "followers"); rather, posted messages are public by default and may also be found by visitors searching the site or tracking the Twitter stream. Each user is thus able to create public posts to initiate discussions, to participate in debates, and to follow the communication of others. To manage these communicative flows and increase the efficiency of public message exchanges, Twitter users have adapted a variety of methods to classify their contributions (tweets)—for example, as a public response (@reply) or a shared message originating from another user (retweet).

Twitter has now become a widely used communications channel across a wide range of applications, from politics, journalism and crisis communication (Bruns & Burgess, 2011a; Christensen, 2011; Larsson & Moe, 2011; Lotan, Ananny, Gaffney, & boyd, 2011; Bruns, Burgess, Crawford, & Shaw, 2012; Mendoza, Poblete, & Castillo, 2010; Palen, Starbird, Vieweg, & Hughes, 2010; Stieglitz & Dang-Xuan, in press) through its use as a backchannel for television shows, cultural and sporting events, and conferences to a wide variety of uses for everyday interpersonal communication (e.g., boyd, Golder, & Lotan, 2010; Deller, 2011; Dröge, Maghferat, Puschmann, Verbina, & Weller, 2011; Marwick & boyd, 2011; Papacharissi, 2011; Weller, Dröge, & Puschmann, 2011). Significant research into some such uses is now emerging, but largely remains in the form of topic-, context-, and event-related case studies that are able to shed substantial light on specific uses of Twitter but do not yet lead to a more comprehensive overall picture of how Twitter is used.

Individuals and organizations may use Twitter to subscribe to the update feeds of other users, as well as to publish their own short messages (to a maximum of 140 characters) about various topics (e.g., from personal and professional updates to press releases and other corporate information). To widely disseminate information on Twitter, the mechanism of retweeting has been adopted by users. By retweeting, users may not only share information but also entertain a certain audience or (by adding comments to the retweets) publicly agree or disagree with someone (boyd, Golder, & Lotan, 2010). As a result, Twitter has become an important platform for users to spread information about topics of shared interest: retweets propagate the original tweet to a new set of audiences, namely, the followers of the retweeting user. Given the growing Twitter user base, the high speed of information dissemination on Twitter, and the significant influence of Twitter as a driver of web traffic, new questions arise about the way it is used to support public information sharing and information search.

Other studies have already made some first steps to investigate how and why certain information items spread more widely than others (Stieglitz & Dang-Xuan, forthcoming [Suh, Hong, Pirolli, & Chi, 2010]). However, so far the literature mainly discusses Twitter activity patterns in the context of individual case studies, while comparative research on a large number of discussions and their dynamics and patterns is missing. By conducting a comparative study of several dozen different cases (including topics such as elections, natural disasters, corporate crises, and televised sporting and cultural events) we have identified a number of distinct types of discussion that can be observed on Twitter. Drawing on a range of communicative metrics, we show that thematic and contextual factors influence the usage of different communicative tools available to Twitter users, such as original tweets, @replies, retweets, and URLs. We also demonstrate patterns in the structure of the user community involved (e.g., number of participants, relevance of lead users). This article presents a first analysis of the overall metrics of Twitter discussions relating to different areas of content, and outlines two standard, stable types of Twitter usage in the context of major topics and events. As such, it represents a significant advance for research that investigates the usage of different communication tools in public discussions.

This article pursues this larger picture by exploring general patterns of Twitter usage, drawing on detailed usage metrics for a wide range of cases and events over the past 2 years. By collating these data points and identifying cases that exhibit similar patterns of activity, we observe a range of common, apparently well-established user practices on Twitter. We suggest that these observations point to regularities in the popular responses to specific themes and events that may also be identified well beyond the Twitter platform itself.

RELATED WORK

In recent years, a substantial amount of literature has been published in the field of Twitter communication. Therefore, we provide a short literature review of those articles that explicitly reflect metrics within Twitter communication in the field of politics, natural and human disasters, and entertainment and brand-related communication.

Politics

In a study of approximately 100,000 messages containing a reference to either a political party or a politician in the context of the 2009 German federal election, Tumasjan, Sprenger, Sandner, and Welpe (2011) show that Twitter is used extensively for the dissemination of politically relevant information and that the mere number of party mentions accurately reflects the election result, suggesting that microblogging messages on Twitter seem to validly mirror the political landscape offline and can be used to predict election results to a certain extent. Conover et al. (2011) examine two networks of political communication on Twitter with more than 250,000 tweets from the 6 weeks leading up to the 2010 U.S. congressional midterm elections. Using a combination of network clustering algorithms and manually annotated data, the authors demonstrate that the network of political retweets exhibits a highly segregated partisan structure, with extremely limited connectivity between left- and right-leaning users. Surprisingly, this is not the case for the user-to-user mention network, which is dominated by a single politically heterogeneous cluster of users in which ideologically opposed individuals interact at a much higher rate compared to the network of retweets. Similarly, Yardi and boyd (2010) find that in a political context Twitter users are more likely to interact with others who share the same views as they do in terms of retweeting, but they are also actively engaged with those with whom they disagree. In addition, replies between like-minded individuals would strengthen group identity, whereas replies between different-minded individuals would reinforce in-group and out-group affiliation. In a large-scale study, Suh, Hong, Pirolli, and Chi (2010) addressed these questions and identified several factors that significantly impact on the retweetability of Twitter messages (tweets), including the presence of URLs and hashtags, as well as the number of followers and the age of the originating user's account. Beside these case-based analyses, Stieglitz and Dang-Xuan (2012) provide a general framework that presents methods for social media analytics in the political context.

Natural and Human Disasters

In recent years, a growing body of literature has emerged in the field of social media and crisis communication (Bruns, Burgess, Crawford, & Shaw, 2012; Hughes & Palen, 2009; Mendoza, Poblete, & Castillo, 2010; Palen, Starbird, Vieweg, & Hughes, 2010). Cheng, Sun, Hu, and Zeng (2011) investigated Twitter as a tool to monitor and capture emerging trends and patterns of time-critical knowledge. They extensively evaluated a diffusion-based recommendation framework and a proposed algorithm using Twitter data collected during the early outbreak of H1N1 Flu. Studies by Bruns, Burgess, Crawford, and Shaw (2012) and by Cheong and Cheong (2011) analyzed Twitter-based communication in the context of natural disasters, focusing on the Australian floods in 2011. By using social network analysis methods, they found that several different groups of actors, including affected locals, emergency services, and mainstream media organizations, played important roles in providing and sharing information about the disaster.

Other studies (Bruns, Highfield, & Burgess, in press; Lotan, Ananny, Gaffney, & boyd, 2011; Vis, 2012) examined uses of Twitter during major civil unrest in the context of the 2011 London and UK riots or the Arab Spring uprisings in a number of North African and Middle East countries. They identified a diverse range of uses of social media for information dissemination alongside and in addition to other media channels and word-of-mouth information, and also highlighted significant differences in activity between local and more distant observers of these events.

Entertainment and Brand-Related Communication

Stieglitz and Krüger (2011) investigated a 2010 brand crisis involving car manufacturer Toyota and showed that, measured by the published number of tweets, crisis discussions are characterized by peaks and quiet periods in the communication of enterprise-related issues. Further, they found that the lead users involved in the Twitter debate played an important role in the discussion, for example by publishing a significantly high amount of all tweets and generating a large amount of retweets.

Park, Cha, Kim, and Jeong (2009) investigated the Domino's Pizza crisis and analyzed the diffusion of bad news through Twitter. They separately classified sentiments in tweets generated by customers and those generated by the enterprise itself, and proved that the diffusion of bad news is faster than that of other types of content, such as apologies.

In a study of users and their behaviors in the Twitter network, Krishnamurthy, Phillipa, and Arlitt (2008) identified three types of users (broadcaster, acquaintances, and miscreants) by analyzing a crawled data set that covered nearly 100,000 users. The broadcasters, also called power-tweeters, are characterized by a large number of followers as well as a large amount of self-created postings. One finding in this study was that these users update their status more often and post more tweets than users of the two other categories.

METHODOLOGY

In order to establish a sound basis for the identification of shared patterns in Twitter-based communication around specific issues, the majority of the Twitter phenomena which we observe in this article are centered around common hashtags (brief keywords included in tweets, prefixed with the hash symbol #). Hashtags are an originally user-generated mechanism for making messages related to a specific topic more easily discoverable and are now well-supported by central Twitter infrastructure as well as by specific Twitter client software; it is now possible for users (and even for nonregistered visitors to the site) to search Twitter for specific hashtags, and to follow the stream of new messages containing specific hashtags in real time. This makes hashtags a useful and an important mechanism for coordinating conversations around identified themes and events, ranging from breaking news (such as #eqnz for the 2010/11 earthquakes in Christchurch, New Zealand) through major media events (e.g., #euro2012 for the 2010 European Football Championships) to viral marketing campaigns (such as #kony2012 and #stopkony for the campaign to bring a fugitive Ugandan warlord to justice). Beyond such world events, hashtags are also used to coordinate much more low-key discussions and user communities, from providing a backchannel for conference delegates to organizing Twitter-based user meetups (such as the long-standing #phdchat, a global discussion for PhD candidates). Finally, a different use of hashtags, which we do not consider in detail here, is as markers of emphasis or emotion, as in, "My bus is running late again. #fail."

Hashtags, then, may emerge ad hoc in response to breaking news and other unforeseen events, spreading virally as more and more users with an interest in the topic see the hashtag in their Twitter feeds and begin to use it themselves (see Bruns & Burgess, 2011b). They may also be used repeatedly for recurring events (such as #ausvotes for Australian federal elections, or #eqnz for each of the four major earthquakes which affected Christchurch in 2010/2011). Alternatively, they may be promoted *praeter hoc* by relevant organizations as the appropriate hashtag to be used for an upcoming event (this is the case for backchannel hashtags for conferences or TV shows, for example). Such diverse hashtags may in turn attract widely varying groups of users. Breaking news events, especially where they are of national or global relevance, may find hundreds of thousands of Twitter users posting or retweeting hashtagged messages, while hashtags related to conferences or TV shows may involve only a much smaller number of users who happen to be attending or watching at the time. Standing hashtags for the discussion of specific continuing topics (from #phdchat to the day-to-day tracking of long-term events such as the popular revolts in #Libya, #Egypt, or #Syria), in turn, may involve only a comparatively small group of committed contributors. At the same time, they may see a temporary influx of a large number of interested users as key developments unfold and are widely covered by mainstream media outlets.

Using the Twitter Application Programming Interface (API), it is comparatively simple to capture comprehensive data sets of the vast majority of all tweets containing a specific hashtag (within limits determined by the reliability of the API and of real-time Twitter tracking tools; cf. Bruns & Liang, 2012). During 2010–2012, as part of a project collaboration between Queensland University of Technology, Brisbane, and the University of Münster, we have done so for some 40 hashtags as well as a number of non-hashtagged keywords (which we discuss later). Individual hashtag data sets for this study were captured using the open-source platform *yourTwapperkeeper* (2012), which utilizes Twitter streaming API and search API functionality to capture, in real time, any tweets containing the keywords (including hashtags) selected by the operator. For more details on Twitter research methods using *yourTwapperkeeper* and alternative technologies, see Bruns and Liang (2012). *yourTwapperkeeper* does not provide for post hoc data gathering; it is able only to capture tweets for set keywords as they are sent. Therefore, the selection of hashtag and keyword data sets used for this study was a function of the long-term research interests of the Brisbane and Münster research groups, which specialize in political, crisis, and brand communication research. In themselves, these over 40 data sets cover a diverse range of uses, therefore, but we also encourage the further extension of this initial work through the addition of hashtag and keyword metrics extracted from data sets gathered by researchers interested in other areas of communication using social media.

To better understand the diversity of uses evident in the present collection of cases, and to identify any common patterns between individual cases, we draw on a catalogue of metrics for describing the communicative patterns which may be observed for each hashtag (see Bruns & Stieglitz, in press, for a detailed introduction of these metrics). In the first place, these included:

- The number of *tweets* in the hashtag data set.
- The number of *unique users* contributing to the hashtag data set.
- The percentage of *original tweets* in the hashtag data set (i.e., tweets that are neither @replies nor retweets).
- The percentage of *genuine @replies* in the hashtag data set (i.e., @replies that are not retweets).
- The percentage of *retweets* in the hashtag data set.[1]
- The percentage of tweets in the hashtag data set that contain URLs.

Additionally, we also divided the total user base for each hashtag data set into three groups, following a standard 1/9/90 distribution (Tedjamulia, Dean, Olsen, & Albrecht, 2005):

- The top 1% of most active *lead users*.
- The next 9% of still *highly active users*.
- The remaining 90% of *least active users*.

For each of these three groups in each hashtag data set, we again calculated the metrics already outlined, taking into account only the tweets sent by that percentile group. Compared across the groups, this provides a measure for each hashtag of how dominant within the overall hashtag conversation the leading user groups were. This enabled us to examine any obvious differences in the Twitter activity patterns of the three user groups.

In the following discussion, we collate and compare these metrics for the range of hashtags which we tracked over the past two years. This enables us to identify communication patterns that are common across these diverse cases, and to develop a typology of hashtagged Twitter usage. First, however, we provide an overview of the hashtag data sets that were used in this analysis, and outline their relevant features.

Hashtag Data Sets

This study draws on a wide variety of data sets, whose key features we outline in Table 1. While the scope of this article does not permit a detailed discussion of the themes and contents of each data set, we note that these cases encompass a wide variety of topical hashtag uses. These range from political themes through natural disasters to entertainment and sports; from

TABLE 1 Overview of hashtag and keyword data sets used for the comparative analysis

Hashtag/ keyword	Description	Theme	Timeframe	Notes on time frame	Total unique users	Total tweets
#0zapftis	Scandal around trojan horse virus developed by German intelligence service	Politics	11–31 Oct. 2011	Three weeks following scandal	6716	26158
#aflgf	Australian Football League 2011 grand final	Sports	1–2 Oct. 2011	Matchday and following day	3793	6135
#angryboys	*Angry Boys*: popular weekly TV sitcom on Australian free-to-air television	Television	12 May to 31 July 2011	Full season	30121	63333
#auspol	Australian politics (general discussion)	Politics	8 Feb. to 8 Dec. 2011	Eight months	26290	854019
#ausvotes	Australian federal election 2010	Politics	20–22 Aug. 2010	Three days around election day	36286	415511
#chch	February 2011 earthquake in Christchurch, New Zealand	Natural disaster	22–28 Feb. 2011	First week after earthquake (initial alternative to #eqnz)	9688	24400
#earth-quake	March 2011 earthquake and tsunami in Japan	Natural disaster	11–24 Mar. 2011	First 2 weeks after earthquake	183794	358737
#egypt	Arab Spring protests	Political unrest	26 Feb. to 26 Nov. 2011	Nine month period since first major protests	281978	6277782
#eqnz	February 2011 earthquake in Christchurch, New Zealand	Natural disaster	22 Feb. to 7 Mar. 2011	First 2 weeks after earthquake	37635	156940
#eurovision	Eurovision Song Contest 2011	Television	9–15 May 2011	Semifinals and and finals broadcasts on 10/12/14 May	137745	520543
#ge11	Irish general election	Politics	26 Feb. 2011	Election day	6151	28468
#gobacksbs	*Go Back to Where You Came From*: weekly reality TV show with political connotations on Australian free-to-air television	Television	21 June to 4 July 2011	Second half of season	8691	29009
#irene	Hurricane Irene along the East Coast of the United States	Natural disaster	27 Aug. to 17 Sep. 2011	Three weeks following first impact	37891	64315
#kony2012	Viral campaign to arrest warlord Joseph Kony	Politics	8–21 Mar. 2012	First 2 weeks of campaign	80874	101425

(*Continued*)

TABLE 1 Continued

Hashtag/ keyword	Description	Theme	Timeframe	Notes on time frame	Total unique users	Total tweets
#libya	Arab Spring protests	Political unrest	26 Feb. to 26 Nov. 2011	Nine-month period since first major protests	363489	3825272
#londonriots	Violent riots in London and the United Kingdom	Crisis	8–21 Aug. 2011	First 2 weeks after riots	127631	212213
#masterchef	*Masterchef*: popular weekly reality TV show on Australian free-to-air television	Television	1 May to 8 Aug. 2011	Whole season	54117	210773
#mkr	*My Kitchen Rules*: popular weekly reality TV show on Australian free-to-air television	Television	13 Feb. to 31 Mar. 2012	Final 27 episodes	12671	63866
#mw3	*Modern Warfare 3*: popular computer game	Net culture	1–30 Nov. 2011	One month around official launch	207858	413922
#norway	Right-wing terrorist attacks in Oslo and Utøya	Crisis	24 July to 9 Aug. 2011	First 2 weeks after attacks	38224	63244
#nrlgf	Australian National Rugby League 2011 grand final	Sports	1–2 Oct. 2011	Buildup and match day	2049	4182
#occupy	Global Occupy protests	Political protests	19 Dec. 2011 to 19 Apr. 2012	Four months of protests	121952	560560
#occupywallstreet	Occupy protests in New York	Political protests	27 Sep. to 27 Nov. 2011	Three months at height of protests	234514	885174
#oscars	Academy Awards 2011	Entertainment	27 Feb. 2011	Event day	236103	639251
#qanda	*Q&A*: popular weekly political talk show on Australian free-to-air television	Politics	21 Feb. to 21 Nov 2011	Whole season	246231	47131
#qldfloods	Major flooding in southeast Queensland	Natural disaster	10–16 Jan. 2011	First week of floods	15553	35658
#qldvotes	2012 Queensland state election	Politics	23–25 Mar. 2012	Three days around election day	5788	17456
#riotcleanup	Cleanup after violent riots in London and the United Kingdom	Crisis	8–21 Aug. 2011	First two weeks after riots	38511	53381
#royalwedding	Wedding between Prince William and Kate Middleton	Entertainment	29 Apr. 2011	Wedding day	492566	926527

#spill	Party room revolt against Australian Prime Minister Kevin Rudd	Politics	23–24 June 2010	First rumors and confirmation of party room vote	11309	46937
#stopkony	Viral campaign to arrest warlord Joseph Kony	Politics	8–21 Mar. 2012	First 2 weeks of campaign	117050	140958
#syria	Arab Spring protests	Political unrest	26 Mar. to 26 Nov. 2011	Eight months since first major protests	229030	5230025
#tdf	Tour de France 2011	Sports	4 July to 26 July 2011	Whole tour (except first two days)	94830	427467
#tsunami	March 2011 earthquake and tsunami in Japan	Natural disaster	11 Mar. to 11 Apr. 2011	First month after earthquake	529913	948640
#ukriots	Violent riots in London and the United Kingdom	Crisis	8–21 Aug. 2011	First 2 weeks after riots	61766	126664
#wikileaks	Political controversy	Politics	26 Feb. to 26 Nov. 2011 + 1–7 Sep. 2011	Nine months + period around Julian Assange arrest in the United Kingdom	119853 16930	422635 35451
bin laden	Death of Osama bin Laden	Politics	2 May to 2 June 2011	First month following bin Laden killing in Abbottabad	1868127	3987919
masterchef	*Masterchef*: popular weekly reality TV show on Australian free-to-air television	Television	1 May to 8 Aug. 2011	Whole season	238689	609714
qantas	Global grounding of flights by Qantas management in response to industrial action	Brand crisis	26 Oct. to 8 Nov. 2011	Two weeks around grounding crisis	42144	98636
steve jobs	Death of Apple founder Steve Jobs	Net culture	7 Oct. to 7 Nov. 2011	One month after death	403321	562411
tsunami	March 2011 earthquake and tsunami in Japan	Natural disaster	11 Mar. to 11 Apr. 2011	First month after earthquake	1936553	4246019

breaking news events through foreseeable, regularly occurring activities to channels for continuous thematic discussion; from local issues to global events; from events that unfolded over the span of a few hours to themes that were discussed for close to a year (and remain active beyond the time span covered in our analysis); and from activities that involve only a relatively small subset of the global Twitter user base, measuring in the thousands, to events that attracted the participation of close to 2 million unique users or generated more than 6 million tweets (see Table 1).

Real-time data collection for these data sets generally commenced as the hashtags related to specific themes and events became prominent on Twitter, especially in the case of acute crisis events. This required researchers to react speedily as news of these crises broke (as in the case of natural disasters such as the Christchurch earthquake or the Japanese tsunami), to rapidly determine the most prominent hashtags (#eqnz, #tsunami), and to add those hashtags to the existing *yourTwapperkeeper* installations for tracking. In other cases (such as #royalwedding, #eurovision, or #ausvotes), hashtags were foreseeable prior to the event and could be added to the tracker in advance. In each case, however, we have further determined appropriate start and end points for the data timeframes to be considered in the present article, in order to focus on the key period of activity for each hashtag or keyword. For natural disaster events, this usually means limiting the analysis to the first days or weeks after the initial disaster event, and for election-related discussion, to the days around election day itself. The specific time frames chosen for each hashtag or keyword are outlined in Table 1. It is necessary to draw on this disparate collection of data sets for our analysis in order to detect any patterns of Twitter use that persist even in spite of such marked differences between individual cases.

In addition to the hashtag data sets (which contain only those tweets about a topic that were explicitly hashtagged—e.g., #tsunami for the March 2011 tsunami), we also include five *keyword* data sets. These were gathered by capturing all tweets that contained only the specific keyword (e.g., "tsunami"), regardless of whether or not the # symbol was prefixed to that term. We discuss these data sets in more detail in the following. Our aim in including them in the following analysis is to examine whether there are any indications that beyond the use of dedicated hashtags, topical communication patterns on Twitter may follow similar principles as we outline them for deliberately hashtagged exchanges.

USER ACTIVITY METRICS

Given the divergence in the number of tweets and unique users for each data set, it is first useful to compare the relative prominence of the leading user groups across these cases. Figure 1 presents the relative number of

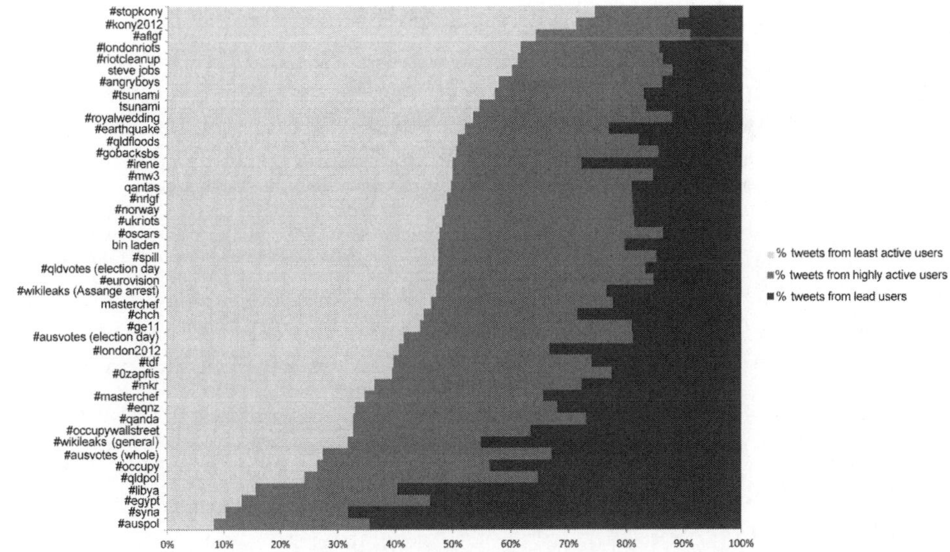

FIGURE 1 Relative contributions from the three user groups.

tweets contributed by each of the three user groups we have outlined already: lead users (top 1% most active users), highly active users (next 9% of active users), and least active users (the remaining 90% of users: the "long tail" of the user base).

Clear distinctions between the cases examined here emerge from this analysis. Roughly half of the cases are comparatively dominated by the two most active user groups, who (in combination) contribute 50% or more of the total number of tweets. For a smaller number of cases, that percentage grows to well above 70%; here, the "long tail" of least active users remains largely silent, while any meaningful exchanges take place mainly within a dedicated in-group of highly active participants.

It is notable in this context that the hashtags that feature the most active groups of leading users are generally also those that cover the longest time frames. In our comparison, the 10 data sets that see the fewest tweets from the least active user group are #syria, #egypt, and #libya (each of which attracted hundreds of thousands of participants and was active throughout 2011); #auspol, a standing hashtag for the discussion of Australian federal politics with a small but highly active contributor community, and #ausvotes (for the discussion of the 2010 Australian federal election); #occupy, #occupywallstreet, and #wikileaks (which serve as key distribution tools for information about global political protest and counterculture movements, over the long term, and attract hundreds of thousands of participants); and #qanda (the hashtag promoted by the Australian Broadcasting Corporation for its weekly political talk show *Q&A*).

By contrast, those hashtags that feature the most active "long tails" of contributors in our analysis are also those that unfold over comparatively short time frames. They include scheduled media events such as #royalwedding (the 29 April 2011 wedding between Prince William and Kate Middleton) or #aflgf (the 1 Oct. 2011 Australian Football League grand final); breaking news events such as the March 2011 Japanese tsunami (in both its hashtag and keyword variants); the August 2011 London riots and the subsequent #riotcleanup initiative organized by affected communities; the death of Apple leader Steve Jobs (which we captured in a keyword data set centered on mentions of "Steve Jobs"); and short-lived viral marketing campaigns such as the initiative to bring Ugandan warlord Joseph Kony to justice (under the hashtags #kony2012 and #stopkony).

From these observations, we suggest that the relative prominence of leading user groups in a hashtag conversation is related to the overall longevity of the hashtag itself (the amount of time during which it was significantly active, and during which we gathered tweets for it). In a comparatively new hashtag, more striated community structures have not yet had a chance to crystallize, while in a long-lived hashtag it is perhaps logical that committed long-term contributors will emerge as lead users as more casual participants come and go. Figure 2, which plots the longevity of hashtags against the relative contribution made by the 90% least active users, supports this finding. Although the possibility is intriguing, it should also be noted that our evidence does not permit us to establish any causal relations between these factors. However, from our data alone it is impossible to determine (1) whether hashtags persist for the longer term *because* a strong group of lead users keeps them going, or (2) whether these lead users inevitably emerge if a hashtag continues to remain active for a long enough time.

TWEET TYPE METRICS

The hashtag data sets examined here also differ widely in their underlying communicative practices, as Figure 3 shows. Here, we examine the relative presence of the three key tweet types we have outlined already (original tweets, genuine @replies, and retweets), as well as the occurrence of URLs in any such tweets. It is again obvious that there are distinct differences in communicative patterns between hashtags: Most obviously, a small number of cases consist overwhelmingly (at 65% or above) of original tweets that neither mention nor reply to other users. These cases (and indeed, all hashtags with more than 50% original tweets) are also marked by the relative absence of URLs in tweets; the vast majority of this group of hashtags contain URLs in less than 20% of all tweets, while the average percentage of tweets with URLs for the remainder of our hashtags is close to 50%.

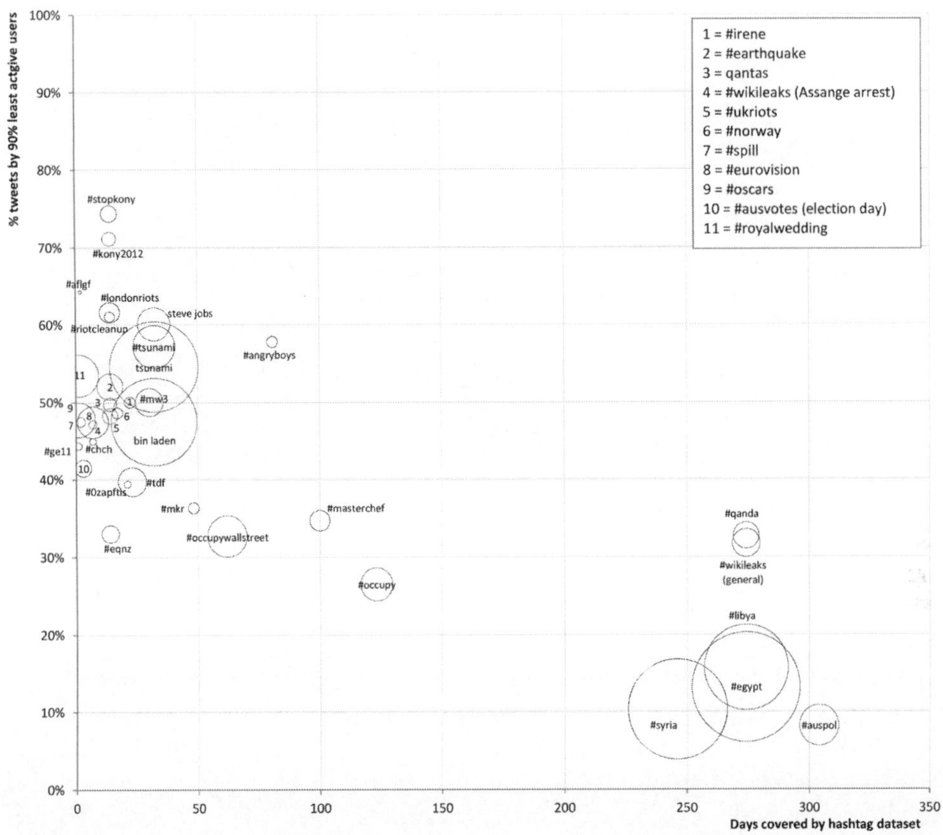

FIGURE 2 Hashtag longevity compared to percentage of tweets contributed by 90% least active users (size of data points indicates total number of tweets for each hashtag/keyword case).

It is notable in this context that hashtags that exhibit a large percentage of original tweets share a number of key contextual characteristics. For the most part, these hashtags relate to major media events, ranging from internationally televised entertainment broadcasts (#eurovision, #royalwedding, #oscars) through important sporting events (#tdf for the Tour de France, #aflgf for the Australian Football League Grand Final, #nrlgf for the Australian National Rugby League Grand Final), to popular daily or weekly television shows (the Australian reality TV programs *Masterchef* and *My Kitchen Rules*—#mkr—the sitcom *Angry Boys*, or the political talk show *Q&A*). Other Australian political events—such as #spill for the 2010 partyroom challenge against Prime Minister Kevin Rudd, or the #ausvotes discussion around election day 2010—also fit this model, as they were (or for #spill, rapidly became) major media events in their own right.

On the other hand, hashtags that saw a substantial amount of retweeting, and comparatively few original tweets, largely fall into a category that

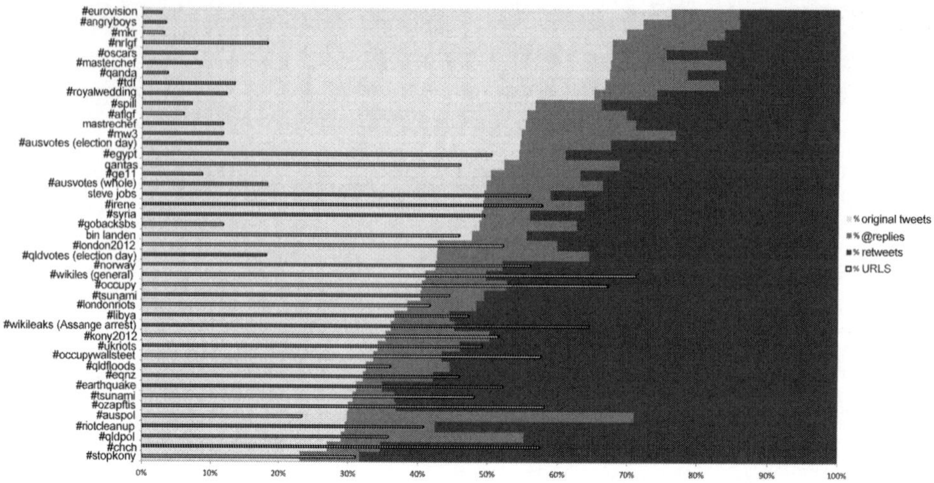

FIGURE 3 Relative percentages of different tweets types across all hashtags. (Note that the percentage of URLs is shown on a separate scale, as URLs can occur across all three tweet types.)

may be best described as "breaking news" or "rapid information dissemination"; they include, most obviously, many hashtags related to natural disasters, from #eqnz (and the alternative #chch, short for Christchurch) through #earthquake and #tsunami (both relating specifically to the March 2011 event in Japan), to #qldfloods, as well as to civil unrest (from #libya through #occupywallstreet to the London #riotcleanup). Additional examples for this category are #stopkony (an orchestrated viral marketing campaign that to some extent behaved like a crisis event) and #0zapftis (a scandal around a Trojan horse virus developed by German intelligence services for covert investigation purposes). Generally, such retweet-heavy hashtags also contain a substantial number of tweets with URLs: On average, half of all tweets in hashtags with more than 50% retweets contain URLs.

Between these two key metrics, patterns in genuine @replies for each case move somewhat more randomly, and this category generally accounts only for a relatively small percentage of tweets in each data set (with @replies constituting more than 41% of all tweets, #auspol is the one major exception to this rule; this may be related to the very well-established, dominant group of lead users in this case). In this context, a limitation of our hashtag-based Twitter research approach must be noted: As users respond to hashtagged tweets, they frequently do not again include the hashtag in their @replies, and such non-hashtagged replies are therefore not included in our data sets. Those users who do include a hashtag in their @replies, by contrast, usually do so explicitly to make their responses visible to a wider audience again; hashtagged @reply conversations are in essence performed in front of a larger public, in other words, but constitute a special case. For this reason, the following discussion largely focuses on the complementary metrics of original tweets and retweets only, as well as on the presence of URLs.

TOWARD A TYPOLOGY OF HASHTAGS

These observations enable the development of a tentative typology of hashtag events, based on the activity metrics which are observable in each case. For the data sets we have examined here, Figure 4 plots the percentage of URLs in tweets against the percentage of retweets in the overall data set, and indicates the combined contribution of lead and highly active users through the size of each data point.

On this graph, two distinct clusters of hashtag cases emerge. At the center of Figure 4 is a cluster that mainly contains hashtags relating to crises and other breaking news events. These range from natural disasters to political protests and civil unrest. This group of hashtags is characterized by both substantial posting of links to further information, and significant retweeting

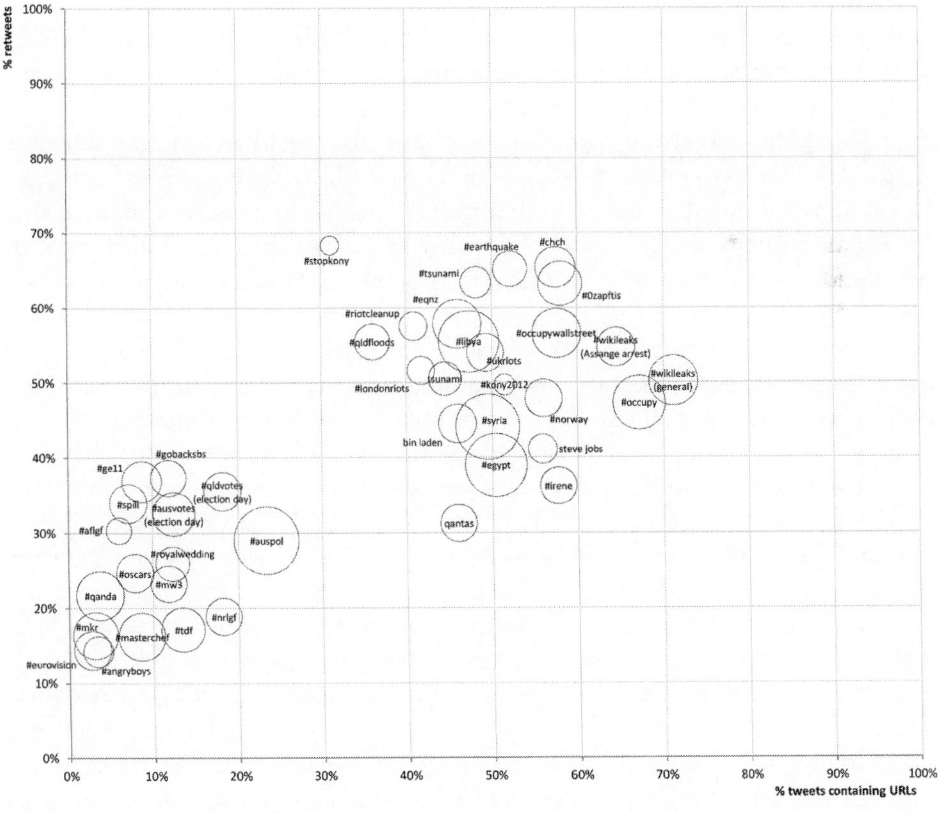

FIGURE 4 Percentage of URLs in tweets versus percentage of retweets among all tweets (size of data points shows combined contribution of lead users and highly active users).

activity. We suggest, therefore, that it is largely centered around a shared practice of *gatewatching* (Bruns, 2005): the collaborative identification, sharing, and passing along of situationally relevant information, here especially in the context of "acute events" (Burgess & Crawford, 2011).

Indeed, it is notable for this cluster of hashtags that most natural disasters, except for the #irene hashtag, for the 2011 Hurricane Irene, are positioned toward the top of the cluster (indicating an especially high percentage of retweets). This may indicate a widespread desire of users to help in sharing key emergency information, and a limited interest in posting comments or other statements about to the unfolding event, while political crises attract a comparatively higher number of such comments in the form of original tweets and @replies. By contrast, on the far right of the cluster we find a number of hashtags that are related to political protest movements (#wikileaks, #occupy, and #occupywallstreet[2]). Their positioning indicates a substantial percentage of URLs being shared through the hashtag, pointing perhaps to contributors' perception of these themes as countercultural issues that are under- or misreported by mainstream media and require constant support through online social networks. In this context, it is notable that #occupywallstreet, which deals more centrally with the struggle between protesters and law enforcement in New York, and the subset of #wikileaks activity around the arrest of Julian Assange share more similarities with the overall crisis cluster than the longer term #wikileaks and #occupy hashtags.

In addition to these hashtags, we have also included metrics for keyword data sets covering mentions of Steve Jobs following his death, for Osama bin Laden after his death in a raid on his Abbottabad compound, and for the Australian airline Qantas during a global grounding of all flights by management in response to an industrial dispute. Of these, the activity metrics for Jobs and bin Laden show strong similarities to other crisis events, pointing to similar gatewatching and news-sharing activities in the context of these breaking news events. The Qantas event behaves somewhat differently, due to a comparatively lower percentage of retweets (and thus a larger number of tweets making original comments). This is in keeping with the significant political implications of the event, beyond the international air transport crisis it caused. Further, we also include the keyword data set for "tsunami" in addition to the hashtag #tsunami, and find a comparatively smaller percentage of retweets for the keyword case. This indicates, not unexpectedly, that hashtagged tweets are more likely to be found and retweeted than non-hashtagged messages, but also points to the likelihood that overall Twitter activity patterns around crisis events, beyond their hashtagged core, are broadly similar to those for the crisis hashtag itself.

Finally, we find the #kony2012 hashtag at the center of the crisis cluster, while its cousin #stopkony is present as an outlier in the overall graph, with a very substantial percentage of retweets but comparatively few URLs. Further analysis must determine the reasons for the latter hashtag's divergent behavior, but it appears sensible that #kony2012, a campaign designed to be disseminated virally and with reference to further information on the campaign Website, and videos on YouTube, would show similar tendencies to the crisis hashtags. In essence, we may understand #kony2012 (and similar viral campaigns) as a deliberately "manufactured" crisis.

A second distinct cluster of hashtags is located in the bottom left quadrant of the graph. The hashtags assembled here are characterized by a very low percentage of URLs in each data set, as well as a comparatively low percentage of retweets. Put differently, these hashtags are mainly used to post original tweets and a limited amount of @replies, with few references to additional information outside of Twitter. The hashtags assembled in the acute events cluster are largely concerned with information sharing, whereas the hashtags in this second cluster are focused on original commentary.

Further, the majority of these hashtags are clearly related to mainstream media events, as we have already seen in the discussion of Figure 3. We therefore interpret these hashtags as cases in which Twitter functions as a backchannel for live events (especially as these events are broadcast by national and international television). These hashtags, in other words, support a shared experience of "audiencing" (e.g., Fiske, 1992): of talking back at the television (or at the live event), along with thousands of other viewers. This sense of temporary, imagined community persists even if—as our data show—actual direct interaction between users through hashtagged @replies and retweets remains relatively rare; it may be sufficient to observe the stream of hashtagged comments, even without engaging with and replying to them. Such a sense of community is further enhanced, of course, if—as is increasingly common practice—television shows include selected tweets from the hashtag stream in an on-screen ticker.

In this cluster, too, further subdivisions can be observed. Interaction through retweets is lowest for sporting and other entertainment events, while political themes attract a somewhat larger percentage of retweets—the #qldvotes, #ausvotes, and #ge11 (for the 2011 Irish general election) hashtags on their respective election days, as well as #spill (for the 2010 Australian political leadership crisis), are located toward the top of this cluster. *Go Back to Where You Came From* (#gobacksbs), while in principle a reality TV show, must similarly be included here, as it thematized the highly controversial theme of asylum seeker policy in Australia. By contrast, it is notable that the hashtag for the overtly political talk show *Q&A* does not show a retweet rate that is comparable to other political backchannel cases, for reasons that remain as yet unclear. Finally, while not immediately connected to any one mainstream media channel or show, the well-established #auspol hashtag, hosting a continuous discussion of Australian political events, appears to operate much like the other hashtags within this cluster. It may be understood, therefore, as an aggregate backchannel to mainstream political news reporting in the country, rather than as collective effort to engage in gatewatching or other citizen journalism activities.

In discussing both these clusters, it is important to note that they emerge from our analysis even in spite of the widely divergent time frames for these individual hashtag cases (ranging from hours and days to close to a year) and the varying sizes of the hashtags' user bases (from less than 10,000 to more than 2 million participants). This points to the fact that these patterns of activity reflect standard uses of Twitter, which participants engage in as the theme and purpose of the hashtag demand it. It appears that the backchannel to a minor television series does not operate much differently from that for a global media event, and the response to a natural disaster does not change substantially as a greater number of people are affected.

Similarly, while (as shown earlier) the dominance of leading user groups appears to be related to the longevity of a hashtag, the activity patterns that we have observed here do not depend on the activities of that leadership group alone, as Figure 5 demonstrates. It explores the presence of any correlations between the combined contributions made by the top 10% of most active users, and the percentage of URLs in the total data set, and finds no significant connections between these metrics. A corresponding graph comparing the contributions of leading users and the percentage of retweets would similarly yield no correlations.

This is an important observation, as it shows activity patterns in a hashtag, as measured by the percentage of retweets or URLs, to be independent of the internal makeup of the hashtag community, as measured through the 1/9/90 distinction between user groups. In Figure 5, the group of backchannel hashtags at the bottom of the graph remains clearly separate from the group of acute event hashtags at the center. The same is true for the percentage of retweets in each hashtag. Leading and peripheral users may be different in many respects, but their understanding of acute events and shared audiencing experiences appears to be similar nonetheless.

CONCLUSION

What emerges from this wide-ranging comparison of participation patterns across a diverse collection of hashtag data sets is that Twitter activities, especially around defined themes and events, are far from random, but instead appear to be governed by a number of standard practices. Of these, the practices of gatewatching and audiencing are most obviously visible in our analysis, and relate clearly to the underlying themes of the hashtags we have examined. A standard response to the emergence of breaking news and other acute events is the tendency to find, share, and reshare relevant information, resulting in a high rate of URLs and retweets. By contrast, for live,

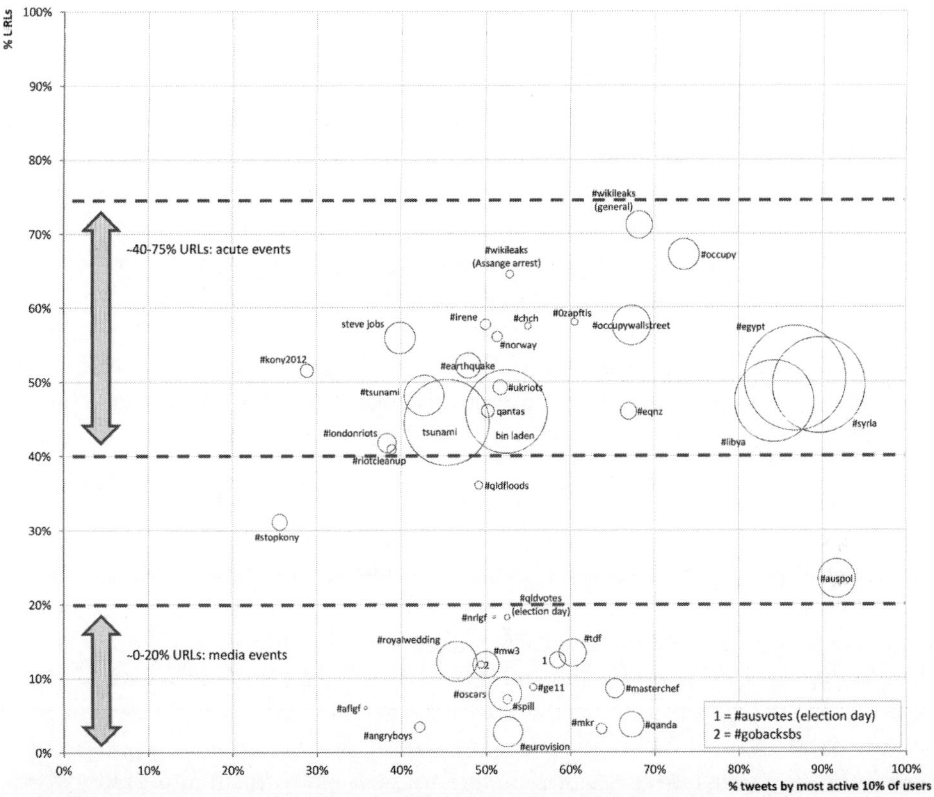

FIGURE 5 Percentage of tweets contributed by lead and highly active users vs. percentage of URLs in tweets (size of data points shows total number of tweets per hashtag).

mainstream media events Twitter acts as a backchannel, containing mainly original commentary that does not engage with the tweets of others or provide a substantial number of links to further information.

For any research dealing with Twitter data, it must be noted that due to the vagaries of working with the Twitter API itself, as well as because of unavoidable disruptions caused by regular maintenance to the university servers on which *yourTwapperkeeper* was run, the data sets thus created do not constitute an entirely comprehensive corpus of all tweets that included the specific keywords. Indeed, it is true that unless the Twitter API can be trusted to deliver all matching tweets without disruption, no study of Twitter that uses these processes can possibly achieve 100% accuracy. Further, as the API is the only access point to large-scale Twitter data which is available to researchers outside of Twitter itself, there is no opportunity to independently verify the quality of the data set. This is a necessary and unavoidable limitation that does not invalidate the findings of studies such as ours, however. Any sufficiently complex system of communication will suffer from a certain level of message loss.

Furthermore, it has to be considered that the types of topical hashtags addressed here are not the only ones that may be observed on Twitter. Further research is required to establish similar metrics for a wider range of Twitter events and to compare them with the metrics we have presented here. For example, it may well be possible that a greater number of counter-culture and protest politics hashtags may exhibit similar patterns to what we have already observed for #wikileaks and #occupy, forming their own distinct cluster of cases. The intracluster distinctions we have noted for both the acute events and the backchannel cluster may also turn out to be more pronounced as more examples are added. Further, it must also be remembered that the uses of Twitter continue to evolve, especially also as a consequence of each major new event. While in combination our data sets cover a period of some 2 years, it remains to be seen whether future events will continue to show similar patterns of activity.

At the same time, if these patterns are indeed consistent across a larger number of cases and for the longer term, then our findings may also open up possibilities to operationalize them in the detection of new Twitter events. It may be possible, for example, to distinguish new acute events from other hashtags by calculating their activity metrics. This could be of use for media monitoring and emergency operations, as it would point to the emergence of crisis events purely on the basis of activity metrics, even if relevant keywords have not yet been identified. Further, if—as our examination of a handful of keyword archives appears to suggest—non-hashtagged keywords behave largely similarly to their related hashtags, this may support the identification of acute events (and their distinction from other trending topics) before users have even agreed on a standard hashtag to adopt.

Finally, our research points to the potential of understanding patterns of Twitter activity at large scale, beyond (but building on) the study of individual communicative events. Such "big data" research (boyd & Crawford 2012), drawing on comprehensive access to user activity data through platform APIs, remains in its infancy but is set to generate significant new opportunities for researchers in the humanities and allied disciplines. Current work on Twitter, such as the research presented here, will be able to be usefully combined and compared with studies of other (social) media platforms in order to develop a more comprehensive and detailed picture of information and communication flows in society. In turn, this may provide the basis for a more sophisticated understanding both of the place of social media in society, and of potential points of leverage for relevant institutions (e.g., governments, media, or emergency services) as they seek to engage with and influence such information flows.

But while this article has focused almost exclusively on the examination of large-scale, quantitative patterns in Twitter data sets of considerable size, this should not be misunderstood to privilege such quantitative research over other approaches. Rather, we close by noting the substantial opportunities for qualitative and combined quantitative/qualitative research that also exist in this field (e.g., Krüger, Stieglitz, & Potthoff, 2012). To begin with, the quantitative approaches to understanding communicative patterns on Twitter that we have introduced here provide an opportunity to pinpoint specific areas for further detailed, qualitative investigation (for a more detailed discussion, also see Bruns & Stieglitz, in press). A focus on the communicative activities of representatives of the different groups of lead, highly active, and least active users that we have introduced in this article enables an examination of a variety of distinct tweeting styles within the same hashtag exchange. For example, representatives of each group could also be studied in much greater detail through in-depth ethnographic work, or engaged through survey or interview techniques, to better understand these diverse approaches to using Twitter in specific communicative contexts.

What must be noted in this context is that the process of generating overall headline metrics for each of these data sets does not destroy the data sets themselves, which remain available for much closer, tweet-by-tweet analysis. So, for example, for data sets that follow the overall gatewatching pattern of collaborative sourcing and sharing information that appears to be common to crisis events, a possible avenue for further research is the qualitative (or mixed-methods) study of how these patterns emerge in each case and of whether these processes of emergence generally follow similar steps. Potential questions to be addressed here include how groups of lead users crystallize from the early participant base; how they come to structure their activities as the acute event unfolds; and how common principles and shared understandings of how to engage with the event are established in each case. Such questions (and similar questions that apply to the noncrisis events among the data sets we have examined here) may be addressed, inter alia, through a close, qualitative reading of the relevant tweets in the data set, through ethnographic studies of user communities, or through other methods drawn from media, cultural and communication studies, anthropology, or the social sciences. The metrics that we have outlined here, and their utilization for a bird's-eye comparison of large-scale communicative events on Twitter, are intended to serve as a useful, necessary starting point for such further research endeavors.

NOTES

1. A number of equivalent user conventions for marking messages as retweets now exist, and are included in this figure; in addition to the most common variant RT *@user* [message], we tested for MT @ *user* [message] (for "manual tweet"), [message] (via *@user*), and "*@user* [message]" (username and original message enclosed in quotation marks), which are also common, with or without added comments from the retweeting user. A second retweeting mechanism was introduced by Twitter itself, by providing a "retweet button" next to each tweet displayed on its Website or in Twitter clients; this mechanism passes along the original tweet verbatim and in full length, without inserting the "RT *@user*" into the message. Many Twitter clients—including the version of the Twitter Website optimized for mobile devices—now

offer a choice between the two formats (cf. Bruns, 2012). Because, contrary to "manual" retweets, such "button" retweets do not result in a new message but simply add to the metadata of the original tweet, they are not captured by our Twitter tracking solution and are therefore excluded from the data sets it captures. This is an unavoidable gap in the data sets, resulting in a systematic underestimation of retweeting activity. It is possible, however, to extrapolate overall retweeting activities from the patterns of "manual" retweeting.

2. We consider such protest movements, which largely remain focused on leading nations in the West, to be distinct from in the civil unrest in Libya, Egypt, or Syria, whose hashtags are located at the center of the cluster.

REFERENCES

boyd, d., & Crawford, K. (2012). *Critical questions for big data. Information, Communication and Society, 15*(5), 662–679.

boyd, d., Golder, S., & Lotan, G. (2010, January). *Tweet, tweet, retweet: Conversational aspects of retweeting on Twitter.* Presented at HICSS-43, Kauai, Hawai'i. Retrieved from http://www.danah.org/papers/TweetTweetRetweet.pdf

Bruns, A. (2005). *Gatewatching: Collaborative online news production.* New York, NY: Peter Lang.

Bruns, A. (2012). Ad hoc innovation by users of social networks: The case of Twitter. *ZSI Discussion Paper* 16. Retrieved from https://www.zsi.at/object/publication/2186

Bruns, A., & Burgess, J. (2011a). #ausvotes: How Twitter covered the 2010 Australian federal election. *Communication, Politics & Culture, 44*(2), 37–56.

Bruns, A., & Burgess, J. (2011b, August). *The use of Twitter Hashtags in the formation of* ad hoc *publics.* Paper presented at the 6th European Consortium for Political Research General Conference, University of Iceland, Reykjavík. Retrieved from http://eprints.qut.edu.au/46515

Bruns, A., & Liang, E. (2012). Tools and methods for capturing Twitter data during natural disasters. *First Monday, 17*(4). Retrieved from http://firstmonday.org/htbin/cgiwrap/bin/ojs/index.php/fm/article/view/3937/3193

Bruns, A., & Stieglitz, S. (in press). Metrics for understanding communication on Twitter. In K. Weller, A. Bruns, J. Burgess, M. Mahrt, & C. Puschmann (Eds.), *Twitter and society.* New York, NY: Peter Lang.

Bruns, A., Burgess, J., Crawford, K., & Shaw, F. (2012). *#qldfloods and @QPSMedia: Crisis communication on Twitter in the 2011 South East Queensland floods.* Brisbane: ARC Centre of Excellence for Creative Industries and Innovation. Retrieved from http://cci.edu.au/floodsreport.pdf

Bruns, A., Highfield, T., & Burgess, J. (in press). The Arab Spring and its social media audiences: English and Arabic Twitter users and their networks. *American Behavioural Scientist.*

Burgess, J., & Crawford, K. (2011, October). *Social media and the theory of the acute event.* Paper presented at Internet Research 12.0—Performance and Participation, Seattle, WA.

Cheng, J., Sun, A., Hu, D., & Zeng, D. (2011). An information diffusion-based recommendation framework for micro blogging. *Journal of the Association of Information Systems, 12*(7), 463–486.

Cheong, F., & Cheong, C. (2011). Social media data mining: A social network analysis of tweets during the 2010-2011 Australian floods. *Proceedings of the Pacific Asia Conference on Information Systems*, Paper 46. Retrieved from http://aisel.aisnet.org/pacis2011/46

Christensen, C. (2011). Twitter revolutions? Addressing social media and dissent. *Communication Review, 14(3)*, 155–157.

Conover, M. D., Ratkiewicz, J., Francisco, M., Gonalves, B., Flammini, A., & Menczer, F. (2011). Political polarization on Twitter. *Proceedings of the 5th International Conference on Weblogs and Social Media*. AAAI Press.

Deller, R. (2011). Twittering on: Audience research and participation using Twitter. *Participations, 8*(1). Retrieved from http://www.participations.org/Volume%208/Issue%201/deller.htm

Dröge, E., Maghferat, P., Puschmann, C., Verbina, J., & Weller, K. (2011). Konferenz-Tweets. Ein Ansatz zur Analyse der Twitter-Kommunikation bei wissenschaftlichen Konferenzen. *Proceedings of the 12th International Symposium for Information Science*. Verlag Werner Hülsbusch. Retrieved from http://ynada.com/pubs/isi2010.pdf

Fiske, J. (1992). Audiencing: A cultural studies approach to watching television. *Poetics, 21*(4), 345–359.

Hughes, A., & Palen, L. (2009). Twitter adoption and use in mass convergence and emergency events. *International Journal of Emergency Management, 6*(3–4), 248–260.

Krishnamurthy, B., Phillipa, G., & Arlitt, M. (2008). A few chirps about Twitter. *Proceedings of the first workshop on online social networks (WOSN ′08)*. ACM publications (pp. 19–24). doi:10.1145/1397735.1397741

Krüger, N., Stieglitz, S. & Potthoff, T. (2012). Brand communication on Twitter—A case study on Adidas. *Proceedings of the 16th Pacific Asia Conference on Information Systems*, paper 161. Retrieved from http://aisel.aisnet.org/pacis2012/161

Larsson, A. O., & Moe, H. (2011). Studying political microblogging: Twitter users in the 2010 Swedish election campaign. *New Media & Society, 14*(5), 729–747.

Lotan, G., Ananny, M., Gaffney, D., & boyd, d. (2011). The revolutions were tweeted: Information flows during the 2011 Tunisian and Egyptian revolutions. *International Journal of Communication, 5*, 1375–1405.

Marwick, A. E., & boyd, d. (2011). I tweet honestly, I tweet passionately: Twitter users, context collapse, and the imagined audience. *New Media & Society, 13*(1), 114–133.

Mendoza, M., Poblete, B., & Castillo, C. (2010). Twitter under crisis: Can we trust what we RT? *1st Workshop on Social Media Analytics (SOMA '10)*. Washington, DC, July 25.

Palen, L., Starbird, K., Vieweg, S., & Hughes, A. (2010). Twitter-based information distribution during the 2009 Red River Valley flood threat. *Bulletin of the American Society for Information Science and Technology, 36*(5), 13–17.

Papacharissi, Z. (2011). Conclusion: A networked self. In Z. Papacharissi (Ed.), *A networked self: Identity, community and culture on social network sites* (pp. 304–318). New York, NY: Routledge.

Park, J., Cha, M., Kim, H., & Jeong, J. (2011). Managing bad news in social media: A case study on Domino's Pizza crisis. *Proceedings of the ICWSM 2012*. AAAI

Press. Retrieved from www.aaai.org/ocs/index.php/ICWSM/ICWSM12/paper/view/4672

Stieglitz, S., & Dang-Xuan, L. (2012). Social media and political communication—A social media analytics framework. *Social Network Analysis and Mining*. doi 10.1007/s13278-012-0079-3

Stieglitz, S., & Dang-Xuan, L. (in press). Emotions and information diffusion in social media—An investigation of sentiment of microblogs and sharing behavior. *Journal of Management Information Systems.*

Stieglitz, S., & Krüger, N. (2011). Analysis of sentiments in corporate Twitter communication—A case study on an issue of Toyota. *Proceedings of the 22nd Australasian Conference on Information Systems*, paper 29. Retrieved from http://aisel.aisnet.org/acis2011/29

Suh, B., Hong, L., Pirolli, P., & Chi, E. (2010). Want to be retweeted? Large scale analytics on factors impacting retweet in Twitter network. *Proceedings of the IEEE International Conference on Social Computing*, IEEE Computer Society (pp. 177–184). Retrieved from http://www.parc.com/content/attachments/want-to-be-retweeted.pdf

Tedjamulia, S. J. J., Dean, D. L., Olsen, D. R., & Albrecht, C. C. (2005). Motivating content contributions to online communities: Toward a more comprehensive theory. *Proceedings of the 38th Annual Hawaii International Conference on System Science*, paper 193b. Retrieved from http://ieeexplore.ieee.org/stamp/stamp.jsp?tp=&arnumber=1385630&tag=1

Tumasjan, A., Sprenger, T., Sandner, P., & Welpe, L. (2011). Election forecasts with Twitter: How 140 characters reflect the political landscape. *Social Science Computer Review, 29*(4), 402–418.

Twitter. (2012, March). *Twitter turns six.* Retrieved from http://blog.twitter.com/2012/03/twitter-turns-six.html

Vis, F. (2012, 24 Jan.). Reading the riots on Twitter: Who tweeted the riots? *Researching Social Media.* Retrieved from http://researchingsocialmedia.org/2012/01/24/reading-the-riots-on-twitter-who-tweeted-the-riots

Weller, K., Dröge, E., & Puschmann, C. (2011). *Citation analysis in Twitter: Approaches for defining and measuring information flows within tweets during scientific conferences.* #MSM2011—1st Workshop on Making Sense of Microposts, Heraklion, Greece, May 30. Retrieved from http://files.ynada.com/papers/msm2011.pdf

Yardi, S., & boyd, d. (2010). Dynamic debates: An analysis of group polarization over time on twitter. *Bulletin of Science, Technology and Society, 20,* 1–8.

YourTwapperkeeper. (2012). Retrieved from https://github.com/jobrieniii/yourTwapperKeeper

Communities of Communication: Making Sense of the "Social" in Social Media

PASCAL JÜRGENS
University of Mainz, Mainz, Germany

As social media usage permeates people's lives, an increasing portion of their daily behavior leaves digital traces to be used by researchers. Social scientists can hope to gain new insight into the previously hidden but digitally recorded aspects of our digital social lives. Beyond aggregate and individual-level studies of user behavior, the digital traces also enable scientific examination of the structure of social interaction through networks. At the same time, the large scale and networked nature of social media data pose a new set of challenges to be overcome through the development of sound methodologies. We take stock of current methodological promises and challenges in social media analysis. Community detection, a set of methods for the discovery of closely knit groups, is then presented as an intermediary step that enables application of existing traditional and network analytical approaches in a smaller setting more suited to social scientific questions. In closing, we argue that this network proximity-based clustering is often more useful for social media analysis than demographic grouping.

INTRODUCTION

In recent years, social media have maturedboth in terms of design and in terms of user adoption rates—to become a platform for rich expression and exchange for a highly diverse user base, attracting intense scholarly interest.

Even so, a large part of their potential is still untapped. The defining elements—the social environment and the interactions within it—are only insufficiently captured by individual and aggregate user data. If we aim at explaining behavior in such a setting, we need to incorporate the social structure itself into research designs and study its influence. Despite recent major advances, an established social scientific methodology for capturing the particular social characteristics of digital observations is only just emerging. So far, the social sciences have continued to rely on small studies with classic content analysis, survey, and experimental designs. The study of online networks, however, remains mostly a domain of the new strand of complexity research that borrows heavily from mathematics (compare Mitchell [2009] and Lazer [2011]). This disciplinary schism leaves social scientists lacking in ways to capture and describe the network structure—arguably the most interesting information provided by social networking sites. Above all, the vast amount of available data poses a challenge even without taking the relational structure into account.

We seek to show how research on computer-mediated communication can nevertheless benefit from employing observational data (digital traces), especially in the form of networks. This discussion is composed of three parts. Following a brief digression of the role of online research in general, we outline the opportunities and challenges that these new data sources harbor. Advantages and pitfalls related to the acquisition and analysis are discussed, especially insofar as they determine the validity of inferences. Next, a very short overview of network analysis and its applications is given. Finally, we argue that a set of computational methods for identifying communities of communication can provide a crucial clustering mechanism that helps to alleviate some of the challenges. It allows researchers to bridge the gap between network and existing approaches by breaking up large data sets into sensible smaller units, whereas traditional methods and theories are joined by working intuition and explorability as well as a canon of rigorous network analytical metrics.

Since it is both somewhat interdisciplinary and touches on a rather new topic, this discussion requires a brief declaration about terminology: We indiscriminately use the terms "social media" and "social networking sites" (SNS) when speaking about technological platforms on the Net that enable and are predominantly used for human-to-human communication. "Social network analysis" is a broad name for any empirical approach to study those. We also skip the discussion of the terminology of "medium" online and employ it alongside "platform" and "channel" to refer to separate services online that differ in structure, user base, and often owner (a newspaper website and Facebook would be two platforms). Unless noted otherwise, "network analysis" refers to the set of quantitative methods (chiefly developed in sociology) that deals with the mathematical analysis of networks and has been summarized by Wasserman and Faust (1994). Finally, the shared attempt to enrich social scientific online research by importing methods borrowed from mathematics, physics and computer science is referred to as "computational social science," even though similar concepts exist with different names (such as the "Digital Methods" approach of Rogers, 2009).

THE VIRTUAL AS REALITY

With Internet adoption in industrialized nations growing closer to saturation level (International Telecommunication Union, 2011, Pew Research Center, 2011, for Germany cf. van Eimeren & Frees, 2012) and time spent online developing alongside, online activity covers an expanding and increasingly relevant part of people's lives. Internet research is no longer constrained to the scrutiny of a small, unrepresentative fraction of media use. At the same time, the wide variety of possible online activities spreads across an even wider variety of platforms, each with its own set of possibly influential technological constraints. So while the formerly encapsulated "virtual" has taken over a meaningful share of people's time and lives, it remains difficult to grasp using traditional research on media use. Representative surveys simply cannot capture the breadth and detail of possible Internet uses and their interactions with "ordinary" daily life, while site-specific research (such as through interviews) lacks generalizability. An alternate approach was proposed by Richard Rogers (2009) in his "Digital Methods" program, in which he argues that it has become necessary to study behavior on the web in its own right and using its own paradigms. Only by performing "medium specific" (p. 11) research, following the deep technological structure and utilizing the web's own "digital objects" (such as links), can the true and potentially new characteristics of digital platforms be entirely understood. Nonetheless, the medium-specific approach needs to offer a way to eventually yield a coherent overall picture. Rogers believes that by closely tracking the technological design with new methods (a strategy he calls "Web epistemology," p.12), results will eventually combine to form a sensible overall picture of society (p. 10ff). His examples include testing hypotheses of language change over time on the Internet and extrapolating to the societal level (p. 9). While we agree that the limited case of testing for change works quite well, our belief is that it does not remove the need for the comparison of results across platforms. Quite the opposite: Web epistemology enables the use of quantitative methods that both attach to and abstract from the web's own digital objects (such as links or "friendship" relations in Facebook).

Motivations for using the digital methods approach, the insights that can be expected, and our argument for the use of network analysis are all closely interwoven with the peculiar nature of digital observational data. In the following two sections, we therefore expand on Rogers's theses and examine the core opportunities and challenges, especially pertaining to the validity of inferences. We hope that this will provide researchers with some background that facilitates both evaluating studies and deciding on methodology for themselves.

OPPORTUNITIES IN SOCIAL MEDIA ANALYSIS

Recent years have seen a surge in the innovative use of digital traces data for all sorts of tasks. Scholars have investigated global mood swings (Golder & Macy, 2011), tracked the use and evolution of phrases in elections (Leskovec, Backstrom, & Kleinberg, 2009), traced political trenches across the blogosphere (Adamic & Glance, 2005) and explained virtual gold exchanges in online games as clandestine networks (Keegan, Ahmed, Williams, Srivastava, & Contractor, 2010), to name but a few. Behavioral data as a by-product of Internet use have opened the way for new methods, for new research designs, and to unexplored phenomena. In many ways, these sources of insight shed old limitations and enable approaches that were impossible before. There are additional advantages beyond the extended scope as well: Several characteristics make digital behavioral data especially attractive for research if properly used. The benefits can be roughly classified into four categories: performance, versatility, economics of research, and epistemology.

1. Performance: Digital traces can exhibit higher measurement precision, higher resolution, and less sampling bias, mainly in cases where large amounts of data are present. As the act of data acquisition is nonreactive, measurement-induced biases (Kreuter, Presser, & Tourangeau, 2008) are eliminated. Given that the technological prerequisites are met, data can be collected from an entire population (such as all users of a web page), eliminating sampling issues. It should be noted that the observations only yield unbiased data *pertaining to user behavior within the respective communication channel*, not unbiased data with regard to human behavior per se. As such, the observations need to be interpreted within the technological constraints of the particular service. As argued earlier, this should not be seen as an impediment but rather as a methodologically necessary consequence of the increasing digitalization of human lives.
2. Versatility: By including "metadata," information not directly related to the original content but to the context of its creation, social media create new dimensions of measurements. For example, the temporal dimension inherently present in logfiles and other automatically captured information allows for time-series analyses (and often causality tests). The proliferation of global positioning system (GPS)-enabled consumer devices has lead Miller (2010) to call for the extension of research in the geospatial domain. Such information—along with self-expressed nationality in profile pages, time zone settings, and so on—can also be put to use for

comparative research: The fixed technological frame creates an artificial most similar systems design that allows for the comparison of different nationalities under identical conditions. Social interactions can be seen as another example of metadata providing new measurement dimensions.

3. Economics of research: The expectation that access to digital phenomena should be easier, faster, and cheaper than nondigital research is only a logical extrapolation from general experiences. Decreasing costs for data storage should help historical research. Also, the cost structure of digital data acquisition includes a high initial investment but—once running—scales slowly. This favors large-scale data crawling projects, which in turn benefits the method's performance (already described).
4. Epistemology: Digital traces vastly facilitate replication studies (see King, 2003, 2007). Furthermore, by basing the analysis on digital objects (technological elements such as links or retweets), the responsibility of recognizing and coding observations shifts from researchers (and assistants) to a deterministic computer, eliminating one level of possible bias.

In summary, research on online phenomena gets both easier and better by following technologically predetermined structures. Before presenting network analysis as an example of such a strategy, some inherent risks should be mentioned.

CHALLENGES IN SOCIAL MEDIA ANALYSIS

Just as "digital methods" (Rogers 2009) facilitate some aspects, they suffer from drawbacks that partly stem from their novelty and are partly inherent. Again, there are four broad categories of issues: unknown distribution of features, unclear relation to offline behavior, ethics, and data logistics.

1. Unknown distribution of features: A large degree of validity issues in social media analytics and online research in general originates in the unknown structures of the net. Without knowing the base population of news websites, for example, it is hard to collect a representative sample and even harder to assess its representativeness. Often, data gathered online are aggregates in dimensions that are not immediately obvious: The observations might include an inappropriately large time span (e.g., news stories across 10 years) and geographically and culturally diverse users. Dave Karpf has pointed out the issue of temporal instability:

> the problems introduced into our research by Internet Time. The first problem is that underlying concepts, such as "The Blogosphere," are not fixed in place. They change even while we study them. The second problem is the impact that these changes can have on the ceteris paribus

> assumptions of our most robust research methods. The third problem is the set of limitations posed by publicly-available online data. Novel research techniques that make use of "Big Data" are often hobbled by the flaws embedded in that data. (Karpf, 2012, p. 17)

Special care must be taken to identify such features and design the data collection accordingly. The same applies to the collection of networks: If the underlying structure is unknown, then collecting a sample that accurately represents the overall network structure is hard (Gjoka, Kurant, Butts, & Markopoulou, 2010; Howison et al., 2011, p. 786).

2. Unclear relation to offline behavior: Clearly, mere observations can only describe phenomena that are exhibited voluntarily. Digital methods have their limits in the willingness of users to disclose information without being asked. As such, some fields, especially those concerned with underlying cognitive and affective constructs, will find little of interest in the available data. Furthermore, the relationships between online and offline behavior are not yet entirely clear and much work remains to be done. As long as it is difficult to relate online findings to existing knowledge and theories, a highly relevant set of questions remains unanswerable. The shaping influence of technology on behavior is a different perspective on the same issue.
3. Ethics: The issue of ethics in online research is twofold. First, a methodological problem arises from the connected nature of the web. Several incidents (Lewis, Kaufman, Gonzalez, Wimmer, & Christakis, 2008; Zimmer, 2010) have shown that users in anonymized datasets can be de-anonymized by linking them to other digital traces they left on the web. The second and central ethical problem is that users (through lack of knowledge, handling errors or carelessness) might make information public to the world, despite wishing to keep it private.
4. Data logistics: Even though the availability of digital data makes acquisition and analysis easier, it also brings new challenges with it. The mere amount of information necessitates powerful computers and software, as well as capable statistical methods. The fleeting nature of content online poses another problem: Information disappears frequently. A systematic approach to the collection and archival of data is required in order not to suffer from unexpected blind spots. In many cases, observational data is owned by private companies that see little incentive to cooperate with scientists, thereby effectively locking out public research (King, 2011). Finally, the technology used to access data—such as crawler programs for scraping web sites or social networks—is often error prone. A conscious effort is needed to understand, document, and test the reliability of data collection mechanisms.

Most of these issues can be alleviated by carefully designing studies with a good knowledge of the respective communication platform. They do, however, remind us that easy "ready-made" solutions, especially the statistical approaches summarized under the label of data mining, cannot produce insights without human interpretation. In practice, researchers frequently need to make (subjective) design decisions that determine a study's outcome. The following section examines how networks can be extracted from Twitter data in order to provide a palpable example of the process that turns digital traces into usable operationalizations.

PUTTING DIGITAL METHODS INTO PRACTICE

In practice, sadly, many modern social networking sites are even less amenable to social scientific research than early computer-mediated communication channels because access restrictions encumber systematic data collection. In this respect, Twitter represents a rather special case. Thanks to its predominantly public nature and the random sample feature of its API (application programming interface, it serves as an easy "test bed" for the application of existing theory and methods. For this reason, we refer to Twitter and use it as an example. This warrants a brief description of its workings. As for all SNS, the service is not without its peculiarities. Although its primary features are the creation and maintenance of lists of friends as well as the exchange of short text messages ("tweets"), its openness led to a classification as "microblogging service" (Java, Song, Finin, & Tseng, 2009), rather than a social networking site.

Four design decisions lie at the root of its difference when compared to other SNS: By default, users' text messages will be pushed to subscribers (called "followers"), but they remain publicly accessible to any inquiring Twitter or web user (for a detailed description of Twitter and the way it works, see, e.g., Huberman, Romero, & Wu, 2008; Jürgens, 2010; Jürgens & Jungherr, 2011). Hence, Twitter is a predominantly public communication channel. This stands in stark contrast to the closed nature of other SNS, where messages are usually accessible only to a small audience. Furthermore, Twitter's relationships (being a "friend" or "follower") do not need to be symmetrical (Gruzd, Wellman, & Takhteyev, 2011). A user can follow her pop idol's Twitter account, but the idol does not need to reciprocate. In such a (quite common) constellation, the user will receive the star's tweets but not vice versa (it should be noted that such asymmetrical relationships have recently been added to other networks as well). Without going into too much detail, there are two more crucial features that must be mentioned. One important aspect of Twitter usage are "retweets," which are quotes of a message that users chose to redistribute to their own followers. These can be thought of as an endorsement of (a) content and (b) the author. Retweets as a link between two Twitter users can be used to construct a network of such endorsement relationships. Finally, messages can be explicitly addressed to a user but remain publicly visible at the same time. If prefixed with the "@" character and a user name, messages are sent directly to that user, bypassing the follower/friend network. These "directed messages" are (in addition to the recipient) only visible to followers of both the sender and the recipient. If a user is mentioned in a message but not at the very beginning, then it remains visible to all the author's followers. A hypothetical example should clarify the difference: If Barack Obama sends "@nytimes I like your style!" to the New York Times then only the New York Times and those who follow both the U.S. president and the New York Times will see the message. If instead he opts to write, "I like the style of @nytimes!," all his followers (even those who do not follow @nytimes) will see the tweet. These three types of relationships (retweets, directed messages/mentions, and the friend/follower relationship) are directly amenable to observation and serve as good examples for the process by which technologically shaped phenomena can be translated into unambiguous constructs (in this case, links of a network).

Among the most drastic changes that digital traces affect in our capability to study communicative behaviors are the improved conditions for the analysis of social interactions. As shown earlier, it has become trivial to identify, classify, and capture certain types of user interactions. Before the advent of digitally logged interactions, the best way of mapping a social network was by relying on self-reported lists of friends. Not only is this an error-prone approach (Eagle, Pentland, & Lazer, 2009; Freeman, Romney, & Freeman, 1987), it is also obviously difficult to obtain enough information in order to map the "whole" network. Contrast this with the links that are constituted by an exchange of Tweets: The measurement is deterministic, and given access to the entirety of Twitter's data, it is comparatively simple to map the entire network of interactions. Ergo, network analysis has become a very appealing methodology for the analysis of social media. Following a short discussion of its uses, we bring together previous conclusions about digital methods and network analysis in order to make a case for community detection.

NETWORK ANALYSIS

Research on social networks has seen a surge in attention, especially due to the increased proliferation of SNS such as Twitter, Facebook, Google Plus, LinkedIn, and others. Studies increasingly include analyses of the network structure as a factor that previously received little attention in the field of computer mediated communication. This doesn't mean that the theoretical and methodological foundation of network studies are new. Networks have among other sources been constructed from Usenet postings (Choi & Danowski, 2006), e-mails (Keila & Skillicorn, 2006), blogs (Adamic & Glance, 2005) ,and long before them from relationships unmediated by technology with influential publications such as Merton (1968) and Granovetter (1983).

Also, compare Lazer (2011) for a short history of network analysis. Consequently, the analysis of social ties in a network-like structure can be performed on many different phenomena within many different settings.

That said, what types of questions can actually be answered by network analysis? There are two outstanding introductions, one by Lazer (2011) and one by Ward, Stovel, and Sacks (2011), both of which attempt to answer this question. They trace the development of network analysis from a political science perspective, an attempt that works quite well as a pars pro toto for social sciences in general. Lazer (2011, p. 62) distinguishes three major strands of inquiry that rely on network analysis: (a) diffusion research (diffusion of innovations, epidemiology, social influence), (b) studies of the effect of network structure on behavior, and (c) the concept of control through positions within the network (exchange theory). All three approaches are indubitably highly relevant for the study of social media. He further identifies five levels of inquiry in networks (p. 64): (a) the positional level (where within a network is one actor?), (b) the dyadic level (what influences and what are the results of a link between two actors?), (c) the triadic level (given that A knows B and C, how probable is it that B also knows C?), (d) the community level (how can one identify dense groups?), and (e) the systemic level (how do various types of networks differ in terms of global attributes such as the average distance between any two actors?). A list of quantitative metrics that are commonly employed can be found in Ward et al. (2011, p. 250). Most of the measures are presented in depth by Wasserman and Faust (1994), which remains the de facto standard work on social network analysis.

Among the simplest types of inferences here are those based on egocentric networks. Some surveys have collected information about the personal network of participants (e.g., Rössler, 1999). Such egocentric data do not map the entire network but instead concentrate on the immediate circle surrounding respondents. They offer aggregate-level insights into questions such as whether perceived issue importance of one's network influences individuals' own perceptions or not (Rössler, 1999). Since the many people and links in between each of the egocentric networks are unknown, in egocentric networks, people and links between each of the individual ego networks are unknown. The data thus cannot reveal positional information about individuals, such as their betweenness centrality, a value that captures how central a person is to information relay across the entire network: "High betweenness often implies that other nodes are dependent for access to information or valued goods" (Ward et al., 2011, p. 250).

Most advanced metrics rely on a complete map of the network. Among them are the average distance between two people, the density and measures of centrality, importance, or prestige, to name but a few. Both approaches—whole network and egocentric—allow valuable descriptions of a network. However, merely singling out the most prominent users or declaring a social network as very dense appears unsatisfactory in that it represents a very high level description of user behavior. Yet even within a single communication platform there may be many entirely separate and different groups with distinct patterns of behavior. Because all interactions are known anyway, aggregation across nonconnected groups may not always be valid. Comparing users' connectedness with respect to a secondary variable is then not enough. Precisely because our knowledge of what's actually happening on SNS is so limited, it is crucial to capture the makeup and structure of communities. Social media's success, after all, is rooted in the deeply human need to belong, to interact with a close group of peers. As Wellman and Gulia (1999, p. 345) note,"To this point, we have considered the ability of the Net to support community ties. Yet a community is more than the sum of a set of ties: its composition and network structure affects how it supplies companionship, supportiveness, information and a sense of identity."

The last part of this article introduces community detection as a method that performs clustering based on connectedness.

COMMUNITY DETECTION

Community detection methods promise to perform a task that is both obviously useful and at the same time appears to require genuine human assessment. The task involves the judgment of whether or not two users within a network structure belong to some (more or less) homogeneous group. In most cases, the methods seek out highly interconnected areas of a network and delimit them from each other. At a closer look, the methods are unlikely candidates for the task. Originating from graph partitioning theories of computer science, community detection algorithms aim to optimize a theoretical value that represents the "goodness" of a given way of dividing up the network into groups of nodes (Fortunato & Castellano, 2009). And indeed, there are several caveats that are to be considered before putting them to use.

As with other explorative aggregation approaches such as clustering, the result is defined by the algorithm. Consequently, a general definition of community remains vague: "Communities are groups of vertices which probably share common properties and/or play similar roles within the graph" (Fortunato & Castellano, 2009, p. 1142). The groups of users that form the result of an algorithm can be defined only from the algorithm's formal goal. Community detection clearly represents an exploratory tool insofar as it accentuates empirical features of the data at hand, rather than defining features such as, for example, the social–psychological sense of community theory (McMillan & Chavis, 1986) does. In most cases, the metric that algorithms attempt to optimize is called modularity (Newman & Girvan, 2004; Newman, 2006). Modularity represents a formalization of the idea that communities should contain many connections within and few outside of the group. Speaking about communities in social media, we can say that community detection identifies densely connected groups of users, that is, groups where members talk to many other members but not many outsiders.

It is important to note that like other clustering approaches (but unlike factor analysis), community detection is not a "destructive" process whose outcome is entirely separate from the original data. Instead, community membership is merely an additional attribute assigned to nodes in the network. Equipped with the results from a community detection algorithm, researchers have new options for the analysis of social media data:

1. Comparison of communities. The network's "composition and structure" (Wellman, 1999, p. 345) is well expressed by a comparison of the communities within. Their size and number indicate the fragmentation of the platform. Comparing their network parameters and topics of discussion yields an even more accurate picture of their role with regard to the entire network. For example, community analysis of Twitter communication can identify closely knit, highly active groups of users, one of which tends to be fans of the teen pop star Justin Bieber (Page, 2012). Not only will the topic composition within this group of fans differ wildly from other communities, but they might also exhibit a much higher degree of self-referentiality. At the same time, the network within will probably be highly centralized with the star occupying the center and fans rarely addressing each other.

   Another beneficial investigation is intercommunity diffusion research. It is now possible to picture the flow of information (or behavior) in terms of communities: Does information spread only internally or is it relayed among them? What is the role of "bridge" nodes?
2. Analysis of single communities: In comparison to the whole network, communities can be small enough to allow labor-intensive methods such as qualitative and quantitative content analysis. The quasi-self-contained nature of a community (as defined by the algorithms) ensure that the entirety of a "public" can be examined without fear of missing crucial aspects of their communication that may not be obvious from the content itself. Even without a full hand-coded content analysis, communities of interest can often be identified by comparing the distribution of topics (such as hashtags on Twitter). An added benefit is that although (as mentioned earlier) unbiased sampling from a network is usually not feasible, communities as the basis of analysis represent an approximately self-contained environment acting as a network of its own. The members' betweenness centrality scores, for example, are still meaningful even if the rest of the network is omitted from the calculations.

To summarize, community detection serves as a clustering step that provides two major benefits. First, it allows for the economic analysis of smaller parts of the network while preserving the social structure instead of aggregating over completely disjunctive individuals. Second, communities work well to reveal the structure and makeup of social networks, including the flow of information between them.

While the detailed design of algorithms is out of the scope of this article, we now briefly discuss two of the most prominent examples that can be easily applied through readymade software. The first is Girvan and Newman's edge betweenness algorithm (GN) (Girvan, 2002). It is based on the concept of "betweenness centrality"—a metric that describes how many (shortest) paths across the network lead through one link. One by one, the links through which the most short connections lead are removed, fragmenting the network. The GN algorithm (and some of its descendants, such as Clauset, Newman, & Moore, 2004) is probably the best known and works well for medium-sized networks. Although there is evidence that it fails to detect sensible communities in very large and dense (well-connected) networks (Leskovec, Lang, Dasgupta, & Mahoney, 2009), data sets beyond several thousand users are too large to compute in a reasonable time anyway. As is the case for most algorithms, GN does not take into account the direction of links. Figure 1 shows the communities that GN detected in a small network of political Twitter users during the German general election in 2008 (for a detailed description of the dataset, compare Jürgens & Jungherr, 2011).

The second algorithm, called "clique percolation" (CP) (Palla, Derenyi, Farkas, & Vicsek, 2005), follows a different design. It utilizes the idea that networks can be said to have choke points that separate two well-connected areas from each other. CP finds cliques, which are completely connected groups of nodes, where every node is connected to every other node, and "moves" them across the network until they reach a choke point. At these

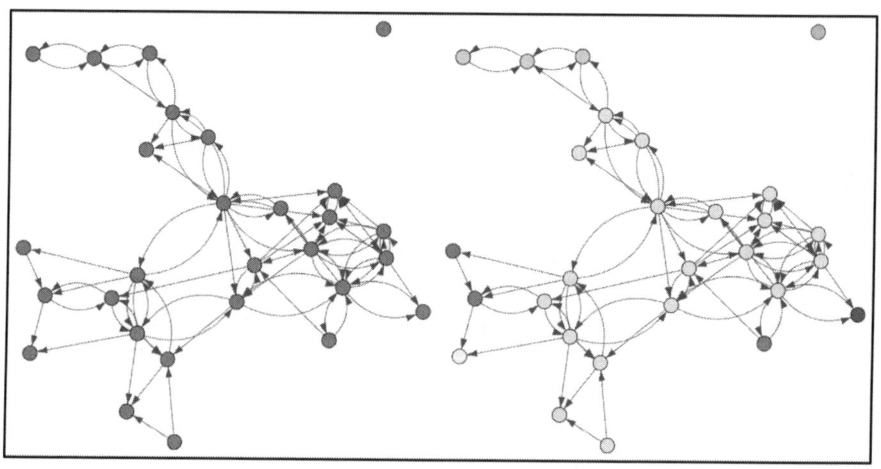

FIGURE 1 Communities detected by the Girvan–Newman algorithm (left: original network; right: colored by communities). (Figure available in color online.)

bottlenecks, the clique cannot move through because of its size. The area of the network that a clique can move to is then defined to be a community. As the algorithm increases the size of cliques, fewer and fewer communities exist. The major drawback is that for every clique size, a separate set of communities is identified and it remains the researcher's task to pick one. On the other hand, clique percolation is not only able to incorporate directed links (where cliques can only "move" in one direction), but it also allows nodes to belong to multiple cliques at the same time. Such a scenario is not only theoretically appealing but also empirically plausible, as Figure 2 illustrates. In Figure 2, a network formed by a small set of prominent Twitter users during the German general election of 2008 is traced by cliques of eight nodes. The algorithm (included in the software package CFinder, available at cfinder.org) quickly identifies an isolated component of users concerned with the uprising in Iran (pink). It also recognizes the main community of Pirate Party supporters (turquoise) and a second community that constitutes a secondary group not entirely merged in.

The field of community detection is of course steadily progressing, with newer and more capable methods developed frequently. Extensive

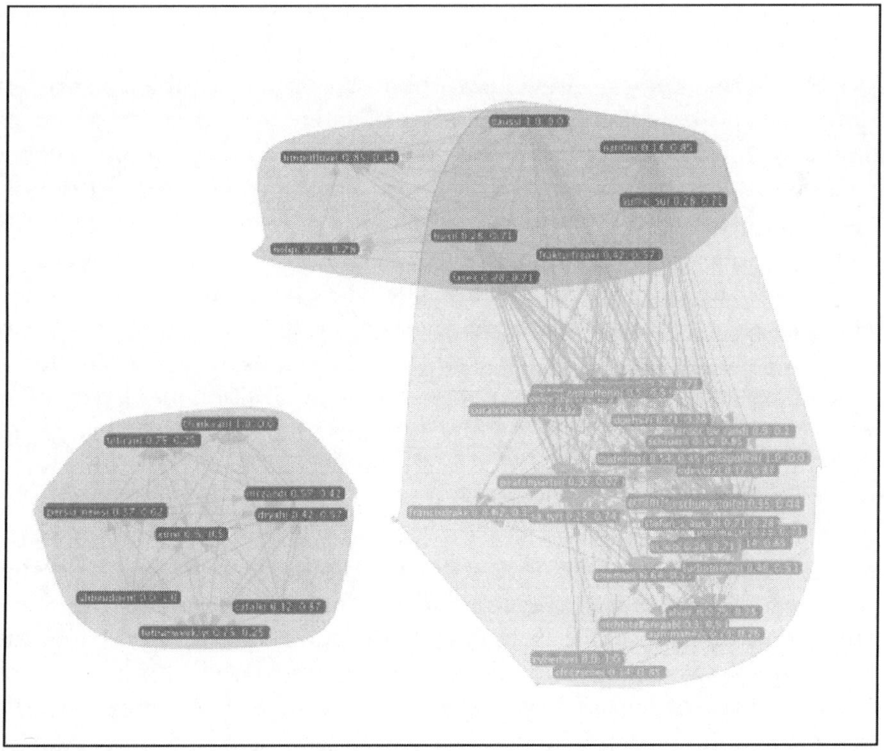

FIGURE 2 Communities detected by the clique percolation algorithm. (Figure available in color online.)

overviews and reviews can be found in Fortunato (2010), Leskovec, Lang, and Mahoney (2010), and Lancichinetti and Fortunato (2009).

As we hope to have shown, community detection is an approach that augments social media analysis by allowing researchers to closely track the empirical reality of user behavior in its networked nature. In the spirit of Rogers's (2009) digital methods program, the approach rests on an epistemological understanding of online research in its own right, merged with the rigorous capabilities of empirical methods. As such, it is not a replacement of traditional social scientific research but rather an orthogonal extension.

Where studies so far have been mainly structured according to well-known variables such as demographics, incorporating the network perspective adds social structure as an additional variable. Rogers (2009, p. 24) calls for a "post-demographic" paradigm. We would like to rather consider it a "super-demographic" paradigm, insofar as existing methods of defining objects of interest are not replaced but merely extended.

CONCLUSION

This article examined how research on computer mediated communication, specifically social media, can draw on features of digital platforms in order to (a) unlock the study of previously unknown or inaccessible phenomena, (b) increase the reliability and precision of inferences, and (c) add to the validity by incorporating platform-specific influencing factors such as technological design and network structure. Based on literature from political science, mass communication, sociology, computer science, and other relevant disciplines, we identified the core challenges and opportunities that set online research apart from traditional social science. In line with Rogers's (2009) program of digital methods, motivations for an extended research methodology were presented. We went on to identify network structure as the most important new paradigm that is made accessible but also amplified by social media. The second part of the text introduced network analysis and briefly surveyed its applications. Special attention was paid to the way in which it integrates into the context of digital methods. Using the example of Twitter, we illustrated this process in practice. The section on community detection marks the last and most advanced argument in our line of methodological advances. Communities formed by communication are an inherent feature of social media. Incorporating them into study designs diminishes some of the issues of digital traces (such as the large amount of data), making the lives of researchers easier. We also argued that they can vastly increase the validity of research where analyses are based on a coherent, relatively homogeneous sphere instead of aggregating over populations whose structure is unknown.

In conclusion, we would like to encourage scholars to make use of the digital features that the web in general and social media in particular have to offer. Even existing research designs can greatly benefit from the addition of a network analytic part. The concept of communities appears especially inviting, since it represents the most promising way of carving meaningful objects of observation from the unknown and ever-changing wilderness that is the web.

There are still many aspects of social behavior on the net that remain undetected. With the help of community detection as a lens that picks out small, meaningful groups defined by actual interaction, research can move on to survey the role of individuals within the group, their involvement in the setting of topics, and other exciting questions.

REFERENCES

Adamic, L. A., & Glance, N. (2005). The political blogosphere and the 2004 US election: Divided they blog. *Proceedings of the 3rd International Workshop on Link Discovery* (pp. 36–43). doi:10.1145/1134271.1134277

Backstrom, L., Dwork, C., & Kleinberg, J. (2007). Wherefore art thou r3579x?: Anonymized social networks, hidden patterns, and structural steganography. *Proceedings of the 16th International Conference on World Wide Web* (pp. 181–190). doi:10.1145/1242572.1242598

Choi, J. H., & Danowski, J. A. (2006). Making a global community on the Net—Global village or global metropolis? *Journal of Computer-Mediated Communication, 7*(3). doi:10.1111/j.1083-6101.2002.tb00153.x

Clauset, A., Newman, M., & Moore, C. (2004). Finding community structure in very large networks. *Physical Review E, 70*(6). doi:10.1103/PhysRevE.70.066111

Eagle, N., Pentland, A. S., & Lazer, D. (2009). Inferring friendship network structure by using mobile phone data. *Proceedings of the National Academy of Sciences, 106*(36), 15274–15278.

Fortunato, S. (2010). Community detection in graphs. *Physics Reports, 486*(3–5), 75–174.

Fortunato, S., & Castellano, C. (2009). Community structure in graphs. In *Encyclopedia of complexity and systems science* (pp. 1141–1163). Springer.

Freeman, L. C., Romney, A. K., & Freeman, S. C. (1987). Cognitive structure and informant accuracy. *American Anthropologist, 89*(2), 310–325. doi:10.1525/aa.1987.89.2.02a00020

Girvan, M. (2002). Community structure in social and biological networks. *Proceedings of the National Academy of Sciences, 99*(12), 7821–7826. doi:10.1073/pnas.122653799

Gjoka, M., Kurant, M., Butts, C. T., & Markopoulou, A. (2010). Walking in Facebook: A case study of unbiased sampling of OSNs. *INFOCOM, 2010 Proceedings IEEE* (pp. 1–9). doi:10.1109/INFCOM.2010.5462078

Golder, S. A., & Macy, M. W. (2011). Diurnal and seasonal mood vary with work, sleep, and daylength across diverse cultures. *Science, 333*(6051), 1878–1881. doi:10.1126/science.1202775

Granovetter, M. (1983). The strength of weak ties: A network theory revisited. *Sociological Theory, 1*(1), 201–233.

Gruzd, A., Wellman, B., & Takhteyev, Y. (2011). Imagining Twitter as an imagined community. *American Behavioral Scientist, 55*(10), 1294–1398.

Howison, J., Wiggins, A., & Crowston, K. (2011). Validity issues in the use of social network analysis with digital trace data. *Journal of the Association for Information Systems, 12*(12), 767–797.

Huberman, B. A., Romero, D. M., & Wu, F. (2008). Social networks that matter: Twitter under the microscope. *First Monday, 14*(1). Retrieved from http://firstmonday.org/htbin/cgiwrap/bin/ojs/index.php/fm/article/view/2317

International Telecommunication Union. (2011, September 6). *Measuring the information society 2011*. Retrieved from http://www.itu.int/ITU-D/ict/publications/idi/material/2011/MIS_2011_without_annex_5.pdf

Java, A., Song, X., Finin, T., & Tseng, B. (2009). Why we Twitter: An analysis of a microblogging community. *Advances in Web Mining and Web Usage Analysis, 5439*, 118–138. doi:10.1007/978-3-642-00528-2_7

Jungherr, A., Jürgens, P., & Schoen, H. (2011). Why the Pirate Party won the German election of 2009 or The trouble with predictions: A response to Tumasjan, A., Sprenger, T. O., Sander, P. G., & Welpe, I. M. "Predicting Elections With Twitter: What 140 Characters Reveal About Political Sentiment." *Social Science Computer Review, 30*(2), 229–234. doi:10.1177/0894439311404119

Jürgens, P. (2010). *Stell' Dir vor, Du twitterst, und keiner hört zu*. Master's thesis, Institut für Publizistik, Universität Mainz, Mainz, Germany.

Jürgens, P., & Jungherr, A. (2011). *Das Internet im Wahlkampf*. In E. J. Schweitzer & S. Albrecht, Eds., (pp. 201–225). Wiesbaden, Germany: VS Verlag für Sozialwissenschaften. doi:10.1007/978-3-531-92853-1_8

Karpf, D. (2012). Social research methods in Internet time. *Information, Communication & Society, 15*(5), 1–23. doi:10.1080/1369118X.2012.665468

Keegan, B., Ahmed, M. A., Williams, D., Srivastava, J., & Contractor, N. (2010). *Dark Gold: Statistical properties of clandestine networks in massively multiplayer online games*. SocialCom '10 Proceedings of the 2010 IEEE Second International Conference on Social Computing (pp. 201–208). doi:10.1109/SocialCom.2010.36

Keila, P. S., & Skillicorn, D. B. (2006). Structure in the Enron email dataset. *Computational and Mathematical Organization Theory, 11*(3), 183–199. doi:10.1007/s10588-005-5379-y

King, G. (2003). The future of replication. *International Studies Perspectives, 4*, 443–499.

King, G. (2007). An introduction to the dataverse network as an infrastructure for data sharing. *Sociological Methods & Research, 36*(2), 173–199. doi:10.1177/0049124107306660

King, G. (2011). Ensuring the data-rich future of the social sciences. *Science, 331*(6018), 719. doi:10.1126/science.1197448

Kreuter, F., Presser, S., & Tourangeau, R. (2008). Social desirability bias in CATI, IVR, and web surveys. *Public Opinion Quarterly, 72*(5), 847–865.

Lancichinetti, A., & Fortunato, S. (2009). Community detection algorithms: A comparative analysis. *Physical Review E, 80*(5), 056117.

Lazer, D. (2011). Networks in political science: Back to the future. *PS: Political Science and Politics, 44*(1), 61–68. doi:10.1017/51049096510001873

Lazer, D., Pentland, A. S., Adamic, L., Aral, S., Barabasi, A. L., Brewer, D., ... Van Alstyne, M. (2009). Life in the network: The coming age of computational social science. *Science (New York, NY)*, *323*(5915), 721. doi:10.1126/science.1167742

Leskovec, J., Backstrom, L., & Kleinberg, J. (2009). Meme-tracking and the dynamics of the news cycle. *Proceedings of the 15th ACM SIGKDD international conference on knowledge discovery and data mining* (pp. 497–506). doi: 10.1145/1557019.1557077

Leskovec, J., Lang, K. J., & Mahoney, M. (2010). Empirical comparison of algorithms for network community detection. *Proceedings of the 19th international conference on World Wide Web* (pp. 631–640). doi:10.1145/1772690.1772755

Leskovec, J., Lang, K. J., Dasgupta, A., & Mahoney, M. W. (2009). Community structure in large networks: Natural cluster sizes and the absence of large well-defined clusters. *Internet Mathematics*, *6*(1), 29–123. doi:10.1080/15427951.2009.10129177

Lewis, K., Kaufman, J., Gonzalez, M., Wimmer, A., & Christakis, N. (2008). Tastes, ties, and time: A new social network dataset using Facebook. com. *Social Networks*, *30*(4), 330–342.

McMillan, D. W., & Chavis, D. M. (1986). Sense of community: A definition and theory. *Journal of Community Psychology*, *14*(1), 6–23.

Merton, R. K. (1968). *Social theory and social structure*. New York, NY: Free Press.

Miller, H. J. (2010). The data avalanche is here. Shouldn't we be digging? *Journal of Regional Science*, *50*(1), 181–201. doi:10.1111/j.1467-9787.2009.00641.x

Mitchell, M. (2009). *Complexity*. New York, NY: Oxford University Press, USA.

Newman, M. E. J. (2006). Modularity and community structure in networks. *Proceedings of the National Academy of Sciences*, *103*(23), 8577–8582.

Newman, M., & Girvan, M. (2004). Finding and evaluating community structure in networks. *Physical Review E*, *69*(2). doi:10.1103/PhysRevE.69.026113

Page, R. (2012). The linguistics of self-branding and micro-celebrity in Twitter: The role of hashtags. *Discourse & Communication*, *6*(2), 181–201. doi:10.1177/1750481312437441

Palla, G., Derenyi, I., Farkas, I., & Vicsek, T. (2005). Uncovering the overlapping community structure of complex networks in nature and society. *Nature*, *435*(7043), 814–818. doi:10.1038/nature03607

Pew Research Center. (2011, December 19). *Global Digital Communication: Texting, social networking popular worldwide*. Retrieved June 7, 2012, from http://www.pewglobal.org/files/2011/12/Pew-Global-Attitudes-Technology-Report-FINAL-December-20-20111.pdf

Rogers, R. (2009). *The end of the virtual. Digital methods*. Amsterdam, The Netherlands: Amsterdam University Press.

Rössler, P. (1999). The individual agenda-designing process: How interpersonal communication, egocentric networks, and mass media shape the perception of political issues by individuals. *Communication Research*, *26*(6), 666–700. doi:10.1177/009365099026006002

van Eimeren, B., & Frees, B. (2012). 76 Prozent der Deutschen online—neue Nutzungssituationen durch mobile Endgeräte. *Media Perspektiven*, *7–8*, 362–379.

Ward, M. D., Stovel, K., & Sacks, A. (2011). Network analysis and political science. *Annual Review of Political Science*, *14*(1), 245–264. doi:10.1146/annurev.polisci.12.040907.115949

Wasserman, S., & Faust, K. (1994). *Social network analysis*. New York, NY: Cambridge University Press.

Wellman, B., & Gulia, M. (1999). Net surfers don't ride alone: Virtual communities as communities. In B. Wellman (Ed.), *Networks in the global village* (pp. 331–366). Boulder, CO: Westview Press.

Zimmer, M. (2010). "But the data is already public": On the ethics of research in Facebook. *Ethics and Information Technology, 12*(4), 313–325. doi:10.1007/s10676-010-9227-5

Talking of Many Things: Using Topical Networks to Study Discussions in Social Media

TIM HIGHFIELD

Queensland University of Technology/Curtin University, Australia

This article outlines a method for studying online activity using both qualitative and quantitative methods: topical network analysis. A topical network refers to "the collection of sites commenting on a particular event or issue, and the links between them" (Highfield, Kirchhoff, & Nicolai, 2011, p. 341). The approach is a complement for the analysis of large data sets enabling the examination and comparison of different discussions as a means of improving our understanding of the uses of social media and other forms of online communication. Developed for an analysis of political blogging, the method also has wider applications for other social media websites such as Twitter.

INTRODUCTION

Social media facilitate the development of conversations online around particular events or topics of interest, where participation is not necessarily limited by geographical or social factors. A message posted publicly on Twitter, for example, is potentially visible to all users of the site, and indeed

---

The initial research informing this article comes from my doctoral research; I thank Axel Bruns and Jason Sternberg for their supervision of this project, and Lars Kirchhoff and Thomas Nicolai for collecting the blog data discussed here. I also thank the anonymous reviewers for their comments and suggestions for this article.

to people without Twitter accounts themselves. Such web-based communication platforms offer ways for opinions, messages, and content to be shared and repurposed quickly and easily. While we might refer to Twitter, Facebook, or the blogosphere as singular entities to identify where discussions are taking place, though, the individuals using these platforms are not the same (and, indeed, the likes of Facebook and Twitter are not used in isolation); their motivations for using these sites vary, and so does their respective interest in a given subject of conversation. The group of bloggers responding to a specific political issue, for example, may be different from the group discussing the previous weekend's sports results. Different discussions will also take varying forms, although occurring within the same space. For instance, responding to crises, publishing live commentary on televised events, or taking part in a conference backchannel may involve different users, interactions, and types of information, but they coexist within the overall activity hosted on sites such as Twitter.

To study how discussion takes place within, and across, social media platforms, researchers might establish long-term projects, tracking a group of users over time. This approach provides important cumulative data for identifying patterns of use—such as how many posts were published by bloggers over time, or which bloggers posted most often. These overall, baseline data are useful for examining *what* the research has found—the overall posting patterns, and the most and least active users, for example. However, it does not easily explain the patterns discovered. As boyd and Crawford (2012) note in their discussion of studies involving "Big Data," the analysis of large data sets from online sources, such as Twitter archives, can lead researchers to find "patterns where none actually exist, simply because massive quantities of data can offer connections that radiate in all directions" (p. 668).

To provide additional insight into online activity, this article promotes the study of *topical networks*: "the collection of sites commenting on a particular event or issue, and the links between them" (Highfield, Kirchhoff, & Nicolai, 2011, p. 341). Using such units of analysis within large data sets is not intended to replace "Big Data"-type studies, but to supplement them by examining the tracked activity in greater detail. Identifying topical networks using these large data sets enables researchers to determine *why* and *when* connections were made, and the context for the discussion of particular topics. This method may also be employed within smaller data sets too, of course; in response to critiques of the quantitative focus of "Big Data," though, this approach can also provide some qualitative exploration of sections of large data sets.

Topical network analysis follows Rogers's (2009) promotion of investigating the "online groundedness" of online activity, where research follows a particular online medium, to track "its dynamics, and makes grounded claims about cultural and societal change" (p. 8). The specific methods used for analyzing data will vary from project to project, depending on the tools used. Due to these differences, this article does not aim to set out a step-by-step process. Instead, it argues at the conceptual level for a mixed-methods approach to gain further value from large, rich data sets. The following sections provide an initial overview of topical networks and the methods for their identification and analysis, and the advantages and limitations of this approach. An example from the Australian political blogosphere is used to illustrate this process. I also outline connections between topical networks and concepts developed around both public communication and online activity, such as issue publics and web spheres, which provide theoretical grounding for this analysis. Finally, I note further directions and applications of this approach.

TOPICAL NETWORKS

Topical networks were initially identified within a long-term research project comparing political blogging in Australia and France (Highfield, 2011), as a way of locating and comparing specific discussions within these blogospheres. The definition cited earlier applied to bloggers' coverage of particular themes and their linking to other blogs and web sources. However, topical networks are not restricted to the blogosphere alone. Rather than referring to "sites," the definition can be expanded to encompass multiple social media platforms, or to concentrate on activity on a single website, such as Twitter. In this latter case, the topical network could feature the different users commenting on a particular issue, such as through a central hashtag. The websites involved will vary between studies, adapting the method in the process as topical networks are examined within a range of contexts, including politics, economics, popular culture, health, and education. Regardless of the research focus, though, the resulting topical network will be oriented around a specific thematic discussion, often within a longer term study of a wider population of sites or users.

In this article, I draw on research using web-based, publicly accessible data, captured from blog posts. However, the same analytical approaches may be used on other data sets. From an education perspective, for example, a collection of *Blackboard* bulletin board posts may be categorized by the subjects covered in the text, providing the initial basis for topical networks within the data set. While this article examines explicit network data through hyperlinks, implied connections may also be used to demonstrate the links between users. Such implied links might appear through replies to other discussion board posts, which might not have a hyperlink to signify the connection. Even without "networked" data, the "topical" approach may be used to examine different types of online communication.

The comparative topical network approach discussed here was developed in response to studies of large, long-term data sets, as a means of examining specific thematic discussions within the wider data collected. The analysis of several months or years worth of data provides valuable information about patterns of use for different websites, such as the extended coverage of Arabic and Persian blogging by, respectively, Etling, Kelly, Faris, and Palfrey (2010) and Kelly and Etling (2008). However, the wider analysis alone does not explain the behaviors tracked, for example, what topics were discussed during a spike or lull in activity or the context for links to external websites.

To answer these questions, topical network analysis takes a multiprocess, mixed-methods approach. First, relevant keywords are used to identify and isolate from the wider data set the data pertaining to a chosen topic, such as blog posts, discussion board contributions, or tweets commenting on specific public figures, organizations, or events. The selected data then form the basis of the topical network. Following the identification of relevant content, a series of quantitative and qualitative processes may be used in combination to examine the discussions and activity represented within the topical network. For example, quantitative methods are used, as with the overall data sets, to determine patterns of activity. Such patterns include the number of contributions per week, day, or hour, the total contributions per user, blogger, or website, and any noticeable spikes or troughs in the discussions.

Depending on the type of data represented within the topical network (tweets, blog posts, and so on), different processes can be used to further analyze the coverage of the chosen topic. Hyperlink network mapping, for example, draws on the networked aspect of the data in question, through explicit hyperlinks to other online sources. Visualizing these connections as network maps can then demonstrate which sources are common references for the participants contributing to the topical network. The visualization process can also help to identify any clusters of users and sources within the overall network, where users in a smaller group link to each other or a distinct collection of websites that are not cited, at least not as frequently, by the rest of the network. However, it should also be noted that while network maps provide important visual cues around the connections between users, and help to make sense of the links present within large data sets, visualization by itself does not provide an explanation as to *why* these connections are made. Similarly, while hyperlinks are often used as indicators of connections between different websites, not all links are the same (see Adamic, 2008; Halavais, 2008).

Topical network analysis also makes use of approaches such as textual analysis to determine the context for the studied discussions. These methods allow studies to take into account different aspects of social media that might not be possible with large-scale, automated data processing, such as differentiating between link type—such as links in blog posts, blogrolls, or comments on posts—and to examine what these links can tell us about online communication. This approach can also negate the question surrounding the longevity of connections between participants in the network. Links featured within blog posts are not necessarily permanent indicators of affiliation or endorsement. A blogger may cite another's work once, in reference to a specific subject, but then never again in his or her later posts. The link from one blogger to another would still appear within the overall data set collected, yet analyzing the total patterns does not provide any context for this connection. Bruns (2012) raises a similar conceptual question around the life span of content and links posted on Twitter, asking how long the connections between users linked by @replies last. The answer to this temporal dilemma is beyond the scope of this article; as is the case for other aspects of these studies, though, the wider context for these links will be important (e.g., the rate of posting per user and overall, the time period covered by the discussion, and any repetition of the links).

Further processes involve analyzing the text of relevant posts individually to provide a qualitative view of the topical network data. Rather than treating the network as a like-minded whole, covering the chosen topic to an equal degree, the textual analysis demonstrates the different responses to the topic, and the context for these comments. While each blog post or tweet contains a relevant keyword for the topical network, the surrounding text might have a different subject as its focus, or the topic in question might be framed around an alternative context. These distinct ways of commenting on a given topic are not as easily identified within quantitative analysis alone, highlighting the value of examining at a qualitative level the activity captured within large data sets to understand the topical networks.

The different discussions tracked by topical networks might also take varying forms depending on the type of event or issue covered. The live-blogging or -tweeting of a sporting event or televised debate may lead to a topical network that is completely dissimilar to that formed in response to a crisis or scandal, with different patterns of posting, linking, and sharing information—even when drawn from the same overall data set. Similarly, the coverage of the same issue on different websites may also vary, depending on such factors as the number of people contributing to discussions and their personal or professional interest in the topic at hand. For example, tracking health-related issues on a specialist forum or discussion board, where health is the main subject to be covered, may depict a debate that is dissimilar to that captured from more general hashtag or keyword archives on Twitter.

Elmer (2006) notes that using a combination of qualitative and quantitative methods allows researchers to analyze in greater detail the dynamics of different discussions (p. 15). This idea guides topical network analysis and its mixed-methods approach to studying large data sets. This method enables the researcher to compare numerous discussions taking place at different points in the data, providing a means for contextualizing overall patterns and accounting for possible variations within "Big Data" projects. Most importantly, topical networks enable researchers to examine how the coverage of a given issue plays out within the wider data, such as how the discussion of a particular person or subject develops over time.

CONCEPTUAL REVIEW

Topical networks have their theoretical roots in several concepts concerning the shape of public debate. Some of these are directly applicable to online media, while others were developed independently and subsequently adapted to this context. Topical networks depict discussions taking place around specific issues. The connections here are not necessarily permanent associations, and the discussions may develop and decline quickly. This idea links to the notion of multiple, temporary issue publics appearing within a more constant, wider scope public sphere (or public spheres). These assemblages may overlap, with people contributing to more than one debate, but each issue public is centered on particular topics or themes (see Dahlgren, 2009). The shape of an issue public will change over time, and the context for each group means these publics will also take different forms in comparison with each other. Different contributors will comment on a range of topics, with no requirement to contribute to all or any debates.

The type and frequency of comments by each person involved in the topical network will also vary based on a number of professional and personal factors. For example, Jang and Park (2012) note the presence of "issue specialists" within discussions, based on the subject in question being an issue of personal relevance. In addition, individuals with a professional background in aspects of the topics covered by the network may be among the most active contributors to the discussion. Within the Australian political bloggers, for instance, different groups of specialists were identified within the wider blogosphere, who would contribute to political debate by adding new interpretations of the issues at hand based on their own economics or polling data analyses (Highfield, 2011).

The discussions featured in this article do not necessarily focus on one particular interpretation of an issue. As Marres (2006) notes, the presence of a group of people in conversation does not mean that participants agree with each other. A great number of voices contribute to public debate overall, with smaller, topical debates taking place among a subset of these participants, each of whom has a varying level of engagement with the topics in question.

While issue publics may develop away from computer-mediated communication, there are Internet-specific concepts that also help develop the ideas behind topical networks. These include web spheres (Schneider & Foot, 2005) and issue networks (Marres, 2006), both of which are formed around issue- or event-driven debates, and include both the individuals contributing to the debate and the resources used within these discussions. Such groups can be platform specific. Bruns and Burgess (2011) suggest that the use of hashtags within tweets "facilitates the *ad hoc* emergence of issue publics made up of interested *Twitter* users around these topics" (p. 38).

Topical network analysis provides researchers with the capability to compare patterns and citations across different events and over time. Each discussion sees the creation of a temporary issue public within the larger group represented in the larger data set, but there is no way of predicting which users will comment on which subject. In a data set containing a known number of contributors, such as tracking the output of several Twitter accounts, topics might be covered by any, all, or none of the individuals concerned. Topical networks then become potentially ideal cases for the study of issue publics. Debates published online are traceable through collections of blog posts, status updates, retweets, and links. Previous studies have examined topical discussions online, focusing on specific cases rather than debates within a wider data set: for example, Bruns's (2007) research into mentions by bloggers of an Australian detainee at Guantanamo Bay, or the analysis of how bloggers responded to Hurricane Katrina by Macias, Hilyard, and Freimuth (2009). Similarly, topical conversations on Twitter have been studied based on individual hashtags or keywords (for example, #ausvotes: Bruns & Burgess, 2011; #wikileaks: Lindgren & Lundström, 2011). Not only are these debates easily searchable and automatically connected through the creation of links for each hashtag, but they can also connect separate discussions around a shared theme—the use of any hashtag is not dependent on following other accounts also posting on this topic. Finally, several studies also track Twitter activity based not on keywords but on a list of user accounts, such as politicians and journalists (Maireder, Ausserhofer, & Kittenberger, 2012); from the collected tweets of these users, keywords can again be used to identify topical discussions within the wider activity captured.

IDENTIFYING AND ANALYZING TOPICAL NETWORKS: CASE STUDY

Topical networks may then be identified within the wider activity on, and across, numerous websites. These networks may be located and analysed from a larger data set of activity, or captured individually as part of an ongoing comparison of online discussions. This process allows researchers to show which subjects attract the widest or most specialist interest among groups of users. Such groups might be genre specific, such as the collection of political blogs studied here, or they might track activity within a local or national user base. For example, Bruns, Burgess, Kirchhoff, and Nicolai

(2012) have mapped how hashtagged discussions representing local and international news stories, sports events, and television programs were distributed across a network of 120,000 Australian Twitter users.

Because of the range of data formats, tools, and methods that might feature within different projects, this article does not seek to list specific, step-by-step processes for the identification and analysis of topical networks. However, this section provides a brief overview of an example from the Australian political blogosphere (Highfield, 2011) to illustrate an approach to topical network analysis. Although aspects of the methods used here might not be appropriate for all studies attempting to track discussions within online communication, the framework guiding the analysis may be applicable to a variety of cases.

The context for the following topical network was a wider research project capturing the published outputs of a sample of Australian and French political bloggers between January and August 2009. During this period, 10,529 posts were archived from 61 Australian political blogs. From each post, data were extracted, such as the date and time posted, links within posts, and the text of each post, ahead of further analysis. The two data sets were then analyzed separately to determine the overall activity represented by the collected posts. This process included identifying the most active sites, most popular sources based on links received, and any peaks or troughs in daily posting activity.

However, these overall patterns cannot show the reactions of bloggers to specific topics. Analyzing just the total posting and linking activity treats these almost as permanent blogging behaviors, where bloggers are active and sources linked to at a constant rate. Within the captured posts, though, myriad topics are discussed, provoking different responses from the bloggers in the sample. Not all bloggers will discuss the same topics, and their own commitments may mean that a blogger does not post for several weeks or months.

These variations can be examined, though, by moving from the wider study of the overall population to the more focused topical networks. This article provides a brief discussion of one such network, formed around the Australian "Utegate" political scandal between June and August 2009. This scandal centered on allegations against the then-prime minister and treasurer of preferential treatment for a Queensland car dealer seeking government assistance in response to the global financial crisis. This case is investigated in further detail, alongside additional political topical networks, by Highfield (2011); for this article, it serves to illustrate the concepts and framework behind topical network analysis.

To locate the topical network, the wider data set was filtered to isolate relevant blog posts. In this case, the data set was filtered at the keyword level (as opposed to limiting the data by a range of dates), in order to track the growth and decline of interest in a topic that had a clear starting point within the collected data. The Utegate topical network was created by searching for posts containing key terms (Utegate, Ozcar) and names specific to the scandal (Godwin Grech). The resulting network drew on data from 52 posts from 17 blogs, published over 8 weeks between June and August 2009.

The filtered data form the basis for the topical network analysis. First, the network was compared to the wider activity during the same period, to evaluate the level of interest in the subject among the bloggers in question. For Utegate, its peak activity on June 21 accounted for more than 10% of the posts published that day. However, within the 2-month period overall, Utegate featured in less than 2% of the total blog posts captured. This suggests that the scandal was not a prominent topic for Australian political bloggers, even though it was a leading story in mainstream media publications at points during the same period.

The topical network analysis then uses different processes to further examine how and why bloggers were discussing the events and issues at hand. Hyperlinks included in each post were extracted to identify which sources were cited during these discussions. Network visualizations aided the process by highlighting the prominence of different sources and bloggers within each topical network. These visualizations were created by representing each link as a directed connection between two sites—*from* the blogger in question *to* the external website. In their coverage of the Utegate scandal, the Australian bloggers contributing to the topical network linked to domestic news sites—as expected, given the local focus of the scandal—and in particular to the websites of News Limited publications.

However, the hyperlink analysis itself is still initially a quantitative process. Here, the context for the links is absent—citing a news article or another blogger is not necessarily endorsement of the views presented, for instance. Textual analysis of the topical network blog posts was then carried out using the Leximancer software to discover the actual subjects featured by the bloggers in the sample. This automated process was supplemented by manually analyzing the posts to evaluate the intentions behind bloggers' choices of links. The Utegate analysis highlights the importance of qualitative methods to topical network analysis. Although News Limited websites were linked to by several Australian bloggers discussing the scandal, these references were not necessarily positive. Instead, bloggers mentioning Utegate commented less on the scandal itself, and more on its disrupting impact on other political issues, or on the way that it was being covered by the mainstream media. In particular, the reporting of Utegate by News Limited publications was criticized by several bloggers, for its content and stance, and also for focusing attention on what the bloggers considered a nonissue. This disapproval was accompanied by links to specific articles that were promoting Utegate instead of political issues that bloggers saw as more worthy or deserving of media attention.

The hyperlink and textual analysis of the topical networks also confirmed patterns from the wider data set; the overall linking patterns between the blogs in the sample suggested that several thematic groups were present within the Australian political blogosphere. These groups were centered on shared topics, including economics and psephology (the study of voting and polling data). While representatives of these groups discussed Utegate, their posts remained within the context of their specialist subjects: for example, analyzing the opinion polls released after the scandal broke, or mentioning Utegate as a contributing factor for rising or falling approval ratings.

These findings further demonstrate the various perspectives and interpretations involved within a single discussion. To illustrate these topical variations within the network itself, composite network visualizations were created. This process drew on both the hyperlink and textual analysis to depict the distribution of different themes through the topical network; Figure 1 shows an example composite visualization, showing the different themes featured, and sources cited, by Australian bloggers commenting on the Utegate scandal.

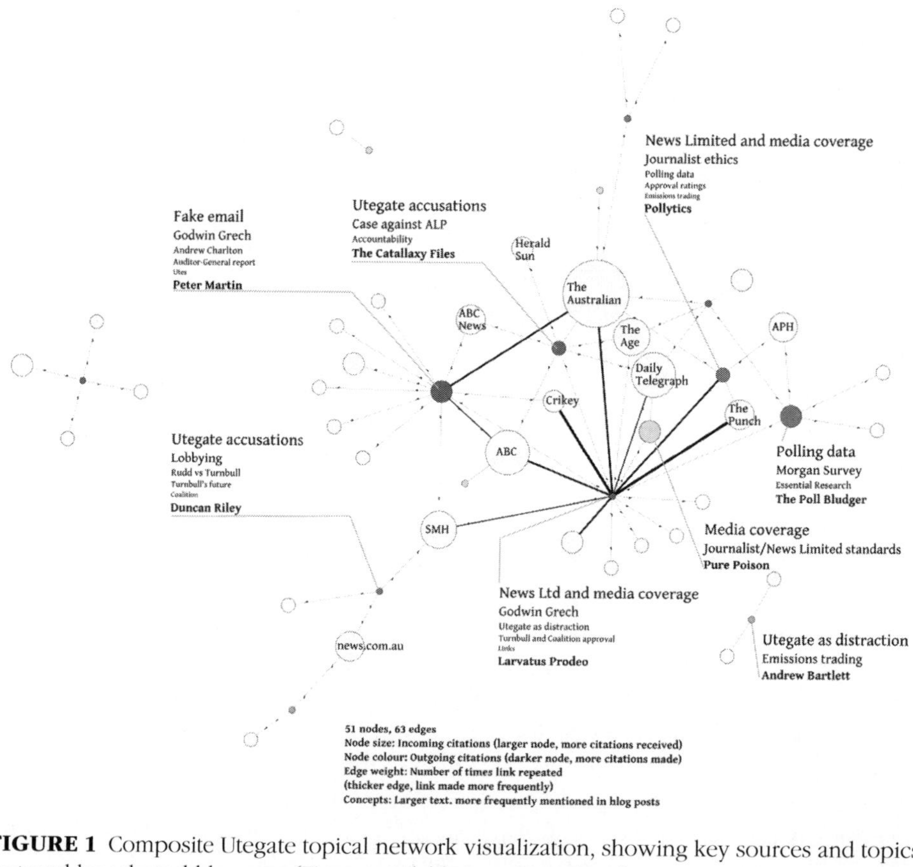

FIGURE 1 Composite Utegate topical network visualization, showing key sources and topics featured by selected bloggers. (Figure available in color online.)

WHY TOPICAL NETWORKS?

As the Utegate case study shows, an advantage of the topical network approach is found in the snapshots extracted from the wider data set. By focusing on temporary groups within a larger population of users or sites, topical networks provide the opportunity to evaluate how public debate takes place online, such as within the blogosphere or social media. For example, different discussions within the political blogosphere might be compared to examine whether bloggers link only to individuals sharing the same political affiliation or ideology, as demonstrated either explicitly on their sites or implicitly through their coverage of issues. Collections of tweets on matters of public interest may be studied to evaluate whether social media users follow the mainstream media in their coverage of issues, or whether they promote alternative interpretations of these themes. However, although topical network analysis method was developed for studying political communication online, the approach has applications beyond this context, as there are many different discussions and uses of social media taking place simultaneously.

The identification and study of topical networks within larger data sets allows for a more nuanced examination of online activity. Patterns and statistics derived from the total data collected provide important contextual information, and serve to introduce the subject of the study—the users or sites tracked. Although the resulting overview of the collected data shows the total activity, though, it does not provide information about the dynamics of discussions within different contexts. The study of topical networks then provides a crucial counterpoint to the analysis of the whole period, composite data set. Instead of viewing the baseline data as the definitive picture of the groups studied, topical networks question the users featured and the connections made between them and other sites. By isolating topical networks within large data sets, the researcher can examine whether the wider patterns are consistent for all contexts, or whether different sites become prominently linked in response to particular themes.

Topical network analysis is still an exploratory method, though, and is not without its limitations. The keyword-oriented method of identifying topical networks does not necessarily locate all relevant material. For research into Twitter activity, for example, more extensive topical networks might be identified around a mixture of keywords and hashtags; in cases where multiple hashtags are used, such as when a central tag has not yet been agreed upon, searching for particular keywords can supplement the filtered data. Posting about a specific subject on Twitter does not also require the relevant hashtags to be included in tweets. Australian political discussion on Twitter often includes the #auspol hashtag, for example, but also encompasses tweets not containing this marker. Similarly, blog posts might include common labels or categories for their posts to note the primary topics featured, but again there is no requirement for this.

As with any study of online activity, especially around Twitter and blogs, it is important to acknowledge the representative limits of the data sets used. While the collected tweets analyzed may number in the thousands or millions, the people involved in the specific discussion on Twitter are not necessarily representative of the total population, nor indeed of everyone using the Internet. Similarly, the presence of links in tweets, blog posts, or on discussion boards does not mean the endorsement of the site linked to, and it certainly does not imply that people seeing the link will follow it. As noted earlier, too, how to define the life span of links and connections between users is a question still to be definitively answered when examining online communication.

The findings from projects tracking a specific group of users or sites, as with the study of French and Australian political bloggers, are also subject to limitations. While the analysis may draw on large data sets, it is highly unlikely that the data will reflect all posts by every political blogger in Australia and France, for example. Although some online communication platforms, such as discussion boards, might provide more closed environments for research, sites such as Wordpress, Blogger, or Twitter, which are not restricted by paywalls or required technical knowledge, have extensive user bases. Instead of trying to track the entire network forming the blogosphere, for example (which, with the presence of locked, and private blogs, is nearly impossible), the research here follows a "partial network" approach (Hogan, 2008). Here, small subsets of the network provide a microcosm of the wider network, with findings and patterns extrapolated upon for more general conclusions about online activity. However, it is still important to note that the research is not studying *all* participants within online discussions. There are also significant ethical questions around collecting online data, and how to use this within research, which have not been definitively answered even for web-based content that is publicly accessible. While it is not the aim of this article to discuss debates of online ethics, these questions will need to be addressed in projects studying Internet-mediated activity.

Limits also apply to the scope of the topical networks themselves; for example, the blogging case study featured here provide an overview of activity within the blogospheres in question. However, it does not take into account any discussions on the same topic published on other websites or social media platforms, or indeed offline. Further topical networks might draw upon multiple websites for their analysis, but this was not the aim of the initial research and is beyond the scope of this article.

Finally, while topical network analysis brings together aspects of quantitative and qualitative methodologies, linking such processes as textual analysis and social network analysis, additional work is required to bring out further detail about who is contributing to the discussion and why. More qualitative work would help to further examine the motivations and rationale behind posting, commenting, or linking. For example, interviewing participants about their uses of online communication and interest in particular topics would provide new, more nuanced information than might be found on the websites in question.

CONCLUSION

The case study outlined here demonstrates how topical network analysis complemented the wider patterns of activity tracked within the total data set used in this project. This example provides an initial account of the use of a method that has important applications for further studies into online communication. As research continues into the dynamics of conversations online, investigating how discussions start and spread, and which topics gain traction where, topical network analysis allows for a consistent approach to identifying, examining, and comparing different discussions within a single data set.

Although it was developed for studying political blogging, the topical network method is transferable across different platforms. By using a mixture of qualitative and quantitative methods, some of which are outlined in this article, research can move beyond the large-scale overviews of analysis into "Big Data," and focus on specific activity within these data sets. This is not to undervalue the insights provided by "Big Data"; topical networks are intended not to replace the analysis of large data sets, but rather to provide additional detail and nuance in examining the online activity tracked in these projects.

There is further scope for developing the topical network method here, particularly by examining multiple platforms concurrently. The discussion of a particular event is not limited to Twitter alone; nor are the participants. Future research may track the dynamics of specific conversations not just within the blogosphere, but across social media in general. As with the single-platform case study outlined here, identifying topical networks within this space will support ongoing research into online activity. By comparing different conversations within a wider data set, the method enables researchers to develop further conclusions than would be possible from looking at a single case study or the baseline data alone. In doing so, topical networks provide more grounded information about how a platform is used, what its users are contributing, and how discussions online may suddenly appear, and just as quickly fade away.

REFERENCES

Adamic, L. A. (2008). The social hyperlink. In J. Turow & L. Tsui (Eds.), *The hyperlinked society: Questioning connections in the digital age* (pp. 227–249). Ann Arbor: University of Michigan Press and University of Michigan Library.

Boyd, D., & Crawford, K. (2012). Critical questions for Big Data. *Information, Communication & Society, 15*(5), 662–679. doi:10.1080/1369118X.2012.678878

Bruns, A. (2007). Methodologies for mapping the political blogosphere. *First Monday, 12*(5). Retrieved from http://firstmonday.org/htbin/cgiwrap/bin/ojs/index.php/fm/issue/view/235

Bruns, A. (2012). How long is a tweet? Mapping dynamic conversation networks on Twitter using Gawk and Gephi. *Information, Communication & Society, 15*(9), 1323–1351. doi:10.1080/1369118X.2011.635214

Bruns, A., & Burgess, J. (2011). #ausvotes: How Twitter covered the 2010 Australian federal election. *Communication, Politics & Culture, 44*(2), 37–56.

Bruns, A., Burgess, J., Kirchhoff, L., & Nicolai, T. (2012, March). *Mapping the Australian twittersphere*. Paper presented at Digital Humanities Australasia, Canberra.

Dahlgren, P. (2009). *Media and political engagement: Citizens, communication, and democracy*. New York, NY: Cambridge University Press.

Elmer, G. (2006). Re-tooling the network: Parsing the links and codes of the web world. *Convergence: The International Journal of Research into New Media Technologies, 12*(1), 9–19. doi:10.1177/1354856506061549

Etling, B., Kelly, J., Faris, R., & Palfrey, J. (2010). Mapping the Arabic blogosphere: Politics and dissent online. *New Media & Society, 12*(8), 1225–1243. doi:10.1177/1461444810385096

Halavais, A. (2008). The hyperlink as organizing principle. In J. Turow & L. Tsui (Eds.), *The hyperlinked society: Questioning connections in the digital age* (pp. 39–55). Ann Arbor: University of Michigan Press and University of Michigan Library.

Highfield, T. (2011). *Mapping intermedia news flows: Topical discussions in the Australian and French political blogospheres*. Doctoral thesis, Queensland University of Technology, Brisbane, Australia. Retrieved from http://eprints.qut.edu.au/48115

Highfield, T., Kirchhoff, L., & Nicolai, T. (2011). Challenges of tracking topical discussion networks online. *Social Science Computer Review, 29*(3), 340–353. doi:10.1177/0894439310382514

Hogan, B. (2008). Analyzing social networks via the Internet. In N. Fielding, R. M. Lee, & G. Blank (Eds.), *The Sage handbook of online research methods* (pp. 141–160). London, UK: Sage.

Jang, S. M., & Park, Y. J. (2012). The Internet, selective learning, and the rise of issue specialists. *First Monday, 17*(5). Retrieved from http://firstmonday.org/htbin/cgiwrap/bin/ojs/index.php/fm/article/view/3888/3206

Kelly, J., & Etling, B. (2008). *Mapping Iran's online public: Politics and culture in the Persian blogosphere*. Berkman Center for Internet & Society: Harvard Law School. Retrieved from http://cyber.law.harvard.edu/publications/2008/Mapping_Irans_Online_Public

Lindgren, S., & Lundström, R. (2011). Pirate culture and hacktivist mobilization: The cultural and social protocols of #WikiLeaks on Twitter. *New Media & Society, 13*(6), 999–1018. doi:10.1177/1461444811414833

Macias, W., Hilyard, K., & Freimuth, V. (2009). Blog functions as risk and crisis communication during Hurricane Katrina. *Journal of Computer-Mediated Communication, 15*(1), 1–31.

Maireder, A., Ausserhofer, J., & Kittenberger, A. (2012). Mapping the Austrian political Twittersphere: How politicians, journalists and political strategists (inter-)act on Twitter. In P. Parycek & N. Edelmann (Eds.), *Proceedings of CeDem12 Conference for E-Democracy and Open Government* (pp. 151–164). Krems, Austria: Danube University. Retrieved from http://phaidra.univie.ac.at/o:154914

Marres, N. (2006). Net-work is format work: Issue networks and the sites of civil society politics. In J. Dean, J. W. Anderson & G. Lovink (Eds.), *Reformatting politics: Information technology and global civil society* (pp. 3–17). Hoboken, NJ: CRC Press.

Rogers, R. (2009). *The end of the virtual: Digital methods.* Amsterdam, The Netherlands: Vossiuspers UvA.

Schneider, S. M., & Foot, K. A. (2005). Web sphere analysis: An approach to studying online action. In C. Hine (Ed.), *Virtual methods: Issues in social research on the Internet* (pp. 157–170). Oxford, UK: Berg.

Researching Communicative Practice: Web Archiving in Qualitative Social Media Research

STINE LOMBORG
University of Copenhagen, Copenhagen, Denmark

This article discusses the method of web archiving in qualitative social media research. While presenting a number of methodological challenges, social media archives (i.e., complete recordings of posts and comments on given social media) are also highly useful data corpuses for studying the social media users' communicative practices. Through a theoretical examination of web archiving as a new method enabled by the web itself, and an example-based discussion of the methodological, technical, and ethical challenges of harvesting social media archives, the article discusses the merits and limitations of using social media archives in empirical social media research.

INTRODUCTION

Given its technical infrastructure, integrating archive, and communication medium, the Internet offers new opportunities for methodological development in media and communication studies. In his review of methods in Internet research, Jensen (2011, p. 52) frames Internet studies as a field in which the Internet is both a tool for and an object of analysis, contending that the Internet as an analytic object to some extent automatically generates and layers its own data. However, to make sense of these data, the researcher must delimit, combine, and contextualize the data at hand in local situations and with theoretical frameworks. Sensitizing the methodological discussion, Jensen distinguishes between "found" and "made" data to delineate differences between data that are produced and archived in digital media regardless of a researcher's interest (e.g., blog or debate forum archives, bit trails, etc.), and data that are created in the interaction between a researcher and a topic of interest (e.g., ethnographic field notes or interview data) (Jensen, 2011, p. 49).

Web archiving is one of the "tools" in the palette of methods for online data collection, enabling researchers to trace and examine how various actors interact with and through the medium of the Internet. The data corpuses generated by web archiving are, in a sense, "found," created through *unobtrusive measures* (Webb, Campbell, Schwartz, & Sechrest, 2000) that simply crawl and harvest what is already online. However, web archives are also "made" insofar as they require a series of methodological choices and considerations to be meaningfully implemented in a research process. In this article, I discuss the potentials and limitations of the method of web archiving for qualitative social media research.

The article aims to provide a methodological discussion of web archiving as a new method enabled by the web itself, and an assessment of its utility in the context of qualitative social media research, and, more broadly audience research. While most research based on web archiving so far has been of a quantitative nature, web archiving may certainly also enrich qualitative research on the contextualised meanings of media use. To anchor the methodological discussion of opportunities and challenges of conducting empirical research based on web archives of social media, I draw examples from an empirical study of ordinary users' communicative practices and meaning-making on blogs and Twitter in everyday life, in which web archives of communication constituted the main body of data (Lomborg, 2011).

The article proceeds in three steps. First, I provide a clarification of the status of social media as an object of analysis for audience studies, arguing that web archiving is a particularly useful method in studies of users' communicative practices. Next, I examine web archiving as a method with emphasis on the methodological, technical, and ethical considerations that tie in with this method. Finally, I discuss the use of web archives in qualitative audience research vis-à-vis two related approaches: online ethnography and classic textual analysis, to clarify the methodological underpinnings, potentials, and pitfalls of web archiving in the systematic study of online communication.

WEB ARCHIVES IN SOCIAL MEDIA RESEARCH

As an object of analysis, "social media" poses conceptual challenges for audience studies: Are we studying texts or are we studying users? On the one hand, social media present themselves as texts (i.e., media products produced by somebody and interpreted by one or more recipients), available for classic textual, production, and audience analysis. On the other hand, the "texts" of social media are only brought into existence through users' communicative practices. Strictly speaking, there is no preproduced "text," just a technological framework or communicative template facilitated by a service provider (i.e., a company such as Facebook or Twitter), which must be "filled" by the communicative contributions of users. Thus, in social media, the text rests on continued user engagement; it is emergent, editable, and undergoing a continuous process of development—often taking the form of interpersonal conversation among users. When looking at social media from an interpersonal perspective, social media prompt us to reach beyond the classic subdisciplines of media studies—production, text, and audience analysis—and incorporate analytical frameworks mainly associated with interpersonal communication, for example, discourse analysis and microsociology. Against this background, social media present an opportunity to rethink established theories and empirical research practices of audience studies.

Web archiving is a method that allows researchers to harvest texts and relevant metadata (e.g., time stamps, sender and recipient profile information, and tags) from the Internet and compile them in data archives for various types of analysis. In social media research, the method has mainly been used for quantitative studies of social media use, including, for example, the patterns and norms of addressivity and collaboration on Twitter (Honeycutt & Herring, 2009), and how users communicate about and form networks around political and other types of events (Bruns & Burgess, 2011; Larsson & Moe, 2012). Web archiving is also well suited for qualitative studies addressing key research questions of audience studies, for instance, concerning the organization of communication and practices of meaning-making of social media use in context, because it involves the generation of a coherent corpus of communications in a given time frame, and in a given networked context online. In other words, social media archives are highly useful data corpuses for the systematic, fine-grained study of naturally occurring, textualized interactions on social media. However, to date, surprisingly little qualitative social media research has relied on web archiving to collect data.

WHAT IS WEB ARCHIVING?

Web archiving can broadly be defined as a method for stabilizing and preserving the ever-changing Internet as an object of empirical research (Brügger, 2005, p. 9). Web archiving originates in the domains of digital preservation and information retrieval (Masanès, 2006), especially in the context of national and international (publicly or privately funded) institutions that serve the function of preserving the Internet as a whole as part of cultural heritage.[1] These domains have played a crucial role in developing and critically discussing web archiving methods, supporting technological infrastructures, and disseminating knowledge of web archiving techniques to public organizations, private companies, and other research fields in which web archiving of specific subsets of the Internet is performed to document and analyze communications and usage patterns.[2]

Archiving websites in general, and social media in particular, poses some significant challenges to researchers. How and to what extent can we adequately capture and fix a highly fluctuating and networked communicative environment? In this section, I examine web archiving as a method in the context of social media research and highlight key methodological, technical, and ethical challenges of using web archiving to study social media.

In a recent article on web archiving, Brügger (2011, pp. 28–29) delineates three strategies for harvesting material on the web. The *snapshot* strategy involves archiving a certain portion of the web at a certain point in time, and is often used to harvest material from a large number of websites. However, snapshots are not well suited to a longitudinal study of websites that are frequently updated, including most social media, because they do not normally capture the deep levels of the website, for example, archives of older posts on a blog. The *event* strategy involves archiving the web (or a specific site or group of sites on the web) in relation to a given event (e.g., general elections, the Olympics, a natural disaster), thereby generating a thematically coherent archive. The event strategy is particularly suitable for research seeking to examine how Internet users communicate about a particular issue, for instance, on particular sites or subsets of the web. A main application of the event strategy in Internet studies is web sphere analysis (Schneider & Foot, 2005). Web sphere analysis is the study of a collection of dynamically defined digital resources spanning multiple websites deemed relevant or related to a central theme or issue. For instance, following a thematic delimitation of the web, Schneider and Foot (2005) studied the U.S. presidential campaign on the web, and Moe (2011) has studied issue-driven temporary web spheres in Norwegian blogs. Furthermore, most existing social media research has used the event strategy of web archiving, typically to harvest and analyze thematically coherent aggregates of tweets using a particular hashtag (e.g., Bruns & Burgess, 2011; Murthy, 2011). The third strategy, known as *selective* archiving, focuses on a small number of preselected websites that are archived continuously, to capture frequent updates and thereby produce a "deep" archive of the given sites. It is not thematically focused, but aims to include all the material that is present on the selected websites at a particular point in time. The selective archiving strategy is not prominent in social media research. However, Lomborg (2011) used data corpuses generated through a selective archiving strategy in her qualitative study of communicative practices as ongoing negotiations of meaning on blogs and Twitter. Full records of interaction on a purposive sample of individual Twitter profiles and blogs over a predetermined time period formed the empirical basis of the study. In the remainder of the article, this study serves to illustrate the methodological discussion of web archiving in qualitative social media research.

Regardless of archiving strategy, the method of web archiving requires consideration for a number of *methodological challenges*, the most fundamental of which concerns the status of the archive as an analytical object. The archived website is not a 1:1 copy of what was actually on the web at a given moment, but an actively created, subjective reconstruction based on choices of what to include, tools used for archiving, and so on (Brügger, 2011). Elaborating specifically on the tools used for automated harvest and analysis of digital media network data, Koed Madsen (2012) notes that software is not neutral, but creates specific "visions" of the web. Additionally, most archives are deficient, either for technical reasons (e.g., errors in the software or hardware used for the archive) or owing to the dynamics of archiving (e.g., if the website is updated while harvesting). Accordingly, when working with web archive data, we cannot rely on the archive providing an accurate copy, a precise and reliable picture of the naturally occurring events on social media. Social media archives are in a sense reconstructed textual records of the actual interactional practices of the users studied. Thus, web archives share with other types of recorded data, including field notes and transcripts, the status of a first analysis and interpretation of the material, although in a somewhat different sense. The production of field notes and transcripts relies on the researcher's firsthand assessment, selection, and interpretation of the "raw data," whereas the labor of the web archivist in the production of data is simply that of defining appropriate boundaries around the object of analysis and then automating a scrape of everything within the perimeters. Hence, although bias in field notes and transcripts may largely be attributed to different interpretations of the material, biases in web archives are consequent—produced by the initial choices of what to include, the "mechanics" of the archiving software, and the process of archiving itself.

For example, the archives created by Lomborg (2011) included the posts and tweets, comments and @replies, the users authoring them, date and time stamps, and the URLs of individual blog threads and tweets, all represented in a program for data analysis called Tatiana (Dyke, Lund, & Girardot, 2009).

As is evident from Figure 1, a screenshot of one of the data archives from Twitter, this representation of a Twitter conversation is very different from how it actually appears on Twitter and on third-party applications for using the service. The interactive features (e.g., the link structure) of the site, the graphics, and the individual profiles were not included, although the links posted in tweets to content elsewhere online were included. What should be included in a concrete social media archive largely depends on the research questions, and there is certainly software suitable for capturing links, graphics, metadata, and so on. However, representing the various

date	time	user	user_to	message	messageurl
01/01/2010	02:57:29	riijaH		Happy new year! http://goo.gl/fb/TD9Y	http://twitter.com/riijaH/statuses/7253705960
01/01/2010	03:07:52	magicmaid	riijaH	@riijaH Happy New Year!	http://twitter.com/magicmaid/statuses/7253968290
01/01/2010	10:03:40	riijaH		morning! dont think i've been up this early before on january 1st ;D happy new years! :D hope your evening was safe and fun <3	http://twitter.com/riijaH/statuses/7264138287
01/01/2010	13:02:32	riijaH	Jinnzor	@Jinnzor im not! :D	http://twitter.com/riijaH/statuses/7266970843
01/01/2010	13:06:12	jinnzor	riijaH	@riijaH Maybe you should! I'm considering it now.	http://twitter.com/jinnzor/statuses/7267022081

FIGURE 1 Screenshot of a Twitter archive.

elements—visual, textual, links, and so on—in their original composition on a given website appears to be a general challenge for web archiving (Brügger, 2011). Hence, at least for qualitative research seeking naturalistic data, basic screenshots may be a good supplement to web archives.

For social media research, web archiving is particularly useful to create an analytically researchable object for the study of textualized communicative practice, which can be registered systematically in a detailed corpus with relevant metadata (e.g., exact time, length of utterance and conversation, geographical location, and application used), as seen in Figure 1. Social media archives—especially those generated through a selective and deep archiving strategy—can reconstruct and make visible a chronology in the communication that would have been almost impossible to access and study otherwise. Particularly in the case of a highly networked and dispersed communicative environment such as Twitter, web archives present the conversations that make up the data much more coherently than would be possible if one had to rely solely on the data as they appear on Twitter. Accordingly, web archiving may be invaluable for obtaining an overview of the data and systematizing the analysis.

On the one hand, web archiving allows the researcher to construct an analytically researchable object that reduces the complexity of the raw data. On the other hand, the web archive also demonstrates one of the grand challenges when studying social media communications, namely, how to document and represent in a valid and reliable way communicative practices that play out in a networked environment and continuously evolve in a process of flux. The validity and reliability of the archived textual corpus for the study of social media use must be addressed. In the translation, or reduction, of actual interaction to textual archive, what happens? What is lost? Apart from the already mentioned lack of 1:1 representation in the web archives of social media profiles as they looked like for their authors, the web archive delimits the object of analysis, social media use, in a very specific way. The web archive only captures that part of social media that manifests itself as text online as users perform certain actions: actual content posted, articulated relationships between content bits (through links) and between users (e.g., follower/followee patterns on Twitter), and the metadata automatically connected to these actions. This means that a very important part of social media use flees the eye of the web archive. The dimension of reading and clicking through other social media profiles is simply lost. In the referred case of Lomborg (2011), for instance, the personalized stream of tweets from the other users that the Twitter profile holder followed was not archived, implying that part of the context of the shifting conversations remained hidden from the researcher's view. To grasp practices of using social media that go beyond the communications that play out on blogs, tweets, Facebook walls, and so forth, one must turn to methods other than web archiving.

In addition to methodological challenges, web archives also present practical–technical challenges in setting up the harvesting of data into the archive with a view to minimize the technical deficiency of the archive. To address technical challenges, basic programming skills (or a collaboration with, e.g., computer scientists) are a prerequisite that is necessary for setting up the software to perform a reliable harvesting, for cleaning the data set, and for making it analytically accessible and presentable. Furthermore, to address practical challenges associated with data access, the researcher may need assistance from the research participants. This is particularly so for social media that are not entirely public by default but require identification through login and password (e.g., Facebook and Twitter). For instance, in the aforementioned Twitter study, the participants' help was needed to capture the @replies that other users had sent to them, because the archive of @replies is aggregated only on the profile holder's personal Twitter homepage. That is, to capture these without the help of the profile holder would require a manual identification of all the other Twitter users who sent an @reply to or retweet of the profile holder during the archived period. Specifically, a piece of archiving software was developed that participants were instructed to access and use to generate an archive file.

To strengthen the validity and reliability of the social media archive and control for technical deficiencies, it may be useful to perform manual checks to ensure that all communications back and forth in the time frame have been archived. Of course, manual reliability checks are only feasible in smaller scale qualitative studies, and are associated with different obstacles for different social media. When studying blogs, reliability checks are relatively unproblematic, as all posts and comments are archived on the blog in separate threads. When studying communication patterns on a service like Twitter, reliability checks are more cumbersome. This is, first, because conversation on Twitter is extremely distributed in the network, that is, tweets are not stored as threads, but as individual statements on the individual author's profile, and in the @replies section of recipients to which a given tweet is addressed. The only link between two tweets in a conversation is the @reply. When harvesting Twitter data from individual profiles, this means that if the profile holder responds to someone else's tweet, and this tweet is not explicitly addressed to the profile holder, then the tweet initiating the conversation is not archived, simply because it is not stored on the profile from which the archive is generated. However, the initial tweet may be traced manually via the URL of the responding tweet, which is archived. Second, unless one has direct access to participants' profiles, it is not possible to verify whether all @replies to a profile holder have actually been archived. The technical challenges may vary considerable depending on the project, the social media service in question (e.g., whether it is public or password protected by default), and the type of archive needed.

On top of methodological and technical challenges, archiving communications from social media presents ethical challenges, and relates to ongoing ethics discussions in Internet research. These challenges are addressed elsewhere in detail (Lomborg, 2012), but they deserve a brief reflection here. While the content of the communications in social media may not be of a strictly sensitive nature, microarchiving of communication entails a detailed tracking of the communications of the specific users sampled for the study and tying of individual utterances (e.g., tweets, blog posts, or comments) to their author. When aiming to do close analysis of actual communicative practice on social media, it becomes quite difficult to anonymize the participants. Simple string search of specific utterances used to exemplify and document the analysis would reveal the original author of the utterance. Hence, the researcher must consider other means of protecting research participants, including, for instance, seeking participants' informed consent. For a general discussion of Internet research ethics, see Ess and AoIR (2002) and Markham and Buchanan (2012).

WEB ARCHIVES AT THE INTERFACE OF METHODS

When considering the methodological issues of constructing web archives just discussed, the status of the social media archive as a data corpus is somewhat ambiguous. The data are "made" through methodological choices of boundary setting between what is important and what can be left out of the "found" data to create a coherent archive with which to address the research questions of a project. In this final section, I address the question of how the archive may be deployed usefully in the qualitative study of social media users' communicative practices and sensemaking. What are its relative advantages vis-à-vis other methods for studying how people engage with media, and what are the limitations to the kinds of inferences possible based on analysis of social media archives?

The method of web archiving to study the textualized communicative practices of users on social media intersects with two core methodological traditions in audience studies, (1) textual analysis as used in reception studies and (2) media ethnography. From an audience studies perspective, using web archives allows for examining in detailed fashion processes of meaning-making in a circuit of production, text, and reception. It also allows for a detailed account of the contextualized practices of interaction and engagement with media and with fellow users that are key constituents in an media ethnographic approach.

Ethnography, broadly speaking, is the closeup study of culture in its everyday unfolding. Ethnographic research mainly deploys participant-observation techniques, interviews, field notes, and immersion in a specific field over an extended period of time to obtain a profound understanding of the "lived experience" of the members of the group or culture under study (Spradley, 1979; Wolcott, 2008). In audience studies, media ethnography denotes a specific line of inquiry that shifts attention from the media text to the context of media use, that is to say, the social activities and cultural practices that evolve around the use of media (e.g., Bird, 2003; Lull, 1980). As a parallel to media ethnography in audience studies, ethnographic research of media use has been—and continues to be—very prominent in the development of the field of computer-mediated communication, including social media studies. Under headings such as "virtual ethnography" (Hine, 2000) and "netnography" (Kozinets, 2010), ethnographic methods have been appropriated by several prominent research projects seeking to document the lived experiences of users, typically, in relatively bounded online communities or specific social media services (e.g., Baym, 2000; boyd, 2008; Kendall, 2002; Markham, 1998).

In contrast to ethnographic research, which leverages the researcher's active and continuous engagement in the field of research to generate first-hand accounts of "the lived experience," web archiving as a method involves the opportunity to generate fine-grained data on "lived communicative practice" without interfering with participants and their ongoing activities during the process of data collection. Hence, the researcher can maintain what ethnomethodology labels a more "disinterested" approach, in which the researcher's often-tacit presumptions about the field site and the members' activities are suspended in the process of data collection (Holstein & Gubrium, 1994, p. 264). In other words, using web archives, it is possible to take a lurking, "fly on the wall" position in the field, close to what Hammersley and Atkinson (1995, pp. 104–107) call a "complete observer," as opposed to engaging in various degrees of participation. From a constructivist-epistemological perspective, this ideal, disinterested position is impossible to attain. However, on the one hand, reliance on a complete record of naturally occurring activities, created through unobtrusive measures, rather than field notes, which are necessarily selective records of data, seen through an ethnographer's prism, arguably provides a stronger basis for systematic and close analyses of the natural organization of communicative practices in social media. On the other hand, the ethnographer's participatory engagement provides for a unique sensitivity to context and to the real-time flow of events on and across social media that is lost in the web archive.

When studying communicative practices, unobtrusive measures may be particularly important. In their methodological and epistemological dissection of the differences between ethnomethodology and ethnography, Pollner and Emerson (2001, pp. 124–125) argue that ethnographic research tends to regard communicative practice not as the object of study, but as a resource for the researcher to get close to the lived experience of the culture under study. Participation in the field is often seen as key to grasping the participants' experience, and communicating with the members "like the members do" is one technique typically drawn upon in online ethnography. While using communicative practice as a resource for interaction with participants provides for the ethnographer's experiencing the culture at first hand, it may also obscure—at least over time—the tacit knowledge and communicative competence implied in participants' communicative practice to make it meaningful in the first place. The practices simply become too familiar. Using web archives, rather than participant-observation, allows for maintaining a distance and unfamiliarity with participants' practices that is needed to question the participants' apparently mundane and habitual ways of using social media, and thus to understand genre negotiation as a practical matter. The archive draws the attention to members' actual activities, and to how particular practices are drawn upon to accomplish the activities and make sense of them in everyday life.

One of the main strengths of web archiving in social media research, in regard to analyzing communicative practice, is that the web archive lends itself very well to detailed examination using textual analysis tools. As Herring and other scholars of computer-mediated communication have long argued, the aggregated textual corpora of participants' communications invite careful analysis of the content, form, and style of communication in various social media contexts—using well-established methods and tools for textual analysis such as content analysis (Herring, 2010a, 2010b). At the same time, given that social media texts are to some extent reminiscent of interpersonal communication, textual analysis of social media goes beyond the classic tools of textual analysis deployed in audience studies and encompasses interpersonal communication concepts such as turn-taking, repair, and facework, which have been developed in analyses of face-to-face communication in micro-sociological and discourse research. Such interpersonal concepts may fertilize the study of communicative practice in social media, when appropriated to suit the study of the mediated, and often spatiotemporally dispersed, communicative environment. For a review of such discussions, see Garcia and Jacobs (1999).

CONCLUDING REMARKS

As a method, web archiving may assist in constructing analytically researchable objects, texts, out of social media. To construct a valid, reliable, and meaningful object of analysis, the creation and use of web archives in social media research depend on the types of research questions asked and the theoretical frameworks applied. The usefulness of web archives in social media research is particularly evident in studies aiming to explore and understand the users' actual communicative practices and patterns on social media. This is so because web archiving techniques can generate full records of naturally occurring communication in context. The web archive constructs social media use as an object of analysis in a very narrow sense, as involving only the activities that manifest themselves in text online, whereas other methods are more suitable if one aims to grasp how communication on social media relates to wider patterns of activity in the users' everyday lives.

In relation to the theoretical toolbox of audience studies, the status of the web archive as a textual corpus made up of users' communicative practices invites researchers to revitalize well-established analytical concepts and frameworks in the study of social media. Along such lines, for instance, Lomborg (2011) has proposed a pragmatic, genre-based framework for studying social media practices based on classic work of television reception and genre. Jensen (2012) has nuanced Raymond Williams's concept of flow to suit the study of digital media networks, and Carpentier (2011) has critically reassessed the concept of participation in audience studies of new media. Because of its history and theoretical baggage, audience studies have much to offer in terms of developing theoretically informed understandings of how ordinary users communicate on and make sense of social media. The use of social media, and the Internet in general, is highly undertheorized. Arguably, a large part of the work that has been done so far has narrowly focused on simply documenting usage patterns in a highly fluctuating and diverse media environment (Wellman, 2004). That is to say, the floor is open for sound theorizing of social media as communicative phenomena.

NOTES

1. In Denmark, for instance, Netarkivet (www.netarchive.dk), a publicly funded agency, preserves the Danish Internet as part of Danish cultural heritage.

2. A comprehensive review of web archiving and its implementation across disciplines is beyond the scope of this article, which focuses exclusively on social media research. For a detailed review of the history and main issues of web archiving, see Lomborg (2011).

REFERENCES

Baym, N. K. (2000). *Tune in, log on. soaps, fandom, and online community.* Thousand Oaks, CA: Sage.

Bird, S. E. (2003). *The audience in everyday life: Living in a media world.* New York, NY: Routledge.

Boyd, D. M. (2008). *Taken out of context. American teen sociality in networked publics.* PhD dissertation, University of California, Berkeley.

Bruns, A., & Burgess, J. (2011). #ausvotes: How Twitter covered the 2010 Australian federal election. *Communication, Politics & Culture, 44*(2), 37–56.

Brügger, N. (2005). *Web archiving*. Aarhus, Denmark: Centre for Internet Research, Aarhus University.

Brügger, N. (2011). Web archiving—Between past, present, and future. In M. Consalvo & C. M. Ess (Eds.), *The Blackwell handbook of Internet STudies* (pp. 24–42). Oxford, UK: Wiley-Blackwell.

Carpentier, N. (2011). New configurations of the audience? The challenges of user-generated content for audience theory and media participation. In V. Nightingale (Ed.), *The handbook of media audiences* (pp. 190–212). Malden, MA: Wiley-Blackwell.

Dyke, G., Lund, K., & Girardot, J.-J. (2009). *Tatiana: An environment to support the CSCL analysis process*. Paper presented at the CSCL 2009, June, Rhodes, Greece.

Ess, C. M., & AoIR Ethics Working Committee. (2002). *Ethical decision-making and Internet research: Recommendations from the AoIR Ethics Working Committee*. Retrieved from http://www.aoir.org/reports/ethics.pdf

Garcia, A. C., & Jacobs, J. B. (1999). The eyes of the beholder: Understanding the turn-taking system in quasi-synchronous CMC. *Research on Language & Social Interaction, 32*(4), 337–367.

Hammersley, M., & Atkinson, P. (1995). *Ethnography. Principles in practice* (2nd ed.). New York, NY: Routledge.

Herring, S. C. (2010a). Computer-mediated conversation: Introduction and overview. *Language@Internet*, 7. Retrieved from http://www.languageatinternet.org/articles/2010/2801/herring.intro.pdf

Herring, S. C. (2010b). Web content analysis: Expanding the paradigm. In J. Hunsinger, M. Allen, & L. Klastrup (Eds.), *The international handbook of Internet research* (pp. 233–250). Dordrecht, The Netherlands: Springer Verlag.

Hine, C. (2000). *Virtual ethnography*. London, UK: Sage.

Holstein, J. A., & Gubrium, J. F. (1994). Phenomenology, ethnomethodology and interpretive practice. In N. K. Denzin & Y. S. Lincoln (Eds.), *Handbook of qualitative research* (pp. 262–272). Thousand Oaks, CA: Sage.

Honeycutt, C., & Herring, S. C. (2009). *Beyond microblogging: Conversation and collaboration via Twitter.* Paper presented at the Proceedings of the Forty-Second Hawai'i International Conference on System Sciences (HICSS-42), January, Los Alamitos, CA.

Jensen, K. B. (2011). New media, old methods—Internet methodologies and the online/offline divide. In M. Consalvo & C. M. Ess (Eds.), *The Blackwell handbook of Internet studies* (pp. 43–58). Oxford, UK: Wiley-Blackwell.

Jensen, K. B. (2012). Lost, found, and made: Qualitative data in the study of three-step flows of communication. In I. Volkmer (Ed.), *Handbook of global media research* (pp. 435–450). Malden, MA: Wiley-Blackwell.

Kendall, L. (2002). *Hanging out in the virtual pub: Masculinities and relationships online*. Berkeley: University of California Press.

Koed Madsen, A. (2012). Hyperlink networks as social metaphors and boundary drawers. In S. Lomborg (Ed.), *Network analysis—Methodological challenges* (Vol. 14, pp. 32–44). Aarhus, Denmark: The Centre for Internet Research, Aarhus University.

Kozinets, R. V. (2010). *Netnography. Doing ethnographic research online*. London, UK: Sage Publications.

Larsson, A. O., & Moe, H. (2012). Studying political microblogging: Twitter users in the 2010 Swedish election campaign. *New Media & Society, 14*(5), 729–747.

Lomborg, S. (2011). *Social media. A genre perspective.* PhD, dissertation, Aarhus University, Aarhus, Denmark.

Lomborg, S. (2012). Personal Internet archives and ethics. *Research Ethics.* doi:10.1177/1747016112459450

Lull, J. (1980). The social uses of television. *Human Communication Research, 6*(3), 197–209.

Markham, A. N. (1998). *Life online. Researching real experience in virtual space.* Walnut Creek, CA: AltaMira Press.

Markham, A., N., & Buchanan, E. (2012). *Ethical decision-making and Internet research: 2012. Recommendations from the AoIR Ethics Working Committee.* Retrieved from http://aoir.org/reports/ethics2.pdf

Masanès, J. (Ed.). (2006). *Web archiving.* Berlin, Germany: Springer-Verlag.

Moe, H. (2011). Mapping the Norwegian blogosphere: Methodological challenges in internationalizing Internet research. *Social Science Computer Review, 29*(3), 313–326.

Murthy, D. (2011). Twitter: Microphone for the masses? *Media, Culture and Society, 33*(5), 779–789.

Pollner, M., & Emerson, R. M. (2001). Ethnomethodology and ethnography. In P. Atkinson, A. Coffey, S. Delamont, J. Lofland, & L. Lofland (Eds.), *Handbook of ethnography* (pp. 118–135). Thousand Oaks, CA: Sage.

Schneider, S. M., & Foot, K. (2005). Web sphere analysis: An approach to studying online action. In C. Hine (Ed.), *Virtual methods: Issues in social research on the Internet* (pp. 157–170). Oxford, UK: Berg.

Spradley, J. P. (1979). *The ethnographic interview.* Belmont, CA: Wadsworth/ Thompson Learning.

Webb, E. J., Campbell, D. T., Schwartz, R. D., & Sechrest, L. (2000). *Unobtrusive measures* (rev. ed.). Thousand Oaks, CA: Sage.

Wellman, B. (2004). The three ages of Internet studies: Ten, five and zero years ago. *New Media & Society, 6*(1), 123–129.

Wolcott, H. F. (2008). *Ethnography. A way of seeing* (2nd ed.). Lanham, MD: AltaMira Press.

Social Navigation on the Internet: A Framework for the Analysis of Communication Processes

MARCO LÜNICH, PATRICK RÖSSLER, and LENA HAUTZER
Department of Media & Communications, University of Erfurt, Erfurt, Germany

The term "social navigation" (SN) refers to media use patterns that are driven by the previous media activities of others. This phenomenon is widely encountered in social media environments, which allow users to easily leave and receive information. However, investigating the variety of SN actions, such as rating, forwarding, and even producing media items oneself, increases the prevalent challenges of empirical research on web content. The article reflects on these challenges and offers possible solutions via the example of a pilot study concerning online news based on a multi-method design with a particular emphasis on online content analysis. Special attention is devoted to the dynamics of online media and online news in particular, data reactivity during research, algorithmic content production, and the impact of relationship-related information.

INTRODUCTION

While searching for information on the World Wide Web, users are increasingly confronted with traces of other users' activities. More and more websites and social media applications allow users to rate content of mass media

---

This article is based on a study conducted at the University of Erfurt, co-authored by Leonie Crayen, Katharina Füser, Anke Grünhaupt, Theresa Hofmann, Anne Müller, and Sebastian Zeitler. The research was supported by a grant of the Thüringer Landesmedienanstalt (TLM), Germany.

online[1] or to forward it to other people. Moreover, users are often able to comment directly or even to blog articles about the pieces of information encountered. This additional information on other users' perceptions is either actively produced (e.g., in the case of a comment) or automatically recorded (by an algorithm that counts the clicks on a link or files the time spent on a certain website). Often, this information is itself edited and published on the websites. In this case, users may assess the additional information that now accompanies the original news item, possibly having an impact on how subsequent users select and retrieve information. This type of orientation on the behavior of other people was earlier labeled "social navigation" (Forsberg, 1998), defined as "navigation that is driven by the actions of others" (Svensson, 2000, p. 1). Today, website operators display these data in the form of toplists (or so-called News Recommendation Engines; Thorson, 2008), which contain evidence on the most popular information on online news websites—usually the "most read," "most forwarded," or "most commented" news articles.

Most research on social navigation (SN) stems from the field of computer science and focuses on building software that supports SN (Dourish & Chalmers, 1994; Forsberg, 1998) and facilitates user orientation in an SN system (Farzan, 2009; Freyne, Farzan, Brusilovsky, Smyth, & Coyle, 2007). Studies from communications scholars are rather scarce and focus primarily on certain parts of the phenomenon of SN. For instance, Walther, DeAndrea, Kim, and Anthony (2010) investigated user comments related to YouTube videos, while Himelboim, McCreery, and Smith (2011) studied the exchange of information within social networks via Twitter. Knobloch-Westerwick, Sharma, Hansen, and Alter (2005) conducted experiments on how people select online news articles that have been enhanced with information about the preceding use by others.

Empirical research on the phenomenon of SN, and especially on the emergence of messages like automatic counts of clicks and likes as well as user comments, can give insight into the origin of SN and its impact on the processes of media and interpersonal communication. However, research on traces of users' activities on the Internet obviously moves beyond conventional methodological standards, and it challenges the instruments of empirical research, calling for new approaches. To obtain reliable and valid results, audience research on the World Wide Web (and using social media in particular) needs to take into account the characteristics of the objects under study. Next to the difficulties that inevitably arise when investigating dynamic and ever-changing web services, the definition and distinction of various actions already described represent another challenge, as they not only differ from website to website but also in the perception of each user who uses them.

This article focuses on these and other problems that come with analyzing SN functions and actions and the audience's use of them in a social media environment with a particular emphasis on online news.[2] To avoid a rather infertile discourse on methodological implications, we argue on the basis of a case study to illustrate the application of both flexible and standardized research instruments, integrated into a multi-method design that incorporates qualitative as well as quantitative research strategies.

THEORETICAL MODELING

Any research on SN requires a full understanding of the underlying communication process. Therefore, it seems essential to structure and define the communicator's and recipient's roles, and to shed some light on how the messages involved are subject to change. For this purpose we briefly introduce a theoretical framework of SN that links various established theories from the field of communication research.

Flexible approaches have proven to be of great use when focusing on online communication processes from a theoretical perspective (Rössler & Legrand, 2012). On the one hand, motivational aspects of SN actions like the rating and forwarding of information or producing content, as well as how people orient themselves based on this information, need to be depicted from a user perspective. On the other hand, the message and its attributes need to be considered as well, because their nature affects the perception of media items and subsequent SN actions. For this it seems helpful to follow the logic of the dynamic-transactional approach (DTA) developed by Früh and Schönbach (1982; Früh & Wirth, 1992). The DTA allows the modeling of communication processes that include factors influencing the user's actions. Moreover, it stresses the relevance of the message, which in our case changes with the (aggregated) information added by the user's actions (SN information; see the center of Figure 1). The DTA also comprises a strong dynamic perspective, conceptualizing the consequences not as "effects" of these messages and the accompanying SN information in a traditional sense. Rather, the fast change of communication roles between a "communicator" and a "recipient" and the internal processing that takes place on each user's part altogether constitute a transactional relationship with mutual influences in the course of time. For a more detailed description see Hautzer, Lünich, and Rössler (2012).

As a basic prerequisite of our model we assume that every SN action features a gatekeeping (GK) dimension (Rössler, 2005). Even a simple click, which unintentionally increases a website's click counter, produces new information—and so does each more or less deliberate action such as rating, forwarding information, or commenting on it. Consequently, these SN actions are gatekeeping decisions, which have implications on the proliferation and diffusion of information (Shoemaker & Vos, 2009).

The permanent adjustment of a user's activation and knowledge levels leads to a selection (i.e., clicking on a link of a news article) and, in case of a positive result, to a perception (i.e., reading the article) of the respective content. During this oscillation of selection and reception, the subjective comprehension of the content (intertransaction) changes, and the same is true for the concomitant interplay of activation and knowledge (intratransaction). As

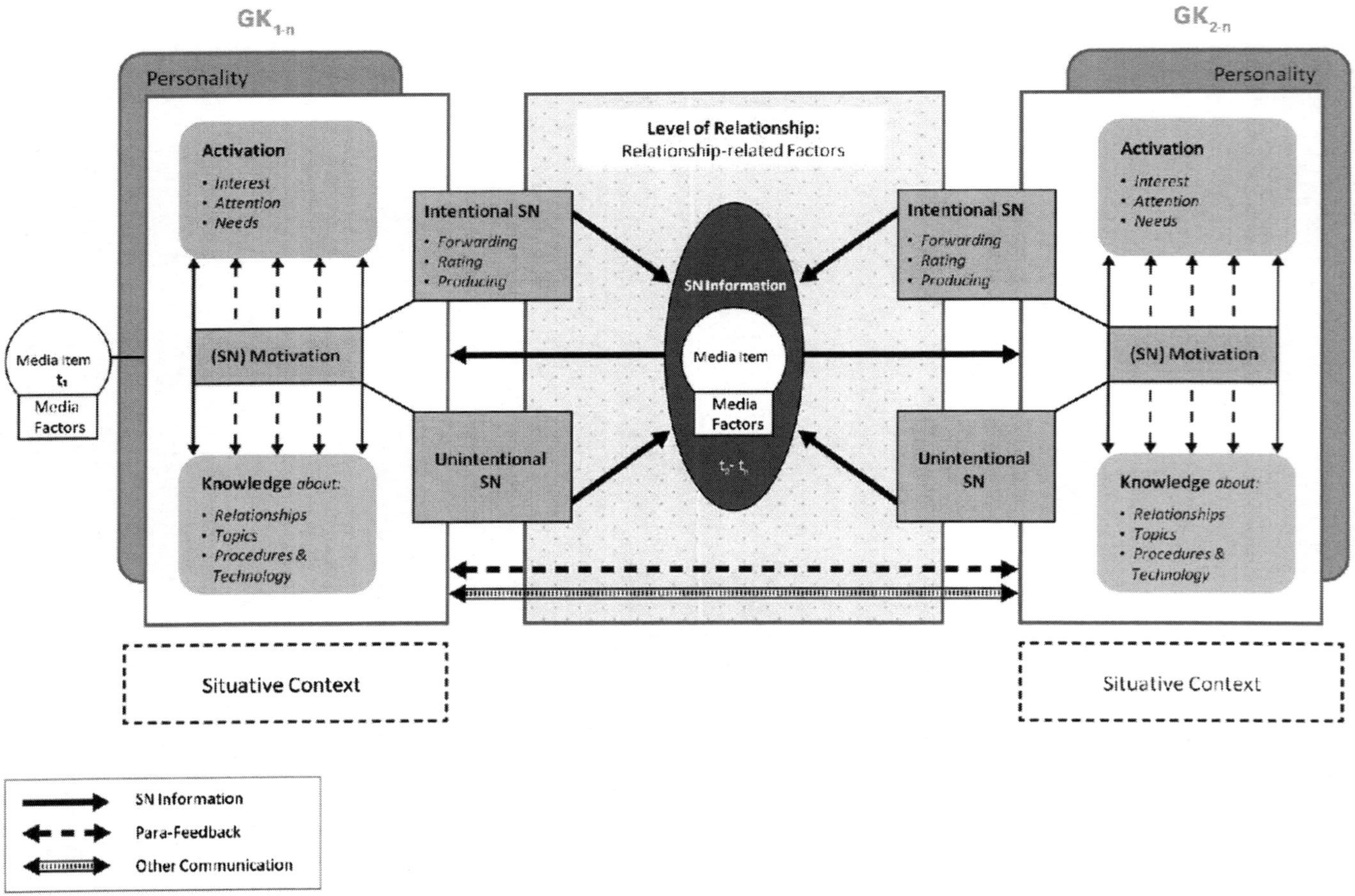

FIGURE 1 Theoretical model of the SN process on the micro level (Illustration based on Früh and Schönbach, 1982).

a consequence, these transactions might result in a motivation to intentionally perform SN actions. The decision to do so is influenced, among other things, by a person's character traits (e.g., opinion leadership) and relationship-related factors between two individuals (e.g., the perceived closeness to a person), complemented by various context factors (e.g., the time available) and factors related to media content (e.g., news values).

Next to the intentional action, each perception leaves behind an unintentional footprint. These data are often processed automatically by hidden algorithms on the news website and subsequently presented in an aggregated manner ("toplists"). The media content is now "enriched" by further information, which may stimulate other users to read a certain article—or even to perform an SN action themselves. By constantly processing the incoming user data through algorithms, the toplists (or other aggregated and published information) are permanently updated. This changes both the media content and its position on a media outlet's website.

Our theoretical reflections on the micro level immediately prompted us to address possible implications on a macro level. Even though we did not investigate possible macro level effects of SN in our pilot study, we want to briefly outline some theory-based assumptions for how individual SN actions and perceptions could affect issue development on a larger scale. Concerning the issue attention cycle (Downs, 1972), the effects of SN might be of high interest, as SN could influence the attention for a single news item as well as the general issue attention. This might explain how topics could proliferate through SN and even unknown issues could spill over to the mass media. In general, the diffusion of issues and events through SN could lead to faster and, eventually, greater public attention than by mass media coverage only. However, SN on a macro level may also impact societal integration and fragmentation (McQuail, 2010).

The consequences of these ongoing changes for any concept of media effects (which is the basis for much empirical research) have already been intensively discussed by Früh and Schönbach (1982). They concluded that an improved concept of media effects does not need to have a new theoretical definition of what an "effect" is, but rather a new suggestion for how a methodological perspective on the "stimuli" could be shaped. Consequently, the aim of our empirical pilot study (based on the theoretical model of the phenomenon Social Navigation as outlined above) was to develop instruments that are able to grasp different parts of its dynamics while contributing to a broader understanding of its nature.

ANALYZING SOCIAL NAVIGATION: A MULTI-METHOD APPROACH

Our theoretical modeling indicates that social navigation as a phenomenon affects the role of the gatekeeper(s) as well as the message itself. A thorough investigation therefore demands a multi-method design. On the one hand, the gatekeeper, permanently switching roles between being a communicator and a recipient of online media content, needs to be investigated by methods devoted to the research on individual cognitions, namely, survey research. The reports of participants contribute to the understanding of media usage, behavior patterns, and personal attitudes (see Fink, 2003) and allow insight into processes of transaction. Thus, as a first step we conducted explorative, semistandardized guided in-depth interviews with experts and regular users, which were later analyzed with qualitative instruments. Subsequently an online survey helped us to gain a better understanding of the patterns identified previously, in particular with regard to the generalizability of our results.

As explained earlier, each analysis of SN also needs to take the online content into account, as it constitutes the foundation of SN. However, the simple application of traditional instruments from content analysis research is often inappropriate. As easy as a plain adjustment appears to be on first sight, it misses the evident characteristics of online content (Rössler, Hautzer, & Lünich, in press; Rössler & Wirth, 2001). As mentioned earlier, the special influence of users and algorithms on dynamic content, especially online news, poses an inherent challenge for the conception of content analysis instruments and their implementation.

In-Depth Interviews

To obtain a first insight into the phenomenon of SN, guided and structured in-depth interviews were conducted, aiming at: (1) a first approach to SN via the assessments of experts from the diverse fields of online communication; and (2) understanding the motives and usage patterns of "ordinary" Internet users.

Interviews with experts

Seven expert interviews were conducted with professionals from the field of online communication (e.g., social network sites, online journalism, online communication research, etc.) and followed a guideline that consisted of general questions concerning SN and focused on the estimation of users' influence on journalistic websites. Experts had to disclose a broad assessment of SN from their own field and expertise; the results were crucial for theorizing and for our research strategy in total.

The interviews confirmed that SN supposedly is a widespread phenomenon relevant for online communication. At the same time, experts anticipated different effects of SN applications on the user, on the audience, on society as a whole—and on media providers themselves, too. The conversations revealed that SN needs to be described in multifaceted ways and that any systematization of SN functions and their implementation in online applications would therefore become a complex task. The interviews also provided speculations about future development in the online environment, such as an increased importance of entertaining and visual content, as well as the relevance of click counters for feedback purposes. Hence our content analysis (see later discussion) included, for instance, entertaining and visual components of news articles, because one expert highlighted that editorial staff may counteract decreasing attention for an article by adding or changing the accompanying picture.

Interviews with Users

Guided interviews with ›regular‹ online users emphasized the motivation for performing SN actions oneself and for perceiving content enriched with SN information. Interviews with 25 savvy online users started with exemplary screenshots to introduce the subject of SN. Subsequently, each participant was asked about the motives for her or his individual usage. These interviews served as a foundation for the online survey and revealed that the users understand SN and its usage differently. As a consequence the questionnaire had to address the various actions and applications of SN in a rather abstract way to include participants' independent from their previous experience with online communication. Due to the importance the participants ascribed to personal relationships with people from whom they receive SN information, a major part of the online survey later emphasized the influence of these interpersonal factors.

The online content analysis benefitted from the guideline-based interviews, too, especially because users reported using SN frequently via social network sites and online news websites. For this reason we focused on the latter to investigate socially navigated content (see later discussion). Participants were also asked to rank the relevance of several types of SN information, leading to the insight that toplists are important to the final decision to take notice of an article. With regard to the type of content that stimulated SN actions, experts generally estimated entertaining content such as funny images and videos to receive particular attention. As a consequence, the coding system for our content analysis on online news also had to include aspects and "news" factors referring to entertainment.[3]

Online Survey

Referring to our SN model on the micro level (see Figure 1), the online survey focused on a standardized analysis of important components of the SN process occurring between two gatekeepers (see Hautzer, Lünich, & Rössler, 2012). Again, it should be emphasized that both perspectives of SN should be considered: the execution of SN actions and the reception of socially navigated media content. From a practical point of view, it makes sense to conduct an online survey constituting fast, direct, and cheap access to an Internet-savvy target group. As an empirical method, the standardized survey captures cognitive aspects and measures behavior patterns of the past, as well as the intentions of actions in the future (Fink, 2003).

Concerning the standardization of the instrument, the main challenges were the operationalization of the SN actions and the perception of socially navigated content, respectively. Every application that enables users to rate and forward content or to produce something new on the basis of existing content has specific characteristics and functions, which result in a certain application configuration and design that a user must deal with. Although all these applications may be reduced to the basic function of "rating something," "forwarding something," or "commenting on something," those response options are, by nature, rather abstract and imprecise. In our pilot study the SN actions were conceived as (1) rating content by a rating scale (e.g., star ratings or Facebook's "like" button), (2) rating content within a comment section, and (3) forwarding content (via e-mail or special applications on a website or social network), which featured two kinds of production—(4) additional remarks referring to the original content via a comment section, or (5) a blog entry. For each of these actions the survey included a nonspecific example; pretests ensured that all those examples were phrased in a way that was intelligible to all. Due to this procedure the questions were not tailored to a certain situation or detached from a particular subject. However, future studies could apply a technically more sophisticated approach employing a flexible design that measures at a random point in time while respondents actually use online content or perform SN actions (see an exemplary conception by Scherer & Schlütz, 2002). Moreover, randomized screenshots could be used as examples to illustrate the single actions and to achieve a common understanding among all participants.

Both the dynamics and the multifaceted nature of an online environment impede the operationalization of relevant survey constructs that probably need to be generated specifically for each new study. While trying to estimate the influence of individual motivations on the frequency of forwarding content, it must be stated that users might also find it difficult to remember their actions precisely. Thus it seems difficult to break down the performance of actions for a typical day or a typical week, which leads to substantial inaccuracies in data collection.

Online Content Analysis

For an online content analysis of social navigation, it seems crucial to develop an appropriate instrument that is flexible enough to accurately measure content that is generated dynamically. However, the methodological approach requires a certain degree of standardization within data collection to ensure a certain quality standard: reliable coding, results that may be compared to earlier findings, and instruments suitable to be transferred to other studies. After a brief introduction to the background of our research, we detail the prerequisites and challenges of an SN online content analysis on the example of our application in a pilot study on online news and reflect on some of the solutions found.

Generally speaking, it seems quite complicated to receive comprehensive data on socially navigated media content, for a simple reason: The population of messages cannot be easily accessed because links forwarded via e-mail and content that is shared, rated, and commented on through Facebook's private user sites are not open to the public. Preliminary solutions could include cooperating with media providers or purposefully recruiting participants, but in both cases only a small number of persons and their SN messages would constitute the sample for some types of case studies.

Instead, the content analysis contributing to our pilot study focused on news articles and the SN information that can be openly accessed on online news websites. Similar to a previous U.S. study conducted by Boczkowski and Peer (2011), we analyzed the similarities and differences between articles selected and published prominently by journalists versus the most socially navigated articles. Many online media outlets currently display News Recommendation Engines (so-called toplists) identifying the most popular news items, for instance the "most read," "most forwarded," and "most commented on" articles. Our research questions looked into the influence of the articles' form and content on the dynamics of social navigation activities (e.g., its news values, including the utility of a news item for a user, the particular topic, and its position on the front page).

Online content analysis design: challenges and solutions

The content analysis of our pilot study was based on a new concept: a process analysis. The sample material consisted of all lead stories and all toplist news items of the German online news website *Spiegel Online*, which was chosen because of its popularity among German online news outlets (IVW, 2011).

For an online content analysis, it appears to be helpful when the sample material is available in digitized form (and therefore machine-readable). However, online content is also transient, nonlinear, hypertextually structured, and reactive (Rössler & Wirth, 2001). The main challenge is to adjust the method of content analysis to this new media environment and its features (see Rössler, 2010, pp. 68–71). The content production, in particular, which increasingly relies on automated algorithms, leads to staggering dynamics of media content mutually dependent on user behavior. In the following we address several of these aspects against the background of our pilot research design.

Multimedia/hypertextuality

The analysis of lead stories on the website and the articles within toplists was limited to the first three news items, respectively. On the Spiegel Online website we encountered two different toplists called the "most read" and "most forwarded" news articles, constituting the unit of analysis for the pilot study (Rössler, 2010, pp. 75–94). A news article was defined as an editorial text, a picture, a picture gallery, an interactive graphic with an associated text, a description, or a video—and the combination of all those elements. Due to the increasing amount of picture galleries and videos on Spiegel Online, a solution was required to appropriately capture those elements that go beyond the ordinary type of textual content. With regard to considerations of external validity, it appeared feasible to include only the first three pictures of each picture gallery (which was to be found above the article or within the text) and the first 30 seconds of a video. Future designs could, however, integrate evidence on the nature of attention distribution while consuming (moving) pictures, which is not available yet. For now, the only option seems to be to capture multimedia elements with flexible solutions for each individual research interest.

Generally speaking, this is actually true for each research process and each sampling unit as it demands its own definition of the unit of analysis—a challenge that is still neglected by many content analysis studies even though a number of problems may arise while coding. In analyzing websites, in particular, it is difficult to transfer tested solutions and definitions from other research objects. Web applications tend to be largely diverse and cause problems with unpredictable changes in page structures and designs, which then require new definitions and adjustments during data collection itself.

Transience

By means of a process analysis, we tried to cover at least partly the dynamics that come with the permanent move of the articles' positions on the front page and within the toplists. The individual rank of each article of the lead stories and in the toplists was recorded every 30 minutes in the course of a natural week. While longer intervals could possibly lead to a loss of information due to the frequency of editorial changes, shorter intervals would have produced additional costs. In a set of pretests the interval length of 30 minutes appropriately covered major changes while allowing for an in-depth data analysis. As we did not detect any changes in editorial content or in the toplists between midnight and 6 a.m., this time period was left out of data collection, taking the risk that in case of breaking news during the night relevant SN actions might be missed.

Methodologically, this proceeding implied a combination of content analysis and observation. Due to the vast amount of data involved, it was impossible to download complete parts of the websites for each interval for coding later. Pretests with Internet crawlers were unsatisfactory and proved to be an option that is rather prone to errors. As a result, we decided to execute the data collection manually and "live" by human coders. However, an investigation with such tight interval periods limits the volume of the coding scheme and needs technical support once it comes to difficult research objects such as news aggregators or microblogs (like Twitter, reddit, or digg). And obviously this approach is hardly appropriate for longer sample periods, given the huge workload involved.

Moreover, the probability of external problems occurring increases with the duration of data collection: An interruption of the Internet connection or technical difficulties in receiving and displaying the news articles are not uncommon, and data collection can be erroneous, too, due to coding errors evoked by stress and time pressure. Small changes within an article can go unnoticed and the coding decision cannot be reproduced. This refers to supposedly the biggest problem of live-coding—its insufficient intersubjectivity, which represents a major criterion for the quality of a content analysis (Rössler, 2010). We expect future research to have access to more intelligent and feasible technical solutions for saving vast amounts of media data, even though researchers usually lack the know-how and funding for developing sophisticated and tailored tools that fit the special needs of the respective study.

The live coding procedure is a step toward flexibility of online content analysis that originally calls for a standardized and highly structured approach of category systems and coding to ascertain reliability and comparability of results. Thus, regarding other aspects we tried to maintain these standards; for instance, all coding was done in the same room on the same computer with a safe online connection to produce a comprehensive and structured data set. At each point in time at least two coders were in charge to cope with unforeseeable situations. Whenever a shift changeover was pending, an overlap of one coding interval was scheduled to exchange all necessary information about the recent coding situation and the current state of media coverage. Next to exhaustive pretesting, an intensive coder briefing and training proved indispensable, where all coders were trained under realistic circumstances and the uncommon flexible elements of the instrument were especially stressed. All coders were integral members of the research group and held a comprehensive knowledge about the theoretical and methodological background of the study. Due to these time-consuming efforts, the process analysis of our pilot study was limited to covering one week, which affected the sample size of 167 coded articles, influenced by the unpredictable functionality of toplist algorithms.

Algorithms

It is crucial for any SN content analysis to cover and take into account the individual characteristics of the websites under study. This is especially true for the toplists and their underlying algorithms, which act as technological gatekeepers filtering the SN information available to the provider. Unfortunately, those algorithms are usually unknown and not accessible to the public, not even for research purposes. A critical evaluation of the role media providers play beyond their obvious editorial functions seems indispensable. At first glance it may seem as if those outlets influence the communication process as an organizing party only (Burkart, 2002, p. 498), but upon closer examination they depend on nontraceable technical distribution services (Neuberger, von Hofe, & Nuernbergk, 2010) with often opaque intentions. A research design can only try to cope with those limitations, as the algorithms are almost impossible to retrieve and call for misinterpretations—for example, if a list of "most clicked" articles does not reflect the sheer number of clicks but is filtered according to the interests of sponsors or of editors who wish to promote a certain issue.

From an empirical point of view, analyzing toplists also entails major problems concerning the position of the individual article: The toplists represent only a small extract of a website's content, namely, the most highly ranked items. The distance among the single list positions, however, is unknown due to the lack of information about the range of clicks (or other data consulted). Hence it remains unknown whether two subsequent ranks differ by several hundred clicks or comments—or, maybe, just two. As a researcher, one can only work with the published ranking information, which is unsatisfying concerning the data level and consequently the precision of data analysis.

Finally, we faced serious challenges posed by the inclusion of data on individual relationships into the algorithms. For instance, social network sites started to personalize the output for each user based on his or her previous interaction with a website—and the usage pattern of the user's designated friends. The underlying mechanisms are even more elusive than the algorithms of frequency toplists and may be understood only by comparisons among individual users (Baresch, Knight, Harp, & Yaschur, 2011). This results in methodological problems for data collection, and furthermore it complicates the interpretation of results: One major finding from our pilot online survey highlighted the relevance of personal relationships with others on the selection of socially navigated content, along with additional factors related to these relationships. In research practice, a content analysis of relationship-filtered SN data would require the support of social network sites, which are substantially constrained by matters of protection of data privacy. Thus, the only option seems a closer linking of survey research and content analysis, which may result in an increasing number of case studies investigating certain topics or individual networks.

Dynamics

Any content analysis that is not itself dynamic will probably fail to record changes of content. A cross-sectional analysis, which works with one particular version of an article only, cannot ascertain the aforementioned reproducibility of results. In our analysis we found, surprisingly, that about 16% of the coded articles were subject to one or more changes by the editorial staff (or, depending on the point of view, almost five out of six top articles remained untouched). As well as possible changes within an article, the permanent move of news articles on a website cannot be grasped by ordinary content analysis instruments. Thus, both dynamic elements were coded for each article—the position and the changes of an article over time. As a result, new categories had to be established and defined (for tapping, e.g., a live ticker or breaking news) to code an individual post from a ticker, as a separate article connected it to the major article with a special key variable updated during the coding process. From our experience, we would conclude that the dynamics of each website need a thorough examination and an individual decision on which options should be incorporated into a study, as there are only a few possibilities for standardizing the recording of dynamic elements.

Reactivity

One significant obstacle for a content analysis of SN information is easily overlooked: Unlike traditional content analysis, the research material is highly reactive. While, for instance, videotapes do not change when they are watched over and over again for coding purposes, aggregated SN counts constituting our research object will constantly change due to the usage of the website in the course of the investigation. This might be problematic when the researcher's clicks lead to ranking changes in situations with low website traffic. Of course, such a manipulation of the research object should be avoided right from the start, and if website content can be downloaded the manipulation is limited to a few clicks. Any live coding procedure, however, should aim at minimizing these distortions—for instance, by observation or, better, knowledge of the algorithmic structure, which might be estimated on the basis of previous testing or insights into the editorial rhythm of updating content.

RESULTS AND CONCLUSION

This is not the place for presenting empirical results of our multi-method design in detail. However, we briefly address a few selected outcomes of our pilot study to provide insight into some opportunities and limitations, as well as ideas for future designs of SN research. First of all, the multi-method approach we pursued served well in answering our research questions in general. As there were hardly any data available, our questions, as briefly mentioned before, focused on general relations between online news articles and social navigation dynamics. The majority of articles from our content analysis sample were lead stories because the editorial part featured a higher frequency of replacements, while toplist articles were ranked longer in average. Interestingly, some articles qualified both as lead stories and "most read" articles, and some articles from the "most read" list were also found in the "most forwarded" list. Much to our surprise, no *Spiegel Online* lead story at all made it to the "most forwarded" list. This indicates that the "forward" toplist mirrors the complementary function of lead stories, as users might prefer to forward original and unusual content that was not already prominently selected and presented at the top of the website by journalists. In all probability we rather assume that the editorial staff or *Spiegel*'s IT department could have defined a particular algorithm to safeguard diversity in rankings and for this purpose prevented articles from surfacing in both categories.

Overall, lead stories focused mainly on politics and current societal debates and were more factual and less entertaining, while articles were more likely forwarded when they consisted of entertaining elements and exhibited a certain utility for the recipient.

Our results also confirm that the "active user" plays an increasingly important role in online communication, and that his or her influence on journalism gradually gains researchers' interest. On the one hand, applications that deliberately allow for user participation (e.g., through ratings and comments) are on the rise, which raises questions about the user's selections and perceptions (Houston, Hansen, & Nisbett, 2011; Knobloch-Westerwick et al., 2005). On the other hand, onliners include aggregated data of previous usage, which is often generated unintentionally, into their decisions. Our interviews reflected the ongoing discussion about privacy protection when data is collected for commercial use. Respondents expressed resentments toward algorithm-based content; they feared a decrease of diversity due to information filters and personalized websites (Pariser, 2011). Serendipities and contact with new and unfamiliar information might decline as behavior patterns become more predictable (Meckel, 2011). However, others argue that chances for diverse experiences increase; they emphasize the additional choices and opportunities for orientation when users and their behavior are actively included in the journalistic process. When people increasingly orient themselves on others, aspects of relationship maintenance gain relevance. The actions of another person whom one knows and probably trusts affect how we allocate attention. We observe a merger between a purely algorithmic processing of data and a media repertoire based on content we are confronted with because other people, among them our friends, saw or used them before us.

As a consequence, recent developments in the online world can only be grasped by academic research by employing the full catalogue of empirical methods. Our preliminary explorative research gave insights into challenges of subsequent standardized data collections, as it incorporated the different perspectives and levels of experience characterizing experts and users of online communication. Our standardized survey of users proved that, in general, existing questionnaire instruments can be transferred and modified to SN research, while a suitable operationalization of single navigation actions remains quite difficult. The diversity of applications offered to online users that refer to SN, therefore, needs to be addressed in a survey that is more abstract and formal, fitting the target group.

A content analysis contributes substantially to our understanding of socially navigated content. Connected with the findings of user research, it permits us to draw inferences on the long-term development of media usage patterns (and, possibly, on concomitant information processing). Methodological challenges include the dynamics, algorithms, and reactivity of the research object, calling for sophisticated solutions in study design and data collection, as suggested here by the "live" coding procedure. Technical developments as well as relationship-related factors recommend a combination of survey and content analysis designs. Therefore, this article opts for multi-method proceedings that flexibly investigate SN phenomena. However, it became evident that the traditional instruments of content analysis are not able to cover essential characteristics of media products based on algorithms. Instead, we favor developing innovative data collection designs that can be tailored to address a particular research question, rather than applying conventional survey and content analysis approaches.

NOTES

1. Even though it clearly belongs to the phenomenon of social navigation, we explicitly do not address and investigate socially navigated content that is subject only to interpersonal communication (timeline posts on Facebook, personal messages on social media sites, etc.) as it is not publicly accessible.

2. This article is not a mere methodological paper on the theory and application of a certain method in a particular area of study, nor is it a research report on a special subject. To give the reader a vivid understanding of the various implications when analyzing social media, we both address general methodological issues and provide ways to tackle those issues at hand. Here and throughout the article the interested reader is referred to the comprehensive report on the study this article is based on. See Hautzer, Lünich, and Rössler (2012) for a depiction of all relevant empirical steps and results and an extensive discussion of both.

3. Note that the survey was aimed at investigating SN behavior in general and was therefore not only focused on online news.

REFERENCES

Baresch, B., Harp, D., Knight, L., & Yaschur, C. (2011, April). *Friends who choose your news: An Analysis of content links on Facebook.* Paper presented at ISOJ: The Official Research Journal of International Symposium on Online Journalism, Austin TX.

Boczkowski, P. J., & Peer, L. (2011). The choice gap: The divergent online news preferences of journalists and consumers. *Journal of Communication, 61*(5), 857–876.

Burkart, R. (2002). *Kommunikationswissenschaft: Grundlagen und Problemfelder; Umrisse einer interdisziplinären Sozialwissenschaft* (4th ed.). Wien, Germany: Böhlau.

Dourish, P., & Chalmers, M. (1994). Running out of space: Models of information navigation. *HCI, Glasgow.* Retrieved from http://www.dcs.gla.ac.uk/matthew/papers/hci94.pdf

Downs, A. (1972). Up and down with ecology—The "issue-attention cycle." *Public Interest, 28*(2), 38–50.

Farzan, R. (2009). *A study of social navigation support under different situational and personal factors.* Retrieved from http://etd.library.pitt.edu/ETD/available/etd-04222009-134348/unrestricted/FarzanRostaApril2009.pdf

Fink, A. (2003). *The survey kit* (2nd ed.), Thousand Oaks, CA: Sage

Forsberg, J. M. (1998). *Social navigation: An extended definition.* Uppsala, Sweden. Retrieved from http://www.nada.kth.se/~forsberg/Documents/SocNav.pdf

Freyne, J., Farzan, R., Brusilovsky, P., Smyth, B., & Coyle, M. (2007). Collecting community wisdom: Integrating social search & social navigation. In *IUI '07: Proceedings of the 12th International Conference on Intelligent User Interfaces* (pp. 52–61). New York, NY: ACM Press.

Früh, W., & Schönbach, K. (1982). Der dynamisch-transaktionale Ansatz 27, 74–88. Ein neues Paradigma der Medienwirkungen. *Publizistik, 27*(1), 74–88.

Früh, W., & Wirth, W. (1992). Looking into the black box: Intolerance of ambiguity and dynamic-transactional processes in the development of issue-related images. *European Journal of Communication, 7*(4), 541–569.

Hautzer, L., Lünich, M., & Rössler, P. (2012). *Social Navigation: Neue Orientierungsmuster bei der Mediennutzung im Internet.* Baden-Baden, Germany: Nomos-Verlagsgesellschaft.

Himelboim, I., McCreery, S., & Smith, M. (2011, May). *Birds of a feather tweet together: Integrating network and content analyses to examine cross-ideology exposure on Twitter.* Paper presented at the Annual Conference of the International Communication Association, Boston, MA.

Houston, J. B., Hansen, G. J., & Nisbett, G. S. (2011). Influence of user comments on perceptions of media bias and third-person effect in online news. *Electronic News, 5*(2), 79–92.

IVW. (2011). *Online data of January 2011.* Retrieved from http://ausweisung.ivw-online.de/i.php?s=1&mz=201101&sall=1&sort=dvisits&angebote=1&netz=1&vgm=1&svisits=1&svisitsiabs=1&svisitsipro=1&svisitsaabs=1&svisitsapro=1

Knobloch-Westerwick, S., Sharma, N., Hansen, D. L., & Alter, S. (2005). Impact of popularity indications on readers' selective exposure to online news. *Journal of Broadcasting & Electronic Media, 49*(3), 296–313.

McQuail, D. (2010). *McQuail's mass communication theory.* London, UK: Sage.

Meckel, M. (2011). *Next: Erinnerungen an eine Zukunft ohne uns.* Reinbek bei Hamburg, Germany: Rowohlt.

Neuberger, C., Vom Hofe, H. J., & Nuernbergk, C. (2010). *Twitter und Journalismus: Der Einfluss des "Social Web" auf die Nachrichten.* Düsseldorf, Germany: Landesanstalt für Medien Nordrhein-Westfalen (LfM).

Pariser, E. (2011). *The filter bubble: What the Internet is hiding from you.* New York, NY: Penguin Press.

Rössler, P. (2005). The myth of the re-invented journalism. Why gatekeepers do not disappear in the Internet environment: Functional and normative gatekeeping of web communicators. In P. Rössler & F. Krotz (Eds.), *Mythen der Mediengesellschaft. The Media Society and its Myths* (pp. 177–203). Konstanz, Germany: UVK Verlagsgesellschaft.

Rössler, P. (2010). *Inhaltsanalyse*. Stuttgart, Germany: UVK-Verl.-Ges.

Rössler, P., Hautzer, L., & Lünich, M. (In press). Online-Inhaltsanalyse. In B. Batinic, N. Jackob, J. Schmidt, M. Taddicken, & M. Welker (Eds.), *Handbuch der Online-Forschung*. Köln, Germany: Herbert von Halem Verlag.

Rössler, P., & Legrand, M. (2012, May). *Political communication in the social web: A process model on the example of user-generated online videos' production and reception*. Paper presented at the Annual Conference of the International Communication Association, Phoenix AZ.

Rössler, P., & Wirth, W. (2001). Inhaltsanalysen im World Wide Web. Probleme und Perspektiven. In W. Wirth & E. Lauf (Eds.), *Inhaltsanalyse: Perspektiven, Probleme, Potentiale* (pp. 280–302). Köln, Germany: Herbert von Halem Verlag.

Scherer, H., & Schlütz, D. (2002). Gratifikation à la minute: Die zeitnahe Erfassung von Gratifikationen. In P. Rössler, S. Kubisch, & V. Gehrau (Eds.), *Empirische Perspektiven der Rezeptionsforschung* (pp. 133–151). München, Germany: Reinhard Fischer.

Shoemaker, P. J., & Vos, T. P. (2009). *Gatekeeping theory*. New York, NY: Routledge.

Svensson, M. (2000). *Defining and designing social navigation*. Licentiate thesis, Stockholm University, Stockholm. Retrieved from http://eprints.sics.se/88/1/thesis.pdf

Thorson, E. (2008). Changing patterns of news consumption and participation. *Information, Communication & Society, 11*(4), 473–489.

Walther, J. B., DeAndrea, D., Kim, J., & Anthony, J. C. (2010). The influence of online comments on perceptions of antimarijuana public service announcements on YouTube. *Human Communication Research*, *36*(4), 469–492.

Employing Creative Research Methods with Tweens in Estonia and Sweden: Reflections on a Case Study of Identity Construction on Social Networking Sites

ANDRA SIIBAK
University of Tartu, Tartu, Estonia

MICHAEL FORSMAN
Södertörn University, Stockholm, Sweden

PATRIK HERNWALL
Stockholm University, Stockholm, and Södertörn University, Stockholm, Sweden

In this article we discuss our experiences from setting up workshops, inspired by creative research methods (Gauntlett, 2005, 2007), on the theme of construction of online identities by young people (aged 13–14 years) in Estonia and in Sweden. Our primary focus is on the opportunities and possible challenges involved when using creative research methods to study the identity construction process of young people by engaging them in participatory, creative activities. Our experiences indicate that such an approach can be especially beneficial when working with young people, as it enabled us to observe the actual construction and usage of gender codes and norms, both in the offline peer group context and in an online setting.

This article is written as part of the project "Construction and normalization of gender online among young people in Estonia and Sweden," funded by the Foundation for Baltic and East European Studies (Östersjöstiftelsen) (2009–2012). Andra Siibak is also thankful for the support of a target financed project from the Estonian Ministry of Science and Education (SF0180017s07) and a grant from the Estonian Science Foundation (8527).

INTRODUCTION

In recent years, social researchers working with qualitative methods have shown a growing interest in "new creative methods" (Gauntlett, 2007), indicating, in the words of Buckingham (2009, p. 633), "a broader move towards 'participatory' research methods." This approach is now being employed within a wide range of disciplines—sociology, psychology, social policy, education, and health—often in research involving children and young people (Awan, 2007; Gauntlett, 2007; Lealand & Zanker, 2006), and in studies concerned with issues of identity and meaning-making (Awan, 2007; Gauntlet, 2007).

Often, creative methods are synonymous with the production of visual material (drawings, photos, videos, and collages, but even three-dimensional artefacts made from clay, Legos, etc.). However, the very idea behind the usage of creative methods suggests that such methodology can help to provide knowledge about aspects of social life that may not be accessible with traditional qualitative research such as focus groups, interviews, or participatory observation techniques (Gauntlett, 2007, p. 182).

"Method" and "creative" are two central concepts in Gauntlett's terminology, words that both are rich in connotation. In this context, "method" refers to the measurements and resources used in finding a systematic way to knowledge production, whereas "creative" should not be read as meaning artistic or tied to cultural evaluation, but rather as referring to making something that did not exist before the creative act. The "new" in Gauntlett's discussion indicates novelty or a need for new impulses—particularly "an alternative to language-driven qualitative research methods" (Gauntlett, 2011, p. 4). This is closely connected to the transformation of our present day media culture into an increasingly multimodal environment with an emphasis on ubiquitous learning (Cope & Kalantzis, 2009) and growing demands for creative competence (Bamford, 2006). Here, school teaching in many countries is falling behind, as not only is it still dominated by analogous and monomedial techniques, but also it remains firm on typographic signs and verbal argumentation.

Simultaneously, in their leisure time and in their contacts with peers, children and young people act and learn within the framework of what Jenkins (2006) has termed participatory culture, where every user and consumer can also be a producer (Bruns, 2006). In fact, young people growing up in late modern societies have become accustomed to using media, social media in particular, in the creation, negotiation, and interpretation of their layers of identity such as gender and age, but also class and ethnicity. As Drotner (2008) puts it, "Leisure is hard work," where various online platforms and social networking sites (SNS) are core spaces. Yet we still know relatively little about the actual practices of young people on the Net when "making gender" or negotiating age. Considering the preceding, we believe that creative research methods can generate new and other kinds of data and offer other perspectives, and hence are a valuable tool for deepening our understanding of young people's online practices.

In this article we discuss our experiences from setting up workshops with young people (13–14 years old) in Estonia and in Sweden, with the research process framed and conducted in line with the ideas underlying creative research methods. Our ambition was to study the construction of online identities among tweens, paying special attention to how they express gender and age in this culturally intense phase of life between childhood and teenage proper. The aim of this article is to reflect upon the experiences gained from the two workshops and to discuss the challenges and opportunities arising from making use of the new creative research methods.

SOME CHARACTERISTICS OF CREATIVE RESEARCH METHODS

Creative research methods are not a totally new phenomenon within the social sciences. In fact, there is a long tradition of using and experimenting with different kinds of action or participatory research (even within the framework of "positivistic" experimentation) in order to arrive at new insights (Denzin & Lincoln, 1994). For instance, creative methods have been actively used in media studies, where numerous researchers have asked children and young people to engage in creative projects either by making drawings (Lealand & Zanker, 2006; Young & Barretti, 2001), shooting videos (Bloustein, 1998; Downmunt, 2001; Gauntlett, 1997; Holliday, 2004), making "scrapbooks" that combine images with text (Bragg & Buckingham, 2008), or mounting collages (Awan, 2007; Williams, 2002). Several researchers (e.g., Perkel & Yardi, 2006; Radley, Hodgetts, & Cullen, 2005) have also made use of photo or video elicitation in which creative (visual) material produced by either the participants or the researcher has been used as a basis for carrying out interviews. Another prominent strand of research comprises studies working with a form known as digital storytelling, where (often disempowered) subjects have the possibility of telling their story in a multimodal fashion based on personal experience (Alexander, 2011; Lundby, 2008).

This latter method is particularly useful when engaging in research involving children and young people. Multimodal or at least visual means have often been used to pinpoint two important aspects that researchers need to take into account when making qualitative studies with young people. First is that the fixation on verbal utterances that comes with interviews and other oral-based methods may not do justice to illustration of the experiences of the young. Second is the fact that the act of interpreting the data gathered also includes a considerable amount of translation of often complex and heterogeneous material into (what is possible to express by) verbal statements; this is obviously a pressing issue, as the modes of communications are often multimodal (cf. Kress, 2010). The uniqueness of the kind of creative and participatory methods that Gauntlett presents, in comparison with other action-oriented and visual approaches, lies in requiring the participants "to spend time applying their playful or creative attention to the act of making something symbolic or metaphorical, and then reflecting on it" (Gauntlett, 2007, p. 3).

In the context of creative methods, it is important to note that the role and skills of the participants are made prominent. This is in strong contrast to more singular visual methods such as photos and drawings, where the visual assignments undertaken by research participants are usually "read" and interpreted by the researchers themselves. The intention of the creative research approach is to give "voice" to the young people participating in the study. In fact, Gauntlett (2007, p. 125) emphasizes that in analyzing the data gathered by means of creative research methods, researchers should not impose *their* meanings on the photos, drawings, videos, Lego constructions, and so on produced by the participants, but follow the classic idea known from visual analysis that "a picture is a statement" (Arnheim, 1969, p. 137).

In social semiotics (sensemaking as a social practice), the meaning of a sign does not reside in grammatical or linguistic structures, but in real-life social situations, where the rhetor (actor) (Kress, 2010) chooses signs from whatever semiotic resources are available in relation to communicative, social, and personal goals. Thus, signs are motivated. Kress (2010, p. 69) writes:

> In signs, sign makers mediate their own social story, their present social position, their sense of their social environment in the process of communication; and this becomes tangible in the reshaping of the cultural resources used in representation and communication. The makers of signs stamp present social conditions into the signs they make and make these signs into the bearers of social histories.

When taking each picture/artifact as a sign, the power balance between the participant and the researcher is considered as shifting into a more collaborative model (Pink, 2003; Toon, 2008).

In this respect, as suggested by Harper (1998, p. 35), "the researcher becomes a listener" whose intention should be to keep "a consequent interest in and acknowledgment of the co-construction of knowledge between participant and researcher" (Toon, 2008, p. 22). Such mutually acknowledged cooperation between researcher and participants in producing new knowledge would "help [researchers] understand how participants see their worlds" (Gauntlett, 2007, p. 107). It is also believed that when participants are given the opportunity to take active part in the study they are able to communicate different kinds of information (Gauntlett, 2007, p. 182) through which the researchers can examine and probe "visible but unseen" everyday behavior (Prosser, 2007, p. 16).

The latter opportunity arises due to the fact that the usage of creative methods implies bodily engagement, as research participants are asked to do something. However, the process of physically creating something—taking photos; making a drawing or forming something out of clay—cannot be separated from the mental processes necessary for creating the artifact or visual expression. This physical and mental involvement is also important since the participants often are asked to orally interpret and comment upon their own work.

One further quality of creative research methods is that they can be used for research both in natural settings and in spaces specifically designed for research. The present study, as shown in the following, is of the latter kind. The arrangements and settings for research of this kind should offer space for flow and enjoyment, and maybe one could speak here of something like a "playful turn" in social research, bearing in mind Gauntlett's (2007) groundbreaking Lego project.

the.GTO.project

The workshops were conducted within the framework of the.GTO.project.[1] Before going on to describe the creative method we used and our reflections upon it, some words on the context in which this study was conducted are therefore appropriate. What we have studied within the.GTO.project are the practices of online interaction among tweens—defined as children aged 10 to 14 years. The main focus of this research is on how societal power structures such as gender and age are constructed in peer cultures on social networking sites (SNS). A central premise for the.GTO.project is that in young people's creation of their life-world of today the online world of social interaction is inextricably intertwined with the offline world.

the.GTO.project (2009–2012) consists of three parts. In the first two parts of the project we used traditional research methods. First we interviewed 10- to 14-year-olds in both Sweden and in Estonia about their practices and thoughts concerning the Internet, gender, age, leisure, school, and so on. In the second and partly parallel phase, we did a form of content analysis with particular focus on visual codes, such as norms for the self-portraits and images of friends that were uploaded. Here the focus was on image sharing sites, such as Swedish dayviews.se and the Estonian counterpart, rate.ee.

The findings of these interviews and content analyses indicate that heteronormativity is a very strict norm that the tweens share and recreate among themselves on these networking sites (Hernwall & Siibak 2011; Siibak & Hernwall, 2011). We also discovered that in identity construction, gender often is portrayed in a very stereotypically and formatted way, and age is an important marker. Furthermore, our studies indicate that girls tend to be more advanced in their online self-portrayal, as they could play with the male gaze and other visual gender norms. In comparison with the girls, the appearance of boys in the photos seems to be less sexualized (Hernwall, 2009; Hernwall & Siibak, 2011; Siibak & Hernwall, 2011).

It was in the third and final part of the.GTO.project that we decided to make use of the new creative methods as a way of getting closer to the young people at the centre of attention. This also gave us the opportunity of testing some tentative hypotheses evolving from the project (such as age being just as important an intersecting power structure as gender; the flow between online and offline; etc.), while at the same time getting not only new empirical data, but also new *kinds* of empirical data. It was furthermore the ambition of these workshops to support the young people's reflections on gender norms and gender values.

In the fall of 2011 we hosted two workshops with junior high school students. The first workshop took place in Stockholm, Sweden, with eighth graders, aged 14 years ($n = 16$, 9 girls and 7 boys). The second workshop was in Tartu, Estonia, with seventh graders, aged 13 years ($n = 19$, 10 girls and 9 boys). In both cases we had rented space outside the school setting for the workshops: in Estonia in an activity center and in Sweden in the local community center.

One dimension of using creative methods is being open about the framing and mission of the research. We therefore visited the young people in their classes before the workshop to present ourselves and the project, and also to introduce the workshop and its theme. We also made sure to have the parents' permission and we were explicit about the fact that the material produced would be used for academic purposes only and that the participants would be made anonymous in our presentations. In both Estonia and Sweden the workshop consisted of students from the same school classes, who therefore knew each other well.

THE TWO WORKSHOPS: MAKING NET PERSONAS

In the first part of the workshop the participants were introduced to the theme: "Construct an online character, aged 10." They were then asked, in groups of four, to make up characteristics for their persona by making drawings, accompanied by written statements/characterizations. Supplied on each group's table to be used freely were paper, pens, crayons, and Post-It notes. We gave no particular instructions; nor did we mention the gender of the persona the students were to construct. All in all, two girl and two boy characters were developed in the Estonian and the Swedish workshops, respectively.

In the next stage of the workshop, the students were to draw and describe the possible social media platforms (social network sites, SNS) that their persona might use. These two stages where then repeated, but with instructions to make the persona 12 and eventually 14 years old, coupled with written statements. After having drawn and written about the 12-year-old persona, the young people were handed laptops with Internet access and asked to continue working on constructing the persona and SNS. All the groups, in both Estonia and Sweden, then decided to construct the 14-year-old persona on the Internet (blog, Facebook, etc.).

All the assignments during the workshops were based on the assumption that sketches drawn and multimodal content produced by the participants are indications of virtual identity constructions and online practices among the young that have caught their attention and have in turn framed particular aspects of the overall (design) message. Therefore, as the participants in our study could delete, add to, or modify all the content they produced during the workshop, we believe that their creative and playful explorations of (online) tween identities contain a mixture of on- as well as offline opinions (e.g., interests from [pop] culture, celebrities they refer to, etc.) and feelings and challenges they associate to and encounter in their everyday lives as tweens. For instance, the drawings and descriptions of imaginary "Net personas" often referred to a number of issues that those on the threshold of adulthood might be facing, for example, exposure to alcohol, drugs, sex, and so on.

In other words, as "the design rests on the possibility of choice" (Kress, 2010, p. 28), we can learn a lot "from the stories that are told and the *way* they are told" (Gauntlett, 2007, p. 103) through such creative processes. In this respect, the "stories" told of these "Net personas" could be "read" almost as a narrative of growing up: starting from seeking one's role and place in life and being expressive about it (skipping school, taking drugs, drinking alcohol), to being more mature and "adult" in one's decisions and choices (earning good grades at school, having a loving relationship with one's girlfriend, etc.).

In fact, when starting off with the hand-drawn sketches we did encourage the participants to take as point of departure their everyday life experiences and associations of online identity work. This proved to be a good strategy. When we handed out the laptops at a later stage of the workshop the focus shifted not just from the collectively created character to fascination with findings on the Internet, but also from the group conversation to interactions with and on the screen. The first phase of the workshop thus gave us an opportunity to witness how peer culture with all its expectations, norms, and values shapes the creation of these imaginary Net personas. For instance, the participants in the Swedish workshop often made use of a patronizing term "*fjortish*" when talking about their characters. Although the term was originally used to refer to age (14), in tween-speak it currently is mainly used to describe the specific way of looking, dressing, and behaving of a person who is considered to be a childish wannabe.

In the later phase of the workshop we could witness how the tweens made use of the content found online as a source of inspiration for developing the characters they had created. A group of Estonian students, for example, made use of Google photo searching and decided that some public photos of Prince Harry would best suit their aims of representing the redheaded boy character called Karl-Mark that they had created. Also among the Swedish students, there were examples of using photos that they already knew about and that were part of their cultural frame of reference.

The Internet was not the only source of inspiration, though. Interaction between the groups increased as the workshops developed. This can perhaps best be illustrated by how the participants became increasingly relaxed and actively took possession of the physical space in the room by moving around more. In fact, as we were interested in exploring the ways in which tweens construct identities in online settings rather than the individual identity process, asking the tweens to work in groups gave us two advantages: (a) The identities constructed were based in a joint reflexive process, and (b) we could take part in this process by talking with the groups, as well as recording their group activities both on video and in audio. Furthermore, we considered it to be important to have the students work in groups, following Gauntlett's (2007, p. 96) argument that group engagement in creative processes has "parallels with how we come to form understandings in everyday life, through interactions with peers."

In the final phase of the workshop we asked each group to present and explain its work to all the others, and a more general discussion on the theme of online identity creation followed. So as not to impose our own adult, researcher interpretations and meanings (see Gauntlett, 2007, p. 125) on the drawings and SNS profile entries of the tweens, we asked each group to interpret its own work. In this respect, we relied on Harper's (1998, p. 35) emphasis on becoming a listener, with intention to keep "the consequent interest in and acknowledgment of the co-construction of knowledge between participant and researcher" (Toon, 2008, p. 22).

REFLECTIONS ON USING CREATIVE RESEARCH METHODS

While some authors have criticized the creative research methods approach for its "naive empiricism" and "naive political arguments" (Buckingham, 2009, p. 635), others have pointed out a number of unique challenges offered by such methods (Bragg, 2011; Piper & Frankham, 2007). In line with this, we end the article with some reflections on the challenges and opportunities that we encountered.

We would like to emphasize that collecting empirical material is just one dimension of the methodology. Another is the reflexivity that ought to follow for both participants and researchers. These two general methodological arguments seem to be of particular importance when it comes to the usage of creative methods. Gauntlett (2011, p. 4) characterizes one of the prime qualities of creative research methods as an "unusual experience (that) gets the brain firing in different ways, and can generate insights which would most likely not have emerged through directed conversation." This obviously does put special demands on the research process, as the results are of *another kind* than usually captured by qualitative methods. It is not possible to state beforehand what kind of data will be produced and hence what kind of data would prove most fruitful and/or informative. There arises a need to weave webs of significance, as Geertz (1973) expressed it in relation to ethnographic studies. Without a doubt, the researcher needs to be present both in the literal sense of the word (being there), to be able to get a feeling of what is happening during the creative experiment, and in terms of mental awareness; one needs to be ready to interact with the participants and the situation as it unfolds, and be ready to update and make changes in the plan. For instance, the students' active and enthusiastic participation in our two workshops led us to ponder the question of whether our young participants were fully aware of the fact that what they were doing, saying, and producing during the workshops was actually part of a research project, and that these kinds of traces were to be scrutinized, discussed, and theorized upon.

We decided to make use of creative methods because we wanted to offer the students an opportunity to reflect upon their own perceptions and practices concerning gender in both off- and online contexts. Furthermore, we wanted to give them the opportunity to take on the role of expert, which is what they are as the first persons growing up online (Weber & Dixon, 2010). For these digital natives (Prensky, 2001), cellphones, cam-phones, laptops, the Internet, and SNS are almost seamlessly integrated in their everyday culture (i.e., Buckingham, 2009, Kress, 2010). In fact, we argue that thanks to creative research methods we were able to follow the actual digital-literacy practices of our workshop participants as they happened (e.g., through their sampling and mashing of images). We were also able to study the flow and liveliness of their online interactions in a way that would otherwise not have been possible.

As creative research methods allow the participants to be in control over their self-expression, we were able to create a more equitable partnership between the participants and ourselves as researcher-moderators. Compared with interview studies, where one's answers are more immediate, creative research methods give young people greater "'editorial control' over the material disclosed" (Holliday, 2004, p. 51, quoted in Gauntlett, 2007, p. 110). In fact, we believe that the group discussion of the works produced during the workshops helped us to establish a "community within which meaning was negotiated and constructed" (Toon, 2008, p. 25). For instance, we could follow how comments, relations, and so on evolved as they were made and how age and gender kept coming back as the central parameters.

The use of what is termed creative research methods, seen in relation to more traditional "word based research," shows that the creative approach can open up spaces for experiences and knowledge otherwise not available, which might prove especially interesting when the informants are young people with other kinds of verbal and written competencies. Our pondering of our experiences of using creative research methods is not to be read as a statement of its qualities in comparison with other methods or traditions, however. Nevertheless, considering the fact that the new media have changed, on a more general level, the way that author, text, and audience relate to each other (and are mutually inspired), creative research methods, which build upon the agency and creativity of the participant, offer an interesting alternative to traditional research methods for studying social media.

NOTE

1. This material is part of a larger empirical study on tweens constructing and normalising gendered identities online in Estonia and Sweden in the research project the.GTO.project (http://mt.sh.se/gto).

REFERENCES

Alexander, B. (2011). *The new digital storytelling. Creating narratives with new media*. Santa Barbara, CA: Praeger.

Awan, F. (2007). *Young people, identity and the media: A study of conceptions of self-identity among youth in southern England*. Retrieved from www.artlab.org.uk

Berger, P. L., & Luckmann, T. (1966). *The social construction of reality: A treatise its the sociology of knowledge*. Garden City, NY: Anchor Books.

Bragg, S. (2011). "Now it's up to us to interpret it": "Youth voice" and visual methods. In P. Thomson & J. Sefton-Green (Eds.), *Researching creative learning: Methods and issues* (pp. 88–103). New York, NY: Routledge,.

Bragg, S., & Buckingham, D. (2008). 'Scrapbooks' as a resource in media research with young people. In P. Thomson (Ed.), *Doing visual research with children and young people* (pp. 114–131). London, UK: Routledge.

Buckingham, D. (2009). 'Creative' visual methods in media research: Possibilities, problems and proposals. *Media, Culture & Society*, *31*(4), 633–652. doi:10.1177/0163443709335280

Denzin, N. K., & Lincoln, Y. S. (Eds.). (1994). *Handbook of qualitative research*. London, UK: Sage.

Denzin, N. K., & Lincoln, Y. S. (1998). *Strategies of qualitative inquiry*. Thousand Oaks, CA: Sage.

Drotner, K. (2008). Leisure is hard work. Digital practices and future competencies. In D. Buckingham (Ed.), *Youth, identity, and digital media* (pp. 167–184). Cambridge, MA: MIT Press. doi:10.1162/dmal.9780262524834.167

Gauntlett, D. (2005). Using creative visual research methods to understand media audiences. *Medien Pädagogik*. Retrieved from http://www.medienpaed.com/04-1/gauntlett04-1.pdf

Gauntlett, D. (2007). *Creative explorations. New approaches to identities and audiences*. London, UK: Routledge.

Gauntlett, D. (2011). *Making is connecting: The social meaning of creativity, from DIY and knitting to YouTube and Web 2.0*. London, UK: Polity Press.

Gauntlett, D., & Holzwarth, P. (2006). *Creative and visual methods for exploring identities—A conversation between David Gauntlett and Peter Holzwarth*. Retrieved from http://www.artlab.org.uk/VS-interview-2ps.pdf

Geertz, C. (1973). *The interpretation of cultures. Selected essays*. New York, NY: Basic Books.

Giddens, A. (1976). *New rules of sociological method: A positive critique of interpretative sociologies*. London, UK: Hutchinson.

Harper, D. (1998). An argument for visual sociology. In J. Posser (Ed.), *Image-based research: a sourcebook for qualitative researchers* (pp. 24–41). London, UK: Routledge.

Hernwall, P. (2009). The space of the body-self. Construction of gender identities online. In F. Deriu, L. Esposito, & A. Ruggiero (Eds.), *Metropoli e nuovi consumi culturali. Performance urbane dell'identità* (pp. 177–197). Roma, Italy: Carocci editore.

Hernwall, P., & Siibak, A. (2011). Writing identity: Gendered values and user content creation in SNS interaction among Estonian and Swedish tweens. *Global Studies of Childhood*, *1*(4), 365–376. Retrieved from http://dx.doi.org/10.2304/gsch.2011.1.4.365

Jenkins, H. (2006). *Convergence culture: Where old and new media collide*. New York, NY: New York University Press.

Kress, G. (2010). *Multimodality. A social semiotic approach to contepmporary communication*. London, UK: Routledge.

Kress, G., & van Leeuwen, T. (1996). *Reading images. The grammar of visual design*. New York, NY: Routledge.

Lealand, G., & Zanker, R. (2006). Dream worlds and media worlds: Using drawings for insights into the lives of New Zealand children. In U. Carlsson & C. V. Feilitzen (Eds.), *In the service of young people?: Studies and reflections on media in the digital age: Yearbook 2005/2006* (pp. 117–128). Göteborg, Sweden: Nordicom.

Lundby, K. (Ed.). (2008). *Digital storytelling, mediatized stories. Self representation in new media*. New York, NY: Peter Lang.

Lykke, N. (2010). *Feminist studies. A guide to intersectional theory, methodology and writing*. London, UK: Routledge.

Manovich, L. (2001). *The language of new media*. Cambridge, MA: MIT Press.

Perkel, D., & Yardi, S. (2006). *Discovering the social context of kids' technology use through photo elicitation*. Retrieved from http://digitalyouth.ischool.berkeley.edu/node/15

Pink, S. (2003). Interdisciplinary agendas in visual research: re-situating visual anthropology. *Visual Studies*, *18*(2), 179–192. Retrieved from http://viscult.ehu.lt/uploads/SARAHPINK.pdf

Piper, H., & Frankham, J. (2007). Seeing voices and hearing pictures: Image as discourse and the framing of image-based research. *Discourse: Studies in the Cultural Politics of Education, 28*(3), 373–387. doi:10.1080/01596300701458954

Poster, M. (1995). *The second media age*. Cambridge, UK: Polity Press.

Prosser, J. (2007). Visual methods and the visual culture of schools. *Visual Studies, 22*(1), 13–30. doi:10.1080/14725860601167143

Punch, S. (2002). Research with children: The same or different from research with adults? *Childhood, 9*(3), 321–341. doi:10.1177/0907568202009003005

Siibak, A., & Hernwall, P. (2011). 'Looking like my favourite Barbie'—Online gender construction of tween girls in Estonia and in Sweden. *Studies of Transition States and Societies, 3*(2), 57–68. Retrieved from http://www.tlu.ee/stss/wp-content/uploads/2011/10/erinumber_Siibak.pdf

Thomson, P. (2008). Children and young people. Voices in visual research. In P. Thomson (Ed.), *Doing visual research with children and young people* (pp. 1–20). New York, NY: Routledge.

Toon, H. (2008). "Deliberately," "explicitly": Redistributing power. An argument for using visual research methods in an educational research project. *Journal of Artistic and Creative Education, 2*(1), 3–39.

Willis, P. (2000). *Ethnographic imagination*. Cambridge, UK: Polity Press.

Young, L., & Barrett, H. (2001). Adapting visual methods: Action research with Kampala street children. *Area, 33*(2), 141–152.

Social Media Use in the Bronx: New Research and Innovations in the Study of YouTube's Digital Neighborhood

MATTHEW CRICK

William Paterson University, Wayne, New Jersey

YouTube has surpassed other social media platforms on a massive scale in application and influence, and has recently begun to impact the way people seek out and use information, learn about the world, and share their own unique perspective often with an international audience. However, this ubiquitous form of social media is perhaps the least scholarly researched form of social media, particularly when it comes to so-called underrepresented and underresearched populations. Generally speaking, formalized social-media theoretical tools and systematic measurement have been lacking as well. YouTube exemplifies the tension between an empowered user and powerful commerce-driven creators in the battle for media control and demands scholarly analysis.

INTRODUCTION

In 1888, Thomas Edison developed the schematics for his Kinetoscope, a device that was designed for one-on-one viewing of short films through a cabinet window (Singer, 2004). Often described as the precursor to home movie projectors and theatre projectors, Edison's Kinetoscope began the relationship between the viewer and the moving image. Actually, his assistant William Dickson is generally considered to have developed the device itself. More than a hundred years later, that early technological experience has mutated into a very personal relationship between human beings and technology through the ubiquitous website YouTube: no longer just a transient, singular experience but a long-lasting community experience that is saved, altered, and reproduced for billions of people. Today, the video-sharing and social-networking website YouTube generates billions of downloads per day, and cofounder Chad Hurley states that "we are at a stage and we give everyone in the world an opportunity to participate and that is being a video platform for creating a solution for people to not only upload and distribute their videos on a global basis but to find and share videos" (http://www.nydailynews.com). In February 2011, YouTube was the second-ranked, most visited website for the week ending February 19 (http://www.hitwise.com) in the category of social-networking websites. Facebook was listed as the number one most visited for that week. Clearly, these statistics indicate that a very large group of people is accessing YouTube, and this fact alone warrants systematic and thoughtful research of the YouTube digital neighborhood. That said, systematic exploration of any group in an online environment presents unique research challenges, as, in the words of Daryl Slack and M. J. Wise, the Internet presents an unstable set of "technological assemblages," which further complicates and demands different research approaches (Slack & Wise, 2005).

Thomas Lindlof and Bryan Taylor (2002) state in *Qualitative Communication Research Methods* that flexibility between research design and expected outcomes is a wise approach to scholarly work in the fluid Internet universe:

> Today, we can no longer be sure that any field site can contain the action we want to study, or that the "field" is even a valid construction ... transnational ethnic migrations, global flows of image and capital, and the explosive growth of media technologies have combined to create worlds of competing discourses and multiple, unstable identities. (p. 99)

Keeping Lindlof and Taylor's suggestions in mind, the Bronx YouTube Study examines through a "cultural studies and uses and gratifications" (UG) theoretical lens one small and underresearched area of the ever-expanding Internet universe and captures how one group interacts, reproduces, manipulates, and understands their world in YouTube's digital neighborhood. Several essential research questions, grounded in the aforementioned theories, frame the research study. Generally, the overall guiding research question for the study was, "How and why are people, specifically those people in the Bronx, accessing YouTube and how does this group feel, behave, and think while active in YouTube?" This overall question was then reduced to several survey and focus-group questions that link to specific conceptual dimensions and provide the framework for the Empirical Model. The following key research questions (RQs) were used in focus groups and on a written survey:

RQ 1: What does posting on YouTube mean to users?
RQ 2: Why do or why don't users post on YouTube?
RQ 3: Do systems of power and surveillance operate within the YouTube digital neighborhood? If so, how do they operate and are users aware of them?
RQ 4: How does YouTube differ from other social networking sites (SNS)?

While each RQ provided new and salient data—never before systematically researched using this group—YouTube RQs 2, 3, and 4 provide the strongest links to the empirical model. While the RQs, Methods, and Results are covered here in detail, it is important to understand some of the current literature in the areas of social networking, cultural studies, surveillance, audience commodification, and uses and gratifications that significantly influenced and shaped the Bronx YouTube Study.

LITERATURE REVIEW

Social Networking Sites (SNS) and Current YouTube Scholarly Research

In 2009, Jean Burgess and Joshua Green released their book on YouTube—one of the few scholarly books written solely about YouTube—advancing the knowledge and the history of SNS into the highest levels of scholarship. In "The Entrepreneurial Vlogger: Participatory Culture Beyond the Professional–Amateur Divide," Burgess and Green argue that historically YouTube has always been a corporately driven service and is a "changing media environment, but it is one where the practices and identities associated with cultural production and consumption, commercial and non-commercial enterprise, and professionalism and amateurism interact and converge in new ways" (Burgess and Green, 2009a, p. 90).

Several international scholars have also written extensively on YouTube and its functions from a cultural studies perspective. For instance, in "The Carnival of the New Screen: From Hegemony to Isonomy," author Bernard Stiegler discusses YouTube as a new form of broadcasting, describing how YouTube has "replaced the television transmitter" (Stiegler, 2009). Stiegler also underscores how young people are using YouTube, vis-à-vis Hayles, describing how the experience of YouTube for younger people—though we don't precisely know how young—ends once they've searched for and found the content they need, as if other textual (not visual) information that can also be found on the Internet would not provide any other useful information (Stiegler, 2009). Stiegler's insights in this regard proved to be somewhat prophetic, as the majority of the survey respondents in the Bronx YouTube Study reported that they used YouTube primarily as a search engine to discover how to do something.

In *Mediated Girlhoods: New Explorations of Girls' Media Culture*, Sarah Banet-Weiser argues that a social networking site like YouTube encourages a new type of self-making. She states, "The construction of the self is not an insular, isolated activity but is rather situate in a media and cultural context that invokes a dynamic between the self and others, or in the case of YouTube, between video content and user feedback" (Weiser, 2010, p. 281). Weiser's important feminist perspective on how young girls' self-concepts are shaped, first by their own hands using tools in the digital and SNS environment, feeds a cultural technology that is both empowering and stultifying. Her study underscores the dynamic tension in the democratized and highly commercialized YouTube environment.

Finally, in the *Video Vortex* article "(MIS)Conceptions about YouTube," noted YouTube scholar Patricia G. Lange comments on the enduring public perception of YouTube as a "source of funny, disturbing, social, amateur and professional content" (Lange, 2010) but asserts that this common viewpoint subordinates and often overshadows the research value of YouTube. Lang's work in YouTube's digital neighborhood, albeit with a different population than the Bronx YouTube Study, shares a similar research perspective that YouTube is a relatively new scholarly research site that offers new and salient data on various groups engaged with social media.

Social media have received a great deal of attention from traditional media outlets ranging from local and national news programs covering suicides involving MySpace and "tweeted" hate crimes, to national commercials touting the value and ease of dating websites like eHarmony, which claims that "eHarmony is responsible for nearly five-percent of marriages in the U.S." (http://www.eharmony.com). In addition, the improvement of online flash technology and the further embedding of YouTube in daily life, as represented by more than 2 billion uploads daily, helped spark political change in Libya and Egypt (http://www.youtube.com). Further, social media, according to many theorists (Jenkins, Poster, and others), has empowered the masses and democratized the Internet: We are no longer a *flattened consciousness* as Gramsci might have imagined. For instance, Burgess and Green (2009) establish YouTube as a legitimate and active research site where participants demonstrate awareness and make choices regarding YouTube as it relates to their daily lives. And Patricia Lange, in a study funded by the MacArthur Foundation, researched YouTube participants less than 20 years of age in an effort to gain insight regarding antagonistic practices on YouTube. She states that "interviewees disagreed about the effectiveness of current solutions to deal with haters and expressed deep concern about mechanisms that may or may not reduce hating behavior but could severely complicate getting access to useful feedback on their work" (Lange, 2007, p. 25). Finally, in John Hartley's chapter in Burgess and Green's *YouTube: Online Video and Participatory Culture*, he argues that

> the origin of meaning has migrated along the "value chain" of the cultural industries, from the author, the producer, and the text, to the citizen consumer, so that "consumption" is a source of value creation, and not only its destination. Media consumption, under such a model, has moved away from being a "read only" activity to becoming a "read-write" one. (Burgess & Green, 2009b, p. 48)

And yet the popular perception of YouTube as a gigantic repository for pet videos and death-defying stupid human tricks continues. For this reason, it is important to direct discussion toward YouTube and its social-networking site characteristics, rather than the content of video uploads. This first step is essential to understanding YouTube's research value. danah m. boyd and Nicole B. Ellison, in "Social Network Sites: Definition, History, and Scholarship," define social network sites as

> Web-based services that allow individuals to (1) construct a public or semi-public profile within abounded system, (2) articulate a list of other users with whom they share a connection, and (3) view and traverse their list of connections and those made by others within the system. The nature and nomenclature of these connections may vary from site to site. (boyd & Ellison, 2008, p. 211)

In Figure 1, from the boyd and Ellison article, we can see that they have defined SNS sites existing since 1997. In 2003, after an increase in SNSs and ultimately a shake-out of many of those new sites, Friendster, MySpace, and Facebook were left as the major competitors. Additional web tools then appeared that enabled SNS's greater functionality and encouraged a deeper involvement on the part of the user. For instance, a user's ability to personalize her/his web page with unique backgrounds, and images and the ability to "copy and paste" code—both developed by MySpace—led to that site's rise in popularity and the demise of the SNS Friendster (boyd & Ellison, 2008). In terms of scholarship, boyd and Ellison point out that a variety of scholarship has been undertaken regarding SNS's. For instance, the bridging of online and offline networks, privacy, and other areas of research such as the work done by Patricia Lange, who "complicates traditional dichotomies between 'public' and 'private' by analyzing how YouTube participants blur these lines in their video-sharing practices" (boyd & Ellison, 2008), have stimulated scholarly discussion.

Scholars Haridakis and Hanson describe YouTube as a space that exemplifies a social environment in which everyone has the potential to be both

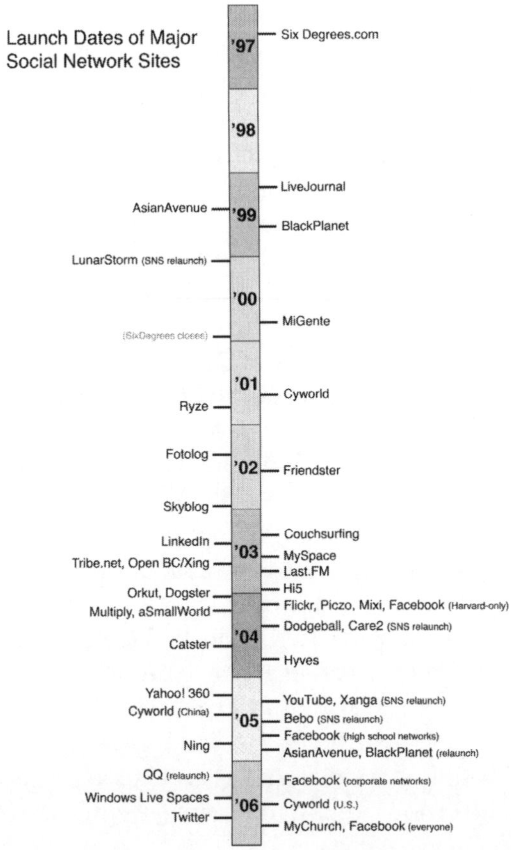

FIGURE 1 boyd and Ellison's SNS track of website launches since 1997. YouTube arrives with Facebook and Yahoo! 360. Reprinted with permission. (Figure available in color online.)

a consumer and purveyor of content (Holtz, 2006), and a place that illustrates the speed with which social networking innovations can achieve widespread penetration and utility (Haridakis & Hanson, 2009).

Cultural Studies

Renowned cultural studies theorist Stuart Hall emphasizes the importance of so-called minority groups in the cultural studies literature. His work on media encoding and decoding formalizes and establishes the position of the reader and how readers interpret the media experience in a variety of ways, often along the reader's specific environment and particular class and racial background. For instance, Hall states that "audiences whose decodings will inevitably reflect their own material and social conditions will not necessarily decode events within the same ideological structures as those with which they have been encoded" (Hall, 1980). Similarly, Haridakis and Hanson (2009) emphasize that, unlike television, the Internet has long been regarded as a medium that is particularly amenable to interpersonal connection and social activities; it follows that Hall's perspective has particular relevance in the Internet environment and in YouTube.

One common view among many cultural studies theorists is that media consumers, YouTubers (people who actively use YouTube) included, are, as writer Lee Siegel proposes, "transforming himself or herself into a product" (Siegel, 2008). Media scholar and activist Sut Jhally, executive director of the Media Education Foundation (MEF) and professor at the University of Massachusetts, has been sounding this alarm along with others for the past several decades in his books and "dreamworld" films. Jhally states in an interview with Carrie McLaren, editor of *Stay Free* magazine, that "Advertising is an active process of creating meaning in which people and advertisers interact. But that is not devoid of power. Again, people make their own messages and meanings, but not in conditions of their own choosing" (Jhally, 2010). Regarding advertising in media, Jhally's point is important. He suggests that people who consume and use popular culture and popular technology like YouTube, which is advertiser supported, do not have power precisely because they are not the ones choosing the conditions in which that power functions. That said, the Bronx YouTube Study adopts a cultural studies perspective slightly different from Jhally's somewhat stricter view of media consumers. Similar to Jean Baudrillard and Mark Poster's perspectives, the theoretical lens that frames the Bronx YouTube Study somewhat embraces Jhally's concerns about how power and surveillance can operate, but in contrast to Jhally's suggestion, the participant is empowered in the Bronx YouTube Study.

Poster states that "The magic of the Internet is that it is a cultural technology that puts cultural acts, symbolizations in all forms, in the hands of all participants; it radically decentralizes the positions of speech, publishing, filmmaking, and radio and television broadcasting, in short the apparatuses of cultural production" (Poster, 2002). Also, Jean Baudrillard's perspective of the subject, although clearly atomizing in some ways, also provides the possibility of a shifting of power from the media to the masses. He writes, "Obviously there is a paradox in the inextricable entanglement of the masses and the media: is it the media that neutralize meaning and that produce 'formless' (or informed) mass; or is it the mass which victoriously resists the media ... are the media on the side of power in the manipulation of the masses" (Baudrillard, 1988).

Baudrillard and Poster describe the Internet as a site where cultural acts are in the hands of all participants and this is an extension of Jürgen Habermas's ideas regarding the public sphere. In "The Public Sphere: An Encyclopedia Article," Habermas states that "by the 'public sphere' we mean first of all a realm of our social life in which something approaching public opinion can be formed. Access is guaranteed to all citizens" (Habermas, Lennox, & Lennox, 1974).

Other scholars, like Nancy Baym in her seminal work *Tune In, Log On: Soaps, Fandom, and Online Community* (1999), focuses on issues of identity in a collective Internet environment. Although Baym's longitudinal study gathered thousands of soap-opera fan Usenet messages, and not video communication as in the Bronx YouTube Study (her work was written several years before YouTube's inception), her critique that Internet communication is really not that unique when compared to other communication technologies, especially when it comes to identity and community, is well taken. Her work also provides somewhat of a through-line with the Bronx YouTube Study in that Baym's study also focused on user-generated content. In the words of reviewer Brian L. Ott, "With much literature on the Internet being theory-driven, one of the unique contributions of this study (Baym's study) is its focus on practice—its detailed attention to the actual activities of users" (Ott, 2002). In addition, in "A Call for Grounding in the Face of Blurred Boundaries," Baym suggests that "We must acknowledge the 'everyday' nature of much human communication and technology ... within a continued focus on the mundane, we should examine how people simultaneously integrate multiple media into their daily communicative experience" (Baym, 2009). This research agenda links well with the Bronx YouTube Study, as it emphasizes participant thoughts, feelings, and attitudes, rather than YouTube's technological features. To sum up, the theoretical constructs, research questions, and resultant data assume that the YouTube participants are not completely powerless and actually restructure and manipulate YouTube through their active involvement. They do this for a variety of reasons and at measurable levels of consciousness.

Having established the present research study's theoretical perspective, it is important to discuss a common cultural studies dialectic that has influenced much of the cultural studies scholarly tradition. This following discussion is not a criticism. In both the Frankfurt and Birmingham schools, a dialectic that pits those who have the means of production, distribution, and power (the capitalists) against the audience and user—who is part of the capitalistic program—is often articulated. However, in the SNS environment this dialectic is different and becomes a shifting of power and production to the audience and/or user, while simultaneously and inextricably connecting the audience/user with more traditional forms of the capitalistic system, its media, and its technology. This particular power shift is reified in surveillance and audience commodification.

Surveillance

As mentioned earlier, in the Bronx YouTube Study, written survey participants' feelings, attitudes, and beliefs were the primary research focus, and their comments included answers to questions about "being watched online"; these questions appeared in both the focus groups and the written survey. Therefore, it is important to introduce current cultural studies research in the area of surveillance to best understand surveillance in online environments.

In "The Work of Watching One Another, Lateral Surveillance, Risk and Governance," Mark Andrejevic provides one perspective for understanding surveillance as it relates to the Internet and social networking websites.

He writes:

> Lateral surveillance, or peer-to-peer monitoring, understood as the use of surveillance tools by individuals, rather than by agents of institutions public or private, to keep track of one another, covers (but is not limited to) three main categories: romantic interests, family, and friends or acquaintances. It also comprises several levels of monitoring, ranging from casually Googling a new acquaintance to purchasing keystroke monitoring software, surveillance cameras, or even portable lie detectors. (Andrejevic, 2003, p. 488)

Andrejevic's conception of "lateral surveillance" and his three dimensions are certainly applicable in the YouTube space, but it is also important to understand that the concept of surveillance, as imagined by Andrejevic as emanating from individuals, is not precisely the same thing as surveillance strategies coming from the institution itself. As a parallel, Stuart Hall's concepts of hegemony and ideology might not manifest in exactly the same way in YouTube as they do in television or radio. The question is, how do hegemony and ideology operate, assuming institutional agents are watching us and influencing our behavior using surveillance strategies? Most participants in the Bronx YouTube Study recognized they were being watched while using YouTube; they were just apathetic to this fact. We can see an example of Andrejevic's form of surveillance—which embeds itself in a kind of audience motivated hegemony and ideology—in user comments, posted videos, and comments regarding each other's posts. For example, in a video posted on YouTube, in the series of posts seen here, YouTubers criticize the United States as well as other users' responses; these are examples of user-led surveillance:

> "Yall can criticize the U.S. all you want, but we've NEVER had a dictator and we've NEVER directly killed our own people for voicing their opinions. We're not perfect, but were pretty damn close."
> "Let's make a deal in the interest of the alliance :
> The better French pilots will execute the operation.
> The British peasants only pay the costs."
>
> "IraQ2.0"
>
> "Us pigs."

> "RON PAUL, RON PAUL!! Screw these western puppets controlled by banksters/oligarchs ... put a real man in charge!"

> "OH shit the US launched 110 tomahawk missiles. Guess you could say they are involved. Btw before anyone mentions it Qaddafi just blew up a hospital and rebel forces have just shot down one of their own. Yes ORDER is needed. another rothchild imperalist operation."

The more common cultural studies interpretation of the term "surveillance" is that it is a manifestation of an overall disciplinary system. YouTube's design and structure do encourage a kind of "panoptic surveillance," as David Lyon states, but YouTube is a place where "postpanoptic surveillance is de-territorialized as well as rhizomic and as such resists exclusionary control strategies" (Lyon, 2006, p. 13). Lyon also points out, and this has particular salience in the YouTube digital neighborhood, that it is "not self-repression, but self-expression (that) characterizes this surveillance, which, importantly, is in the terms of the watched, not the watcher. Theoretically, panoptic ideas are radically destabilized and complexities of power relations are fore grounded" (Lyon, 2006, p. 167). Hille Koskela, in Lyon's edited volume, writes in her paper "The Other Side of Surveillance: Webcams, Power and Agency" that "People do not submit to the passive role of 'the observed' that surveillance offers them but, instead, play various active roles with 'surveillance' equipment'" (Koskela, 2006, p. 172). Koskela, a researcher particularly interested in webcam surveillance, explains that one significantly different aspect of surveillance (pre-YouTube) relates to the amount of visual material that circulates throughout the Internet. She suggests that "the roles of representations have multiplied. The visual material is circulated through various channels and often runs out of control of those responsible for the original purpose of surveillance" (Koskela, 2009, p. 175). This observation characterizes surveillance in YouTube very well as a place where users regularly submit footage originally recorded for real-life surveillance, which then becomes appropriated for entertainment or so-called "whistleblower" evidence. For example, a simple search in YouTube using the phrase "surveillance footage" yielded almost 4,000 results ranging from humorous in-store footage from Target Stores to color, high-quality footage posted by the Washington County Sheriff's office in Oregon asking the public for help in identifying two suspects in a convenience-store robbery. (http://www.youtube.com).

These three views of how surveillance can be expressed in YouTube—as a peer-to-peer monitoring activity, as a phenomenon in the form of self- expression, and as a tool for participants who use surveillance footage in unanticipated ways—are all part of the YouTube experience. Beyond SNS surveillance strategies, the SNS audience also functions as audience commodity, although in ways dissimilar to traditional forms of media like television and radio.

Audience Commodification

The concept of audience commodification, as it relates to mass communication, is not a new idea; however, an in-depth discussion of audience commodification and its deep connection to Marxist perspective and Smythe's "blindspot" argument are beyond the scope of this article. Articulated in his 1981 work *Dependency Road: Communication, Capitalism, Consciousness and Canada,* Dallas W. Smythe describes the audience commodity as "a material base of work which people must do under monopoly capitalism" (Smythe, 231). However, Smythe's foundational views of capitalism and its relationship with audience labor and his specific definition of audience power have implications in the YouTube environment. In addition, Rick Maxwell (1991) and his interrogation of Jhally and Livant's view that the audience is working and creating commodity *while they watch* and Fisher's (2012) position that exploitation and alienation are inextricably connected in the social-networking environment significantly expand and broaden Smythe's original argument and bring audience commodity theory into the present day and YouTube. Smythe states that "At its base, work is doing something creative, something distinctively human—for the capacity to work is one of the things which distinguishes human beings from other animals" (Smythe, 1981, p. 26). He continues, vis-à-vis Rinehart (1975):

> By changing the world they live in through labor, human beings *at the same time* alter their own nature, for the lives of people *are both influenced by what they* produced and how they produce. (emphasis added)

Smythe connects labor, human nature, and production, and this also links with his definition of audience power, which is a force that flows from audience commodity. Audience power is "literally a commodity" (Smythe, 1981). He equates viewers watching television as producing power in relation to the capitalist system and that material form of power—the audiences' views aggregated and packaged for advertisers—represents power that advertisers get "dirt cheap" (Smythe, 1981). If we imagine YouTube users from Smythe's perspective, we can see how Google has perpetuated the television production and advertising model Smythe developed and linked to his audience commodity theory. For example, YouTube users' videos are given ratings and advertising is embedded into the videos themselves. However, as they pertains to YouTube, Smythe's observations only go so far. Audience members in YouTube are also content creators and partners, so they can share in profits and also share in the surveillance and policing of other YouTubers. This is something that was never part of early broadcast television's structure. Rich Maxwell (1991) describes audience commodity as a theory

> that proposes that modern demand management institutions—the so-called business services of advertising, mass media, product design and so on—transform the qualitative differences among the myriad viewing and consumption activities into objects of equal value that can be bought and sold on market. (p. 74)

It is important to recognize that Maxwell is writing in response to Smythe's ideas about audience commodity and also regarding television viewing, considered a relatively passive audience activity during this historical period. However, while Maxwell accepts audience commodity generally, he disagrees that an audience is necessarily producing labor when its members are not watching television, partly because "the audience carries a price and can be bought and sold for profit, it appears as though money grows out of watching; it assumes the form of commodity" (Maxwell, 1991, p. 83), and this form represents capitalism and can therefore shift as capitalism does. He also believes that the cultural industries or "consciousness industry" according to Smythe (1981) are dominated by the audience commodity and they do not necessarily represent a "fount of value production for these institutions" (Maxwell, 1991). Maxwell suggests that the audience, as a commodity form, may provide surplus value for an advertiser, or for Google in the case of YouTube, but this is not something that is inextricably linked to the act of watching television. Eran Fisher, offering yet another perspective of the audience commodity, states that the audience in a social networking environment are producing audience power through "high-levels of participation, by user-generated content, and by the ability to create varied channels of communication: one-to-one, one-to-many, and many-to-many" (Fisher, 2012, p. 174). Fisher's perspective marks a shift in thinking about the audience as active, rather than passive, and this is a more appropriate conception of the audience, as it applies to SNS, than Smythe's and Maxwell's ideas.

Essentially, Fisher dialectically links, as Marx does, the ideas of alienation and exploitation. Fisher suggests that these trends provide a connected and evolving interpretation of what happens with the audience, or user, in the SNS environment. So, for instance, the more a user posts on Facebook, the more commodity she/he is creating for Facebook but also the less alienated and more satisfied she/he will be. Fisher's SNS exemplar is Facebook, but his discussion of production relations and information as ephemeral shows up as particularly evident in the YouTube universe. He states, "Facebook epitomizes a new form of production relations, where value is created not primarily by workers of the company, but by the audience. And the most important thing that Facebook users produce—the primary source of Facebook's value—is communication and sociability" (Fisher, 2012, p. 176).

His articulation of production relations fits YouTube well, as YouTubers are also communicating (through video responses, videos, and textual responses) and they are the primary producers. YouTube also offers an environment that is not, in Fisher's words, "spatially fixed and temporally limited" (Fisher, 2012). YouTube users are well aware of the "work" they do, but they do this work for a variety of reasons ranging from personal enjoyment to a desire to create their own media brand and attain stardom. Fisher summarizes the audience in SNS this way: "The audience in SNS is a commodity (sold to advertisers), a labour power (producing communication), and media (a means of communication) through which commercial messages are distributed" (Fisher, 2012, p. 172). Fisher believes that in order for capitalism to be successful in SNS, the user must feel de-alienated; what follows is increased and harder work inside the SNS, in the form of pictures and social interaction on Facebook and videos on YouTube. Once this occurs, user exploitation and advertising increase and, finally, real monetary value is added.

Finally, scholar Philip Napoli, in "Revisiting 'Mass Communication' and the 'Work' of the Audience in the New Media Environment," describes audience commodification as a process that begins with Web 2.0 users that are "involved in the processes of production and consumption as they generate and browse online content, as they tag and blog, post and share" (Napoli, 2010, p. 509). For instance, in the YouTube environment users are audience members whose behaviors, that is, online clicks, videos watched and posted, and textual comments, become data that the "institutional communicator" (Google) can then aggregate and sell. That is, by participating in YouTube and agreeing to the website's terms of service, every YouTuber is providing work product for Google, through their labor. In addition, according to Napoli, "Increasingly, not only are audiences contributing content that can be monetized by content providers, but it is also increasingly the case that audiences engage in the work of the advertisers and marketers who traditionally support these content providers" (Napoli, 2010, p. 512).

Uses and Gratifications

Simply put, "uses and gratifications" is concerned with the ways in which people use media for their own purpose which may flow from social or psychological needs of the individual. Uses and gratifications (U&G) has a long history in more traditional media, specifically television; this theoretical tool offers a useful beginning for understanding the ways in which those who use media experience that media. The dearth of relevant U&G literature regarding the Internet notwithstanding, Alan Rubin, in his 1981 paper "The Interactions of Television Uses and Gratifications," describes how a researcher might generally approach a mass communication technology. Rubin states that "mass communication uses and gratifications studies followed a path of explaining single variable relationships. In other words, the various uses of television would be initially observed and measured, and then each use or motivation would be independently and separately related to other variables in the investigation" (Rubin, 1981, p. 4). Rubin goes further and describes how these studies provide "heuristic knowledge concerning reasons why individuals use a mass medium," and it is these core ideas that make U&G research techniques a logical choice for the Bronx YouTube study.

Paul Haridakis and Evonne Whitmore, in their work on Rubin's contributions to the field of uses and gratifications, provide a roadmap for understanding the U&G trajectory:

> Uses and gratifications gradually evolved "from psychological and sociological models of indirect media effects" (A.M. Rubin & Rubin, 1985). It "incorporates several variables from these models, including the psychological disposition of the individual and the social structure and relations of media consumers" (p. 6).The origins of U&G can be traced to early gratifications studies from the 1940s, a time when Researchers such as Lasswell (1948) were seeking to identify the functions media serve for people. In U&G studies, people are seen as purposive, goal directed, and motivated in their use of the media (and other communication activities) to satisfy their social and psychological needs and want. (Haridakis & Whitmore, 2006, p. 767)

Katz, Blumler, and Gurevitch, in *Uses and Gratifications Research,* articulated five major characteristics of the U&G model: (a) The audience is conceived as active, (b) in the mass communication process the linking of need gratification and media choice lies with the audience member, (c) the media compete with other sources of need satisfaction, (d) methodologically speaking, many of the goals of mass media use can be derived from data supplied by individual audience members themselves, and (e) value judgments about the cultural significance of mass communication should be suspended while audience orientations are explored on their own terms (Katz, Blumler, & Gurevitch, 2007, pp. 15–17).

Thomas E. Ruggiero, in his article "Uses and Gratifications Theory in the 21st Century," explains some of the historical and present-day criticisms of U&G: "U&G continued to be challenged by four serious conceptual problems: (a) a vague conceptual framework, (b) a lack of precision in major concepts, (c) a confused explanatory apparatus, and (d) failure to consider audiences perceptions of media content" (Ruggiero, 2000, p. 6). In an attempt to address the aforementioned concerns in the Bronx YouTube research study, regarding methodological approach, the researcher mitigated the typical criticism of U&G as lacking precision. Through highly structured research protocol employing qualitative data collection techniques, specifically focus groups and interviews, qualitative data collection was blended with a more typical U&G quantitative survey data collection approach (Ruggiero, 2000).

Ruggiero also remarks that scholars predict a "move beyond studying single users, two-person ties and small groups, to analyzing the computer-supported communities (Garton, Hahthornthwait, & Wlelman, 1997)" (Ruggiero, 2000, p. 29). The Bronx YouTube Study is one of the first attempts to move beyond researching a single person to researching an online community of users, in an attempt to systematically analyze behavior, attitudes, and beliefs in a large scale social-networking environment.

Rubin (1981) describes media use, from the perspective of U&G, as "people's needs and motives to communicate, the psychological and social environment, the mass media, functional alternatives to media use, communication behavior, and the consequences of such behavior" (p. 19). Finally and most recently, Sarah Banet-Weiser describes YouTube as a social-networking site where the media community is active and producing videos (Banet-Weiser, 2010, p. 282). And scholar Carolyn Lin states that "personal computer users outside of the work environment also appear to fit the self-motivated, goal-oriented, and gratifications-expected audience definition" (Lin, 1996).

Finally, in an SNS research study by Urista, Dong, and Day that relied on U&G as its model, the researchers analyzed young adults in the MySpace and Facebook digital environments. Vis-à-vis Rubin, the researchers defined U&G as "a psychological communication perspective which focuses on how individuals use mass media and other forms of communication such as interpersonal communication to fulfill their needs and wants" (Urista, Dong, & Day, 2009, p. 218). The researchers used the qualitative method of focus-group interviews and content analysis to describe outcomes. However, what was lacking in their work was a basic descriptive analysis of the respondents; this might have illuminated or even helped structure the focus-group questions and revealed interesting research directions.

The U&G approach, articulated through Rubin, McQuail, Ruggiero, Banet-Weiser, and other scholars, served as an important tool in the Bronx YouTube Study and linked conceptually with the study's larger theoretical model. Further, U&G framed the study's empirical model and subsequent respondent survey, thus driving the data collection and ultimately any assumptions, conclusions, or observed relationships articulated in the larger research study.

WHY THE BRONX?

There appears to be a tradition of collecting and reporting communication research, which may not accurately represent the larger human population. This assumption has merit when considering that, for instance, at the time research began for this article, no published data on YouTube or social media use in the Bronx, or with any minority population, was represented in any of the major communication scholarly databases. To see whether this research assumption was accurate, race/ethnicity data from Harvard, Georgia State, Ohio State, and Rutgers universities and the University of Southern Californa based on total student enrollment were collected and aggregated; the total student enrollment figures are published on each University's Institutional Research website.

This nonrandom demographic data sample represents distinct geographical locations and provides somewhat of a cross-section of the United States. These highly regarded institutions are also listed as among the top communication programs in the country by the National Communication Association (NCA) doctoral program reputational study. In particular, the Annenberg School is rated as one of the top five communication schools along six separate areas of communication specialization (www.natcom.org, 2010). Each university's total enrollment of self-reported Hispanic or Latino students was combined and then expressed as an overall percentage of total students at all of these universities. The results show that less than 15% of each university's total students report their race/ethnicity as "Hispanic" or "Latino." Specifically, in the cases of Harvard (http://www.provost.harvard.edu, 2011), Georgia State (www2.gsu.edu, 2011), and Ohio State (www.osu.edu/osutoday, 2011), the Hispanic student enrollment was below 6%. At the University of Southern California (USC), where the general nonstudent population is 47.7% Hispanic—according to the U.S. Census Bureau—only 12.1% Hispanic students were enrolled in USC in 2008 (www.usc.edu/private/factbook, 2008). Logically, it then follows that any communication research utilizing the undergraduate populations at these universities—representing institutions that generate a significant portion of the top communication research in the world—may underrepresent minority populations in the United States. This assumption could be confirmed by analyzing the demographic information from specific research studies at these institutions.

Based on the Pew Project's research on Internet use, 61% of Hispanics reported using the Internet in 2008 (www.pewInternet.org). This suggests that a disproportionate number of Hispanic Internet users nationwide most likely represent the subjects for research in the field of communication, when considering the aforementioned data from USC, Rutgers, Harvard, Georgia, and Ohio State student populations. Therefore, it can be argued that *communication research in terms of the Internet*, often conducted using undergraduate university students from large communication programs nationwide, may not adequately represent the attitudes, beliefs, and feelings of students in the Hispanic population or the perspective of people in the general human population. This makes the Bronx YouTube Study particularly relevant. There is current scholarly research regarding the issue of ethnic and racial representation in research.

In their paper "The Weirdest People in the World?," scholars Joseph Henrich, Steven J. Heine, and Ara Norenzayan, all faculty in the Department of Psychology at the University of British Columbia, provide some startling data—from the field of psychology—that support the assertion that the people used for research studies in their field of psychology might not represent the larger human population very well. The authors suggest that the results from numerous studies may not be generalizable at all in the larger world and that American undergraduates typically used in research studies are problematic for several reasons, including scoring higher in the areas of uniqueness and self-actualization (Henrich, Heine, & Norenzavan, 2010). The authors also describe how U.S. undergraduates are more autonomous, are high self-monitors, and are more subject to attitude change than non-undergraduate populations (Henrick et al., 2010). Because of these differences, the authors contend that researchers should take care to avoid generalizing data to the larger human population.

METHODS

The Bronx YouTube Study was a mixed-method exploratory study completed in the Bronx, New York, in the fall of 2011. Using written survey data, each respondent's answers were collected and analyzed using descriptive statistics. Focus-group interviews were also completed and these data were reported as verbatim text and used to illustrate specific conceptual areas, as articulated in the Empirical Model, from the participants' perspective. The Bronx YouTube Study research data originate with a primarily Hispanic group, providing systematic data gathering in a social-networking environment. A majority of focus-group participants and survey respondents self-reported as Hispanic, Latino/a, and African-American (www.bcc.cuny.edu), as can be seen in Figure 2. This group has never been researched from a cultural studies perspective in the context of the YouTube, and yet YouTubers and other video-sharing website users represent 71% of online adults in the United States, with minorities more likely to visit a video sharing website like YouTube than whites, according to the 2011 PEW Research Center's Internet and American Life Project (http://www.pewInternet.org/Press-Releases/2011); this is expressed in the Figure 3.

The qualitative and quantitative Bronx YouTube case study measures YouTube users' attitudes, beliefs and feelings about their YouTube experience. As mentioned, areas of inquiry—articulated as research questions, not hypotheses—include participant perception of YouTube and its function, whether YouTube works in a "top-down" fashion like television and radio, whether YouTube is a place where immaterial labor is encouraged for corporate gain, and how surveillance and monitoring operate in YouTube from the perspective of the participant. The exploratory Bronx YouTube Study research results do not attempt to establish inviolate quantitative relationships between theoretical constructs and empirical data; nor are the quantitative data statistically random and generalizable. The exploratory nature of

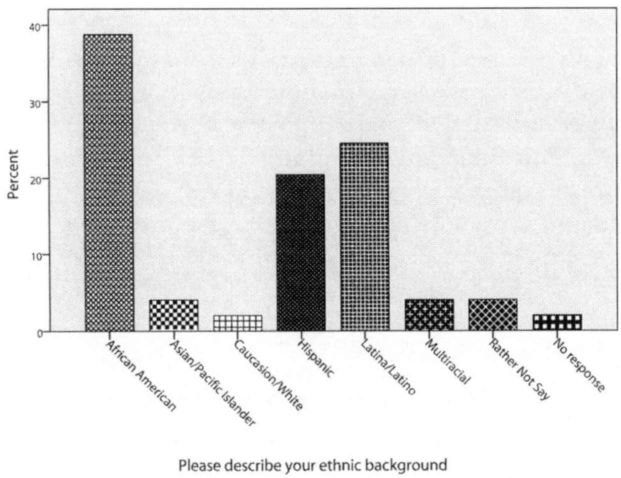

FIGURE 2 Nearly 50% of the respondents self-reported as Hispanic or Latina/Latino and nearly 40% self-reported as African-American. From Crick (2010), with permission.

this specific research precludes hypothetical results testing. However, the research gathered and analyzed in this study paves the way for more robust, experimental and deeper qualitative and quantitative measurement and comparisons in the future.

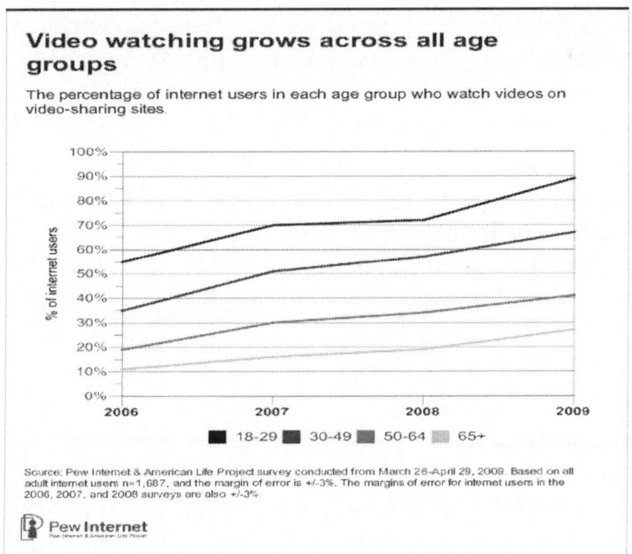

FIGURE 3 Pew Internet Video Watching Growth demonstrates that video watching increases over time overall and within the group 18–29 years old, the majority age group in the Bronx YouTube Study. From "Pew Internet and American Life Project," survey conducted March 26–April 29, 2009, with permission. (Figure available in color online.)

Given the aforementioned data, it can be theorized from a cultural studies perspective that so-called Hispanic users—which are in the majority in the Bronx—might offer unique and important perspectives regarding content creation and reading of texts, particularly in terms of portrayals of power, attitudes, beliefs, and feelings. Examining YouTube in this way offers valuable and new research that contributes to overall scholarly understanding of this group. Further, generally YouTube-specific research is lacking in the current scholarly body of SNS research.

Survey Instruments, Sampling, and Procedures

The written YouTube survey questions were developed over a period of a year and pretested in a class at a community college in the Bronx. Initially, it was hypothesized that an online survey tool would be most convenient, as data could be more easily managed and, Schutt reports that "data entry errors are almost eliminated and results can be reported quickly" (Schutt, 2009, p. 176). However, the researcher learned through further investigation that in online surveys, specifically surveys that are sent via e-mail (as the Bronx YouTube study survey was to be sent), response rates are declining and that techniques used in mail-in surveys to increase response rates don't seem to work in an electronic environment (Sheehan, 2001). Subsequently, an anonymous and confidential written survey was developed. The significance of developing and administering the Bronx YouTube survey should not be underestimated in terms of its heuristic value. As of this writing, no quantitative data have been gathered for this particular population and little or no quantitative or mixed-method research has been done in the YouTube SNS space compared to other SNS like Facebook or MySpace. In fact, a thorough search through the academic database *Communication and Mass Media Complete* using the search terms "Facebook," "YouTube," and "MySpace" demonstrates a significant difference in the highest number of academic journals, periodicals, and newspapers, and popular press publishing work on SNS. The *Communication and Mass Media Complete* search using "Facebook" as a term yielded 901 results and "YouTube" yielded 628 search results. A search using "MySpace" as a term generated 306 results.

In the Bronx YouTube exploratory research study, the qualitative data articulated in the focus-group interviews were privileged over the quantitative data from the written survey; the statistical data analysis was critically important in detecting possible relationships between and within dependent variables (DVs) and independent variables (IVs), but this analysis was only exploratory and not statistically generalizable. It was most important to the researcher and integral to the overall research plan that participant comments would provide the best evidence for potential future research directions and subsequently drive the study's research. Regarding population size, the total student population from which the convenience sample was taken, at the time of the research study, was 10,740. Written surveys were distributed to a convenience sample of 465 students at a 2-year institution in the City University of New York. Using the online sample determination calculator at www.surveysystem.com/sscalc.htm, with a confidence level of 95% and a $p < .05$, 371 truly random cases would be needed to achieve confidence. According to Bartlett, Kotrilk, and Higgins, in *Organizational Research: Determining Appropriate Sample Size in Survey Research* this survey response rate provided a sample large enough to gain a 95% confidence level given the total population of Bronx college students and given a random sample (Bartlett, Kotrilk, & Higgins, 2009, p. 49). Bartlett, Kotrik, and Higgins also point out, regarding influences on sample size, that "researchers should report both the appropriate sample sizes along with the sample sizes actually used in the study, the reasons for using inadequate sample sizes, and a discussion of the effect the inadequate sample sizes may have on the results of the study" (Bartlett et al., 2009, p. 49). Recall that the Bronx YouTube Study was exploratory, not experimental, and no hypotheses were articulated—research questions were formulated, instead; therefore a truly random sample, while desirable, was not necessary for this study.

Out of the 465 surveys distributed, the 362 complete, usable surveys were then numbered 1–362 randomly; a Microsoft Excel program generated 50 of the numbers 1–362 randomly and those surveys were used for data analysis. Regarding the 50 cases chosen for the sample, Wimmer and Dominick in *Mass Media Research: An Introduction* state that "A primary consideration in determining sample size is the research method used … samples with 10–50 subjects are commonly used for pretesting measurement instruments and pilot studies, and for conducting studies that will be used only for heuristic value" (Wimmer & Dominick, 2011, p. 102). Wimmer and Dominick (2011) also state that a sample size of less than 30 in a given cell produces unstable results (p. 104). For the Bronx YouTube Study, the research proceeded partly on Wimmer and Dominick's recommendation that the research investigation would more appropriately work as an exploratory study, given the primarily heuristic value and considering the time, financial resources, and project management concerns. Finally, relatively current YouTube U&G research studies rarely provide statistical information of the type in the Bronx YouTube Study, revealing a possible qualitative bias in what *Video Vortex* calls "YouTube Studies" and a need for even the most basic quantitative work.

Focus-Group Procedures and Sampling

For the focus groups, e-mails were sent to approximately 230 of the anonymous written survey participants; this was the number of legible e-mail addresses returned on the written surveys. Of this group, approximately 45 students responded and only three respondents were able to meet for a focus group. As this number was inadequate for meaningful focus-group data analysis, a convenience sample of 10 students was selected. The focus-group comments were then professionally transcribed and grouped along the Empirical Model's DV dimensions of perceived *convenience, surveillance,* and *necessity.* Then the most appropriate responses for each dimension were selected for analysis. Again, as this study was exploratory and utilized research questions to drive analysis, the focus-group participant comments were selected based on how well the researcher felt the comment linked with a particular overall research dimension, like surveillance or power, rather than using a content analysis or some other methodology; capturing the tone and authenticity of the focus-group participants was paramount.

The following five questions were asked in order to gain some sense of demographic information for capturing a "snapshot" of this group: "How many years of college have you completed?" "How old are you?" "How would you describe your ethnic background?" "What is your gender?" "How long have you lived in New York?" It should be noted that the focus-group participants met the criteria of YouTube users. The participants self-reported as being Hispanic, multiracial, Caucasian, and African American. The group consisted of seven males and three females ranging in age from 20 to 36 years of age with 80% in the 20–26 years old range: nearly exactly the same percentage as in the survey group and exactly the same age range. All focus-group participants had completed some college. Similar to the RQs, the focus-group questions fit the conceptual areas articulated in the Empirical Model. The most relevant focus-group questions are listed here, while other focus-group questions like "Tell me a little bit about the kinds of things you do on the Internet" and "Some people say YouTube has a lot of videos to share, but they aren't very good. What do you think?" didn't generate any significant discussion amongst the participants. However, that material was transcribed and can be found in the original research. The focus-group questions were:

a) What kinds of concerns do you have, if any, about someone you don't know monitoring your activities while you are on the Internet?
b) What does the term *surveillance* mean to you?
c) Who do you think controls *YouTube*?
d) When you're looking at videos, what types of videos do you like to watch?
e) Are you aware of any risks when posting on *YouTube?* If so, what are they?
f) If there are risks in posting on *YouTube,* how do you protect yourself?
g) When you're on the *YouTube* website, what kinds of things do you do?

As the study's empirical model drove the focus-group and written survey questions, a brief discussion of this model and Figure 4 further guide this discussion.

Empirical Model

To date, the Bronx YouTube Study represents the only original YouTube research engaging a largely non-white, college-age group. In Figure 4, the Bronx YouTube Study's theoretical research dimensions are operationalized. These research dimensions, articulated as the *independent variables* "gender, age, language, ethnicity, and type of Internet connection" were measured against the *dependent variables* "perceived necessity, surveillance, and convenience," as well as the *dependent variable* "number of YouTube videos shared or viewed." This model served as a good analytical tool that could be useful in different social-networking environments. When used with a truly random sample, this model would, perhaps, provide strong and potentially generalizable statistical results.

RESULTS

As previously mentioned, the Bronx YouTube Study is an exploratory study. No hypotheses were articulated and the study was not experimental in nature. However, methodologically speaking it was also important to establish a

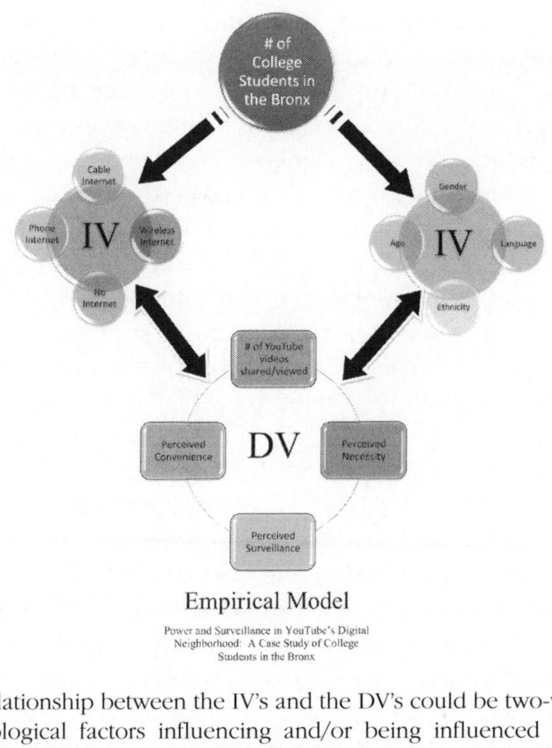

FIGURE 4 The relationship between the IV's and the DV's could be two-way, with socioeconomic and technological factors influencing and/or being influenced by perception and videos shared or viewed. From Crick (2010), with permission. (Figure available in color online.)

"picture" of the YouTube participants in the study, for the reasons already given, and a written survey provided statistical data like demographic and Internet use information that could then be compared to the dependent variables articulated in the empirical model. While admittedly the quantitative measurement was not derived from a completely random group and any statistical results cannot be generalized to a larger population, the IV and DV comparisons suggest interesting future research. Simply put, the non-socioeconomic and demographic data reported by survey respondents, compared with data derived from survey questions that represent the conceptual areas in the Empirical Model—perceived convenience, perceived surveillance, and perceived necessity—represent valuable research. And the individual focus-group questions, linked to the specific conceptual areas, complete the mixed-methods research approach and offer valuable and systematically collected and measured participant perspective in the form of verbatim focus-group comments. The following section details some of the most salient RQ results.

Selected Research Questions (RQs)

RQ 2: WHY DO OR WHY DON'T USERS POST ON YOUTUBE?

It seems reasonable to expect that there would be a positive correlation between time spent on YouTube and importance of YouTube in daily life, suggesting that the more "important" YouTube is to a person, the more time that person spends on YouTube. If this is true, then in the DV "perceived necessity" we might see a significant relationship between variables. However, when the "time spent" and "importance of YouTube" responses were correlated, the results showed the two questions were independent of one another with correlations well below significance. Further, when controlled by the "Internet connection type" IV, illustrated by Table 1, Pearson's chi-squared reveals the same sort of independence, indicating perhaps that regardless of the speed of the Internet connection the time spent on YouTube and the perceived importance of YouTube to the Bronx survey respondents have little influence on the perceived need for YouTube. When using YouTube, overall, survey respondents indicated high levels of interest in searching for certain kinds of information, like entertainment (music videos for instance), but didn't appear to be that impacted by the speed of the Internet connection when Internet surfing. Those with phone-line Internet connections appeared to be most impacted, but still only at a .316 significance level.

There are several possible reasons why there was not a strong correlation between the IV and DV in this case. In this study, since almost 100% of the respondents possessed some type of cable-based Internet connection the ability to access YouTube videos might be considered "easy" or "expected," which suggests that perhaps the concept of "need" wouldn't even be part of the respondents' thinking. Also, the concept of need might bring to the

TABLE 1 Relationship between Internet IV and perceived necessity DV Spearman rho correlations

			How much time per day would you estimate you spend on YouTube?	How important would you estimate YouTube is in your daily life?	What type of Internet connection do you use?
Spearman's rho	How much time per day would you estimate you spend on YouTube?	Correlation coefficient	1.000	–.196	–.145
		Sig. (two-tailed)	—	.173	.316
		n	50	50	50
	How important would you estimate YouTube is in your daily life?	Correlation coefficient	–.196	1.000	.221
		Sig. (two-tailed)	.173	—	.123
		n	50	50	50
	What type of Internet connection do you use?	Correlation coefficient	–145	.221	1.000
		Sig. (two-tailed)	.316	.123	—
		n	50	50	50

Note. From Crick (2010), with permission. Sig., significance.

respondents' minds other ideas like "purpose," and "use/value." That is, the respondents might not think YouTube has much purpose for them. In terms of the IV "Type of Internet Connection" we can see in Table 1 that there appears to be no positive correlation with either of the variables in the *perceived necessity* DV.

Between the variable "time per day spent on YouTube" and "importance of YouTube in daily life," we can see a negative correlation. While it is difficult to know precisely what this negative correlation means, we know that the larger values of the variables that create the DV *perceived necessity* are somehow associated with smaller values in the IV of *type of Internet connection*. In Figure 5, we can also say that the low levels of importance of YouTube in daily life are associated with similarly low levels of time spent on YouTube daily.

Figure 5 also depicts the two variables in the DV *perceived necessity* measured against the variable "how much time would you estimate you spend on YouTube"; we see that the relationship between the variables is not linear, as the relationship occurs primarily in the 0–1 and 1–2 hours per day subcategories, and not across much of the other categories. Survey

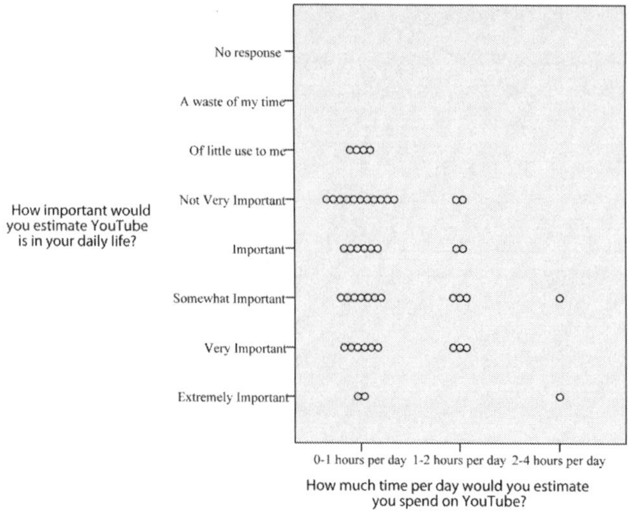

FIGURE 5 Respondents spent few hours on YouTube but also estimated that YouTube had some importance in their lives. From Crick (2010), with permission.

respondents who spent only 0–1 hours per day on YouTube represented 72% of the sample; however, 64% of the respondents thought that YouTube was at least "important" to them. This was an unusual outcome, as it would be expected that a person who did not use YouTube that often—0–1 hours per day—would not consider YouTube very "important" at all. Conversely, when looking at the histograms, Figures 6 and 7, respectively, for each dimension in these DVs, we can see that there is a fairly normal distribution in the "importance of YouTube" variable. In the "time spent" variable

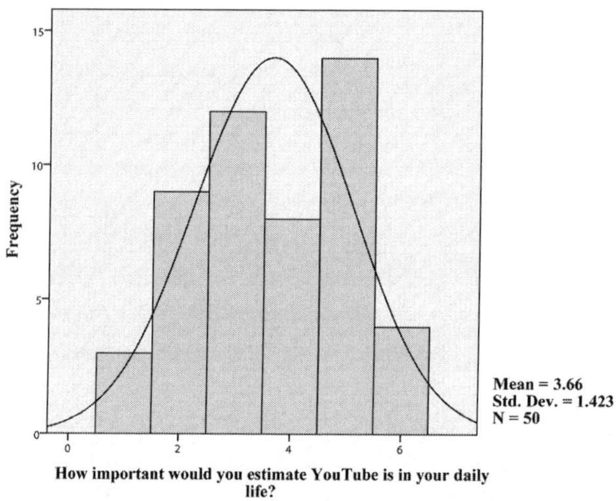

FIGURE 6 Respondents indicated YouTube has some level of importance in daily life. From Crick (2010), with permission. (Figure available in color online.)

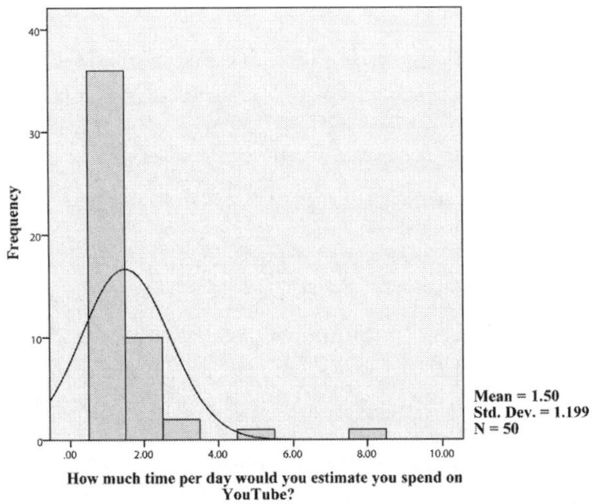

FIGURE 7 Within the "time spent" dimension, most respondents indicated spending 0–2 hours on YouTube daily. From Crick (2010), with permission. (Figure available in color online.)

histogram we can see that the distribution is positively skewed, indicating that many survey respondents spend very little time on YouTube daily.

RQ 3: DO SYSTEMS OF POWER AND SURVEILLANCE OPERATE WITHIN THE YOUTUBE DIGITAL NEIGHBORHOOD? IF SO, HOW DO THEY OPERATE AND ARE USERS AWARE OF THEM?

Perhaps more than any other research question, RQ 3 generated the richest and the clearest survey and focus-group results. For instance, along the lines of the concepts of *power* and *surveillance,* three survey questions provided thought-provoking data. Question 16 asked, "In general, how active are you in protecting the following information submitted by you on *YouTube*?" Question 17 asked, "While using YouTube, how much do you worry that people you don't know are watching what you do?" Finally, question 18 asked, "While using YouTube, how much do you worry that the company that owns YouTube might be using and/or selling your information (like the types of video you upload/download or advertisements you click) without your knowledge?"

RQ 3 generated focus-group comments regarding the concepts of power and surveillance and what participants understood those words to mean; this information provided an important contribution to a deeper understanding of the user's relationship to YouTube and to those who own and control YouTube. It should be noted that written survey respondents were not asked to define surveillance and power, as the researcher felt more value would be gained from broaching the topic of defining terms in a focus-group format, rather than in a survey format. Still, as focus-group participants were also sometimes survey respondents it can be argued that a general understanding of power and surveillance in YouTube might be shared by a majority of study participants, although this was not established statistically.

The Bronx YouTube study participants' perspective regarding the concept of *surveillance* within YouTube is paramount. Generally, focus-group participants believed surveillance meant "being watched." Here is an excerpt from a representative conversation, from the Bronx YouTube Study, between focus-group members:

Interviewer: Okay. Okay. All right. So there are two key terms that I'm interested in finding out what you guys think they mean. One of them is surveillance. So what does the word *surveillance* mean to you? Anyone can start.

Honda: To me, it's—uh ... the first thing that comes to mind is security.

Interviewer: Security. Surveillance means security.

Honda: Well, not directly security, but like a type of or some derivative of it. But uhm ... I guess surveillance when it comes to the Internet could be people monitoring what you're doing every second and—but honestly I feel a little uneasy about that just because I do a lotta things on the Internet, like I'm sure everybody does, and I don't even have to mention specifically what comes to mind, but, you know, let your mind roam.

Interviewer: What about you, Tiffany? What were you going to say?

Tiffany: I was saying that surveillance basically means that you're being watched, yeah. So like if you're on the Internet, even though like if you go to Facebook or Twitter, I think there's somebody—I think there's somebody watching you. I think there's like something monitoring what you're doing.

Interviewer: So how do you feel about that, the fact that you're probably being watched, if you're correct?

Tiffany: Uhm ... it's whatever, because I still—like I do my banking online, like I pay my credit-card bill, but I feel like I'm being watched just like to a certain extent like, you know, something like that.

Interviewer: Okay. Walt.

Walt: Sometimes uhm ... you do wonder if, you know, these sites that you're on, how much of your own information they're releasing to anyone else, 'cause a lotta these sites are built on advertising, and you're like—you know, they're trying to make as much money as they can, and how much of your information are they releasing?

Note: Focus Group transcriptions from Crick, 2010, p. 154.

On the written survey, when considering respondents' feelings about surveillance and their active protection of financial and e-mail information,

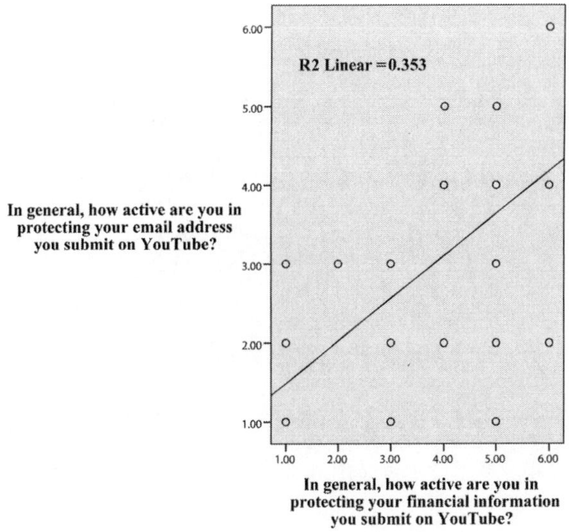

FIGURE 8 Protecting financial and e-mail information while on YouTube are positively correlated. From Crick (2010), with permission.

we see a positive correlation. Given the small sample size and ordinal scale, correlations were calculated using Spearman's rho method and a two-tailed significance test. Regarding Spearman's rho method, in *Reasoning with Statistics,* Williams and Monge emphasize the efficacy of this statistical choice (Williams and Monge, 2001). When looking at the potential relationship between *actively protecting e-mail* and *actively protecting financial information* variables, there is a positive and significant correlation between the two variables. However, we do not know exactly why that relationship is positively correlated and significant. We can see in Figure 8, the scatterplot, that there is a positive but relatively weak statistically relationship between these two variables.

The data in Figure 9 suggest that survey participants in this study were concerned about surveillance when it comes to their financial and e-mail information and this concern is echoed in the focus-group comments; YouTube participants are active in protecting that e-mail and financial information. Finally, these particular research variables are strongly associated with the concept of surveillance when measured individually.

RQ 4: HOW DOES YOUTUBE DIFFER FROM OTHER SOCIAL NETWORKING SITES (SNS)?

In "Branding the Post-Feminist Self: Girls' Video Production and YouTube," scholar Sarah Banet-Weiser writes about YouTube as a powerful social-networking tool, particularly in the area of self-branding. She writes, "Developing a self-brand on commercial social networking sites, such as YouTube, means that girls reference brands not simply as commodities but as the context for

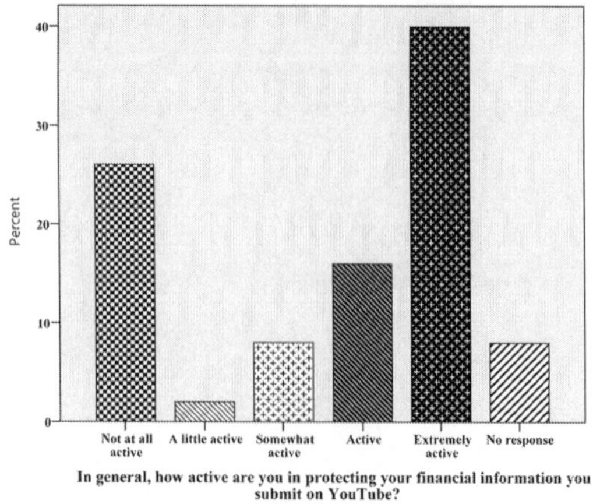

FIGURE 9 A large majority of respondents are active in protecting financial information while on YouTube. From Crick (2010), with permission.

everyday living" (Banet-Weiser, 2010, p. 285). Banet-Weiser's observation regarding self-branding applies to the Bronx YouTube Study, as respondents using the video comment feature in YouTube shape how others see them. Due to the aforementioned difficulties with the focus groups in the Bronx YouTube Study, the qualitative data for RQ 4 are not as strong as the other research question data. RQ 4 was not asked on the written survey, but was discussed in a focus-group interview. It is important to note that focus-group information gathered in relation to RQ 4 occurred during an interview with only one respondent and then again in an interview with only two respondents. After these two instances, the researcher determined that a third focus-group interview was required and all other RQ focus-group data came from the large, 10-person focus group.

The following excerpts represent a sample of comments from the Bronx YouTube study 10-person focus group.

Interviewer: Why would you consider it a social networking web site?

Respondent 1: Because you're able to upload your photo, uhm ... you can share—uh ... you can share information with people and uh ... I think you can even meet people on YouTube and say like, oh you know, maybe we can work on this video together or if you sing, I dance, or something like that. But as far as you can, you know, I don't think it has the avail—the availability that you can chat with someone like Facebook does, or AIM or whatever, but you can email each other back and forth, and people can see your likeness and see what you do and comment on videos and say, "Oh I think it's cool, call me, this is my number." So yeah, I think people can meet that way.

Interviewer: What would you say?

Respondent 2: Yeah, definitely part of that social platform. It may not be up as high as Facebook or MySpace or Twitter or stuff like that.

Interviewer: You mean like as much of a social network?

Respondent 2: Engaging, yeah, engaging; it's not as—you know it's not as real time engaging where you can chat with someone life, you know? Uhm … but it's there, somewhere in the podium, in the middle, somewhere, where you can, you know, you could socialize with people that you don't know, and people you do know. So, that's another good thing about it, I think. You know? You could definitely step outside of yourself for those who need to do that, and then there's also the people that get addicted and then they probably just step back into themselves, so I mean there's—either way you could look at it. Yeah I do think it's part of the social.

In the focus-group comments regarding what posting on YouTube means (RQ 4), some participants felt like YouTube had SNS features, but was still dissimilar to more comprehensive SNS's like Facebook. In the following, a participant describes his or her reasoning behind using YouTube for its SNS features:

Respondent 2: I only use the social network, you know, features of YouTube when it's, you know, prevalent to a video. Like, okay, "I like this video, let me hit this person up and see if, you know, we can do some work together." Or, "Hey, you know, I like that shot!" Like, you know, film director, "What did you do to get that?" <inaudible> because I don't have their Facebook or any other way to contact them. And usually if you get an email from a stranger, like actually in person, even when <inaudible> to click on it. But if they see it on the YouTube, <inaudible> reply to this video, they will be more inclined to see it. And then, you know, network and connecting can come out of that. But those are the only ways I see myself using that.

DISCUSSION AND IMPLICATIONS

Although the results of the Bronx YouTube Study cannot be generalized to the larger population in the Bronx, three important observations can be made. First, respondents are not uploading videos very often. This may be as a result of technological barriers, time constraints, or lack of interest. Second, focus-group participants believe that they share in the types of *power* that exist in the YouTube space. They claim rights to manipulate, repurpose, and re-edit videos, desire payment for work they do (videos they have produced and uploaded to their own channels), and actively control the YouTube environment to a certain degree. YouTubers are at least on some level aware of the policies and procedures of YouTube, LLC, and generally speaking accept these policies as long as there isn't too much of an obvious intrusion into the YouTube experience. For instance, respondents are generally at least a little bit concerned about being watched ("surveilled") on YouTube, but only when it comes to personal information like credit-card numbers or e-mail. Interestingly, respondents didn't care if their gender was somehow revealed online. Finally, and most surprising, respondents are using YouTube to learn about how to do things; they search for knowledge in the form of downloadable videos. Several of the focus-group participants spoke about how they learned to do something on YouTube, and in one instance a participant talked about learning how to tie a necktie because his father wasn't around to teach him. Figure 10 illustrates that seeking out information on YouTube is common among YouTube Bronx Study participants. Sixty-six percent reported searching for information on "how to do things" on YouTube. This particular result is important as it uncovers a heretofore hidden research value in YouTube. Prior to this study, YouTube as a valuable and dynamic *learning space* had not been explored scientifically. Therefore, not only does YouTube represent a new frontier in research on learning in a specific technological environment, but the Bronx YouTube Study data on searching for information on "how to learn to do something" directly contradict popular notions of YouTube's cultural presentation as a gigantic repository of useless videos. The implication here is that beneath the surface of

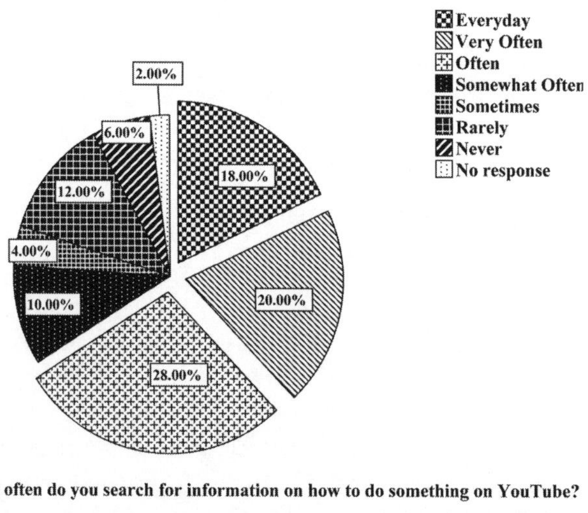

FIGURE 10 A significant portion of the Bronx YouTube Study participants search YouTube for information on how to do something. From Crick (2010), with permission.

YouTube's pet videos and mash-ups, YouTubers are also using the website to learn about their world and might perhaps be changing that world at the same time. This point is significant as it confirms in a qualitative and quantitative way what media scholars have always believed about media, that media has power and influence beyond the features and functions of the delivery technology.

The Bronx YouTube Study explored some of the attitudes, beliefs, and behaviors of Bronx college students regarding their YouTube experiences. The research data, collected and analyzed from focus-group and survey information, establish that YouTube is an online space where users experience concerns about surveillance, believe they have power, but also recognize they don't possess all the power. The Bronx YouTube Study quantitative data also establish a positive relationship between, for example, a person's desire to protect her/his credit card and e-mail information, overall surveillance concerns, and the potential capturing and aggregation of sensitive information by YouTube. In addition, Bronx YouTubers did not upload videos very often. These results will, perhaps, stimulate more SNS research with typically underrepresented groups in communication scholarship, particularly in rapidly growing populations like Latinos/Latinas, and, given recent events at foreign embassies around the globe, the issues of protected speech and government control of potentially dangerous speech posted on YouTube necessitate a better understanding of YouTubers and their motivations and thinking about YouTube, as well as government's role in our everyday lives along the lines of creative freedoms.

BRONX YOUTUBE STUDY LIMITATIONS

Survey Limitations

One limitation with the written survey is the number of questions linking to each specific theoretical dimension, as well as some lack of precision in the language of the survey and focus group questions. An additional limitation is that the design of the survey instruments may have been cumbersome for some respondents. Several surveys were returned completely blank, for instance, and some questions were not answered. Although the Likert scales were generally strong, providing good distance between points and offering a variety of points from which to choose, words and phrases like "could care less" and "concerned" and "worried" might have meant different things to different people.

Data Collection and Analysis Limitations

The use of a sample that is nonrandom limits the data generalizability. In addition, the homogeneity of the sample, while providing excellent insight into the Bronx participants' attitudes, behaviors, and beliefs, influenced research outcomes and statistical generalizability; sample size was also a contributing factor along these lines. A future YouTube study, along similar theoretical lines but utilizing a truly random sample, would perhaps provide more generalizable data and represent better the population as a whole, assuming of course that the population was not in the aforementioned "weird" group.

FUTURE RESEARCH

Scholarly research on YouTube continues to grow, with recent qualitative and quantitative work published in edited volumes like *Video Vortex* and Patrick Vonderau's *The YouTube Reader.* YouTube's connection with Google deepens and the website looks ever more like an advertiser-driven website. Economically, YouTube's projected and continued profit and its status as a rapidly growing SNS suggest an even greater influence in the U.S. and international media landscape. However, even given these facts, YouTube remains

FIGURE 11 This retro version of YouTube emphasizes its status as a transcendent repository for everything video. Reprinted with permission from www.momapropaganda.com.br (Figure available in color online.)

relatively underresearched in terms of systematic mixed and /or single method scholarly research approaches when compared with SNS like Facebook. New research methodologies are required in the online world and certainly the perspectives of those underrepresented in the current Internet and mass media universe need to be heard. YouTube hasn't achieved the influence of Edison's Kinetoscope yet, but it is easy for us to imagine YouTube's "digital neighborhood" as international designers from Momapropaganda have in the retro advertisement in Figure 11.

REFERENCES

Andrejevic, M. (2002). The Work of watching one another: Lateral surveillance, risk, and governance. *Surveillance & Society, 2*(4), 479–497.

Banet-Weiser, S. (2010). Branding the post-feminist self: Girls' video production and YouTube. In M. K. Kearney (Ed.), *Mediated girlhoods: New explorations of girls' media culture* (pp. 277–291). New York, NY: Peter Lang.

Bartlett, J. E. II, Kotrik, J. W. H., & Higgins, C. (2001). *Information Technology, Learning, and Performance Journal, 19*(1), 43–50.

Baudrillard, J. (1988). The masses: The implosion of the social in the media. In P. Marris & S. Thornham (Eds.), *Media studies: A reader* (2nd ed., pp. 528–531). New York, NY: New York University Press.

Baym, N. K. (2009). A call for grounding in the face of blurred boundaries. *Journal of Computer-Mediated Communication, 14*, 720–723.

Baym, N. K. (1999). *Tune in, log on: Soaps, fandom, and online community*, vol 3. Sage Publications Incorporated.

Blumler, J. G., & Katz, E. (1973–1974). The uses of mass communications: Current perspectives on gratifications research. *Public Opinion Quarterly, 37*, 509–521.

Boyd, D. M., & Ellison, N. B. (2008). Social network sites: Definition, history, and scholarship. *Journal of Computer-Mediated Communication, 13*, 210–230.

Bronx Community College Demographics. (2010). Retrieved from http://www.bcc.cuny.edu/InstitutionalResearch/_private/Profile/Fall_2010_profile.pdf

Burgess, J., & Green, J. (2009a). The entrepreneurial vlogger: Participatory culture beyond the professional–amateur divide. In P. Snickars & P. Vonderau (Eds.), *The YouTube reader* (pp. 99–108). Stockholm, Sweden: National Library of Sweden.

Burgess, J., & Green, J. (2009b). *YouTube: Online video and participatory culture.* New York, NY: John Wiley and Sons.

Crick, M. R. (2010). *Power and surveillance in YouTube's digital neighborhood: A case study of college students in the Bronx.* Unpublished doctoral dissertation, Rutgers: The State University of New Jersey, New Brunswick, NJ.

eHarmony marriage statistics. (2012, August). Retrieved from http://www.eharmony.com/?cid=66103&aid=1001&kid=GOGsUOYJlqP8&keyword=eHarmony&pcrid=20196630219&mt=e&gclid=CIbAopL6868CFQjf4Aodp1N6VQ

Fisher, E. (2012). How less alienation creates more exploitation? Audience labour on social network sites. Triplec (cognition, communication, co-operation): Open access. *Journal for a Global Sustainable Information Society, 10*(2), 171–183.

Georgia State Demographics. (2011). Retrieved from http://www2.gsu.edu/~wwwire/numbers/2009%20Spring%20numbers.htm

Google Earnings. (2011). Retrieved from http://investor.google.com/earnings/2010/Q2_google_earnings.html

Habermas, J., Lennox, S., & Lennox, F. (1974). The public sphere: An encyclopedia article (1964). *New German Critique, 3*, 49–55.

Hall, S. (1973). *Encoding and decoding in the television discourse*, vol 7. University of Birmingham, Centre for Cultural Studies.

Haridakis, P., & Hanson, G. (2009). Social interaction and co-viewing with YouTube: Blending mass communication reception and social connection. *Journal of Broadcasting & Electronic Media, 53*(2), 317–335.

Haridakis, P. M., & Whitmore, E. H. (2006). Understanding electronic media audiences: The pioneering research of Alan M. Rubin. *Journal of Broadcasting & Electronic Media, 50*(4), 766–774.

Henrich, J., Heine, S. J., & Norenzayan, A. (2010). The weirdest people in the world? Federal Ministry of Education and Research, RatSWD, Working Paper No. 139. Retrieved from http://ssrn.com/abstract=1601785 or http://dx.doi.org/10.2139/ssrn.1601785

Koskela, H. (2006). The other side of surveillance: Webcams, power and agency. In D. Lyon (Ed.), *Theorizing surveillance: The panopticon and beyond* (pp. 163–181). Cullompton, UK: Willan Publishing.

Lange, P. G. (2007, March). *Commenting on comments: Investigating responses to antagonism on YouTube.* Presented at Society for Applied Anthropology Conference, Tampa, FL.

Lin, C. A. (1996). Looking back: The contribution of Blumler and Katz's Uses of Mass Communication. *Journal of Broadcasting & Electronic Media, 40*(4), 574–582.

Lindlof, T. R., & Taylor, B. C. (2002). *Qualitative communication research methods* (2nd ed.). Thousand Oaks, CA: Sage.

Lyon, D. (2006). *Theorizing surveillance: The panopticon and beyond.* Portland, OR: Willan Publishing.

Maxwell, R. (1991). The image is gold: Value, the audience commodity, and fetishism. *Journal of Film and Video, 43*(1/2), 29–45. Retrieved from http://www.jstor.org/stable/20687928

Musser, C. (2002). Introducing cinema to the American public: The Vitascope in the United States, 1896–7. In G. Waller (Ed.), *Moviegoing in America: A sourcebook in the history of film exhibition* (pp. 13–26). Malden, MA: Blackwell.

Napoli, P. M. (2010). Revisiting 'mass communication' and the 'work' of the audience in the new media environment. *Media, Culture & Society, 32*(3), 505.

National Communication Association Reputational Study. (2011). Retrieved from http://www.natcom.org/NCA/files/ccLibraryFiles/Filename/000000001566/A%20Study%20of%20the%20Reputations%20of%20Doctoral%20Programs%20in%20Communication%202004.pdf

Ohio State University. (2011). Demographics. Retrieved from http://www.osu.edu/osutoday/stuinfo.php#enr_min

Ott, B. L. (2002). Identity and the Internet: Mapping Scholarship on Cybercommunity, book review of Nancy K. Baym's *Tune In. Log On: Soaps, Fandom, and Online Community. Review of Communication, 2*(1), 44–47.

Pew Internet and American Life History. (2011). Retrieved from http://www.pewInternet.org/Static-Pages/About-Us/Project-History.aspx

Pew Internet and American Life Project. (2009). Retrieved from http://pewinternet.org/Reports/2009/13--The--Audience--for--Online--Videosharing--Sites--Shoots--up/2-Demographics/Online-video-view-has-grown-across-all-age-groups.aspx

Pew Internet and American Life Project. (2011). Retrieved from http://www.pewInternet.org/Press-Releases/2011/Video-sharing-sites.aspx

Poster, M. (2002). Visual studies as media studies. *Journal of Visual Culture, 1*, 67–70.

Rubin, A. M. (1981, August), The interactions of television uses and gratifications. Presented at 64th Annual Meeting of the Association for Education in Journalism, East Lansing, MI.

Ruggiero, T. (2000). Uses and gratifications theory in the 21st century. *Mass Communication & Society*, *3*(1), 3–37.

Schutt, R. K. (Ed.). (2009). *Investigating the social world* (4th ed., pp. 139, 228–230). Sage Publications.

Sheehan, K. (2001). E-mail survey response rates: A review. *Journal of Computer-Mediated Communication*, *6*(2), 0–0. Retrieved from http://onlinelibrary.wiley.com/doi/10.1111/j.1083-6101.2001.t600117.x/full

Siegel, L. (2008). *Against the machine: Being human in the age of the electronic mob*. New York, NY: Random House.

Slack, D. J., & Wise, M. J. (2005). *Culture and technology: A primer*. New York, NY: Peter Lang.

Smythe, D. (1981). *Dependency road: Communication, capitalism, consciousness and Canada*. Norwood, NJ: Ablex.

Stewart, D. W., & Shamdasani, P. (1990). *Focus groups: Theory and practice*. Thousand Oaks, CA: Sage.

Stiegler, B. (2009). The carnival of the new screen: From hegemony to isonomy. In P. Snickars & P. Vonderau (Eds.), *The YouTube reader* (pp. 40–60). Stockholm, Sweden: National Library of Sweden.

Sut Jahally. (2011). Interview. Retrieved from http://www.sutjhally.com/articles/jhallyvstwitchell

University of Southern California. (2011). Demographics. Retrieved from http://www.usc.edu/private/factbook/2009/all_byethnicity_09.pdf

Urista, M., Qingwen, D., & Day, K. (2009). Explaining why young adults use MySpace and Facebook through uses and gratifications theory. *Human Communication*, *12*(2), 215–229.

Williams, F., & Monge, P. (2001). *Reasoning with statistics: How to read quantitative research* (5th ed.). Belmont, CA: Thomson Wadsworth.

Wimmer, R. D., & Dominick, J. R. (2011). *Mass media research: An introduction* (9th ed.). Boston, MA: Wadsworth Cengage Learning.

YouTube. (2011). Washington County surveillance footage. Retrieved from /watch?v=-3vw-OaxResearcherbA)

YouTube. (2012). Libya uprising. Retrieved from http://www.youtube.com/watch?v=6sNAlcj_W-k

Digital Media Stories Through Multimodal Analysis: A Case Study of Erahoneybee's *Song About a Child Welfare Agency*

TARA LA ROSE

University of Toronto and York University, Toronto, Ontario, Canada

Tuber Erahoneybee's digital media story Song About a Child Welfare Agency *provides YouTube audiences with a glimpse into a student intern's experience of human service work. This article uses Erahoneybee's story as a case study in the application of multimodal analysis with digital media story texts. Application of multimodal analysis in this way supports multiple and open readings of these texts, which highlight meanings made from the multiple communication modes and the convergence of these modes as present in this digital story. The analysis suggests the complex and political nature of personal stories of human service work and the need for additional research into the possibilities of digital media stories in the field.*

INTRODUCTION

Erahoneybee's digital media story *Song About a Child Welfare Agency* provides YouTube audiences with a glimpse into a student intern's experience of human service work. This story serves as an example of the potential uses of digital media in the field. Across the sector, technology-based story-making

The author thanks thank Nancy Jackson, Donna Baines, Peter Sawchuck, James Coyle, Barbara Heron, Gary Dumbrill and Maureen La Rose for their support with her work.

practices are becoming alternatives for client engagement, professional development, and critical reflection. These practices are being utilized to achieve a range of goals from therapeutic intervention, to consciousness raising and empowerment, to community engagement, popular education, and critical reflective practice (Brushwood-Rose, 2009; Lambert, 2008; Lundby, 2008).

In an effort to support research activities using digital media stories, this article seeks to extend the traditional uses of multimodal analysis as adapted by Baldry and Thibault (2006). Through a case study approach, using Erahoneybee's text as a model we can consider her experience of human services work in more detail by using multimodal analysis to deconstruct her text. Deconstruction of this story demonstrates how multiple meanings can be identified and evaluated (Baldry, & Thibault, 2006; Rosenfeld Halverson, Bass, & Woods, 2012; Woods & Dempster, 2011) and how this process further supports our development of a more complex understanding of the potential role that the Internet, Web 2.0, and digital media technologies as social media processes may play in human service knowledge generation and mobilization (Boler, 2008; Brushwood-Rose, 2009; Fitch, 2005; Thumim, 2008). Readers may want to watch the 53-second YouTube story now to help in their understanding of this analysis; the video maybe accessed through the link http://youtu.be/uA9PPndeZIA.

Baldry and Thibault's (2006) method allows for consideration of a wide range of texts from books, to brochures and posters, to websites and film texts. While multimodal analysis is not applied to digital media stories in Balrdy and Thibault's work, their application of the method to a wide range of texts suggests extension to digital media stories is a meaningful form of experimental analysis. Other examples, including a study of youth video making projects by Rosenfeld Halverson, Bass, and Woods (2012) and analysis of complex texts completed by Woods and Dempster (2011), also support creative use of this method.

POST-STRUCTURALISM, POST-MODERNISM, AND MULTIMODALITY

Digital media stories are understood to facilitate multimodal and multivocal meaning making (Brushwood Rose, 2009; Lambert, 2008; Lundby, 2008; Thumim, 2008). Meaning is made in these stories through multiple communication modes and the convergence of modes, which may in turn produce multiple voices in the text (Kress, 2003; Lundby, 2008; Thurmim, 2008). Multimodal analysis acknowledges, explores, and legitimizes the presence of multiple meanings and voices within singular texts and thus is highly useful in analysis of digital media stories (Baldry & Thibault, 2006; Rosenfeld Halverson, Bass, & Woods, 2012; Woods & Dempster, 2011).

Multimodal analysis and digital media storytelling share a common paradigmatic orientation with post-modernism and post-structuralism. Both areas of scholarship center notions of holism, multiple truths, open readings, and representation (Brushwood Rose, 2009; Davies, 2006; Hutcheson, 1989; Kress, 2003; Lundy, 2008; Rosenberg, 2004). Multimodal analysis allows us to deconstruct and consider more closely the roles these complex elements may play in meaning making within stories while allowing links to be made across contexts closely related to these stories.

REPRESENTATION, SYMBOLS, AND LAYERS OF MEANING

Representation and the politics of representation (Hutcheson, 1989; Kress, 2003) become key elements in story analysis. The use of symbols and audience members' interpretation of symbols used support the meanings made within the story (Baldry & Thibault, 2006, p. 19; Hutcheson, 1989; Kress, 2003; Lundby, 2008). In some cases, representations activate particular discourses within the texts that may or may not be held in the conscious awareness of story makers and/or audience members as they each approach their engagement with the narratives (Brushwood Rose, 2009; Kress, 2003; Lundby, 2008).

Symbols concentrate meaning and may be used to reinforce dominant/normative understandings or to challenge normativity, and/or to demonstrate alternatives (Hutcheson, 1989; Kress, 2003; Rosenberg, 2009). For example, Erahoneybee uses child welfare assessment triage codes and practice jargon to reflect her experience of working as an intern in a child protection services agency. She uses these codes in unintended ways extending meaning beyond the intended location and context. She illustrates how acts of "challenging" may be demonstrated through performances of tensions and contradictions, as well as through the use of irony, parody, wit, and humor, methods recognized as particularly effective in challenging taboos and abject subjectivities (Baldry & Thibault, 2006; Davies, 2004; Hutcheson, 1989).

These processes are strengthened by the multimodal and multivocal capacities of digital media storytelling (Lundby, 2008; Thumim, 2008). Multimodal texts allow us to use some communication layers to "say" one thing while other layers "show" another (Kress, 2003; Lundby, 2008). These contradictions, disconnections or disjunctures can signal the need for deeper consideration leading audiences to potentially seek out explanations that may extend beyond the text (Baldry & Thibault, 2006; Lundby, 2008; Thumim 2008).

DECONSTRUCTION AND TRANSCRIPTION

Multimodal analysis leans heavily on the process of deconstruction to facilitate the examination of meaning. Deconstruction creates layers in the text or what we might understand as "contrast" between meaning-making modes; these contrasts support our capacity to analyze these layers as separate and yet connected elements that remain a part of a whole story (Baldry & Thibault, 2006; Rosenfeld Halverson, Bass, & Woods, 2012; Woods & Dempster, 2011). Consideration of these layers requires analysis informed by relevant disciplinary knowledge, as well as epistemological and ideological understandings as activated by the content(s) and context(s) of the text (Baldry & Thibault, 2006). As a researcher I may identify and apply a wide range of supporting materials to the analysis in order to explore and articulate the meanings I find there. In some cases these meanings may reflect what is understood as "the author's intent" but may also reflect what post-structuralists present as "open readings," potentially bringing to life meanings "beyond the author's intent" (Baldry & Thibault, 2006; Davies, 2009; Rosenberg, 2004).

This contrast is facilitated through transcription, which in the case of multimodal analysis serves the dual function of defining elements to be analyzed and serving as a layer of analysis in and of itself (Baldry & Thibault, 2009; Woods & Dempster, 2011). Multimodal transcription describes and interprets multiple elements of the text, as well as elements that are *external to* but clearly *related to* the central body of the text—for example, the YouTube channel environment or the story-making method, two elements that are discussed later in this article.

Multiple kinds of transcripts are created each reflecting a layer of analysis and/or category of communicative activity (Woods & Dempster, 2011). These layers reflect researchers' decisions about what to analyze in the text (Baldry & Thibault, 2006, p. 6). Transcripts can focus on a wide range of elements such as: "sequence of events ... gestures ... camera angle ... soundtrack ... words spoken, [or] the relationship between time and use of space" (Baldry & Thibault, 2006, p. 6). Many other kinds of transcripts are possible; researchers must decide what and how to transcribe, depending upon the content and context of the story (Baldry & Thibault, 2006; Rosenfeld Halverson, Bass, & Woods, 2012; Woods & Dempster, 2011).

CONTEXT AND POLYCONTEXTUALITY

Context is seen as an important element of meaning making (Baldry & Thibault, 2006, p. 2; Kress, 2003). Multimodal texts like digital media stories are polycontextual texts (Neiworth & Wilson, 2009). Polycontextuality supports the notion of meaning as situated and open to multiple readings and interpretations based on the standpoints from which they are read. Context and content can be understood to be co-constitutive processes, each making and reinforcing one another, contradicting and confounding one another (Baldry & Thibault. 2006, p. 17). Analysis of these complex elements requires consideration of "how" situated meanings and generalized meanings are made from these texts as they are read.

Further, polycontextuality allows us to consider how meaning is created by the layers in a text inviting us to consider layers of context which can in turn produce more layers and (potentially) more contexts (Baldry & Thibault, 2006, p. 21). These meanings may also have broader cultural meanings, linking us into new systems of contextualization nested within wider sociocultural and political meanings. For example, Erahoneybee uses triage codes to describe her internship experience. We might also read the use of the codes as symbolic of neo-liberalism and thus read her experience as symbolic of neo-liberal outcomes in human service work.

MAKING AND SHARING STORIES

As we apply multimodal analysis to Erahoneybee's story we may contrast a number of different layers within this short 54-second story. Analysis of the YouTube environment, notions of genre, phase, soundtrack, and discourse activation each provide independent meanings while creating more complex meanings through convergence.

To begin, the fact we can be an audience to Erahoneybee's story warrants consideration (Lundby, 2008). Digital media stories are described in much of the literature as narratives authored by people who have a story they wish to tell (Brushwood-Rose, 2009; Lambert, 2008; Lundby, 2008). Some story makers use an inductive "organic" process using technology and their creativity to tell a story, or mimic stories they have seen online. Other stories may be created through the use of particular story-making approaches learned in workshops or course environments or through do-it-yourself manuals (Brushwood-Rose, 2009; Lambert, 2008; Thumim, 2009).

Sharing stories relies on the capabilities of digital media and Web 2.0 technologies (Lambert, 2008; Lundby, 2008). The built-in sharing capacity of these environments supports popular notions of sharing as a conclusion to a creative process (Lange, 2009). Trends of social media use normalize personal sharing practices in public Internet spaces and are linked to positive social status, which reinforces the desirability of sharing (Boler, 2008; Brushwood Rose, 2009; Lange, 2009; Snicker & Vanreau, 2009; Thumim, 2008). Story sharing brings to life many empowerment goals common in human service work, including breaking silences, gaining voice, making change, making connections, building affinity, and sharing knowledge, which activate discourses of popular education and "grass-roots" social change engagement (Boler, 2008; Brushwood Rose, 2009; Lambert, 2008; Lange, 2009; Lundby, 2008; Snicker & Vanreau, 2009; Thurmim, 2008).

Song About a Child Welfare Agency does not use a storytelling "method" or "technique" but rather reflects a personal or "organic" approach. Erahoneybee's story is shared publicly through YouTube. As a digital media sharing "platform," YouTube provides Internet users with a global stage for sharing and a database of archived digital texts accessible through a "keyword" search inside the YouTube environment and through Google (Snicker & Vanreau, 2009). Sharing in this environment requires the creation of a personalized database commonly referred to as a "channel." Channels provide a unique space for organizing materials and may be "customized" through the use of display templates, permissions, and functions available through the service (Snicker & Vanreau, 2009; *YouTube Essentials Guide*, 2011).

Channels may be designed to reflect their owner's aesthetic "style" limited by a predetermined set of choices (Thumim, 2008). Erahoneybee's channel reveals how the standard categories in YouTube create a portrait of the user. For example, we know Erahoneybee is a "20 something" college student from somewhere near Boston, Massachusetts. *Song About a Child Welfare Agency* is one of her most popular stories, receiving 1472 views (as of February 9, 2012), while most of her 76 other stories have received less than 100 views. We also know that Erahoneybee hasn't been online using this channel for almost a year.

QUESTIONING AS ANALYSIS

In analyzing Erahoneybee's story, the Baldry and Thibault (2006) notion of "questioning" as an analytical technique within multimodal analysis is a helpful consideration (p. 16). Framed as a researchers' attempt to make "logical meaning" from the materials available within the texts, questions make (some of) the researchers' internal considerations explicit through externalization (Baldry & Thibault, 2006, p. 16). Questions also articulate intertextual knowledge utilized by the researcher, allowing us to try on meanings activated by Erahoneybee's work without foreclosing other meanings.

Readings and analysis of texts supported by questions may utilize "in the text" and "intertextual knowledge" to "fill in" ambiguities or "missing" elements of a narrative (Baldry & Thibault, 2006, p. 16). For our purposes, intertextuality is broadly defined as the "systems of meaning relations which are common to some set of texts however large or small in some community" (Lemke, 1985, as cited in Baldry & Thibault, 2006, p. 55). In the human service sector, intertextuality opens up the possibility for connections between digital media stories and formal knowledge, as well as other interdisciplinary materials.

The nature of ambiguities and missing pieces could itself be another focus of analysis allowing for consideration of these practices as ideological. Multiple questions also provide us with the opportunity to experiment with multiple meanings and to consider different categories of information that might support "logical" meaning-making (or sense-making) without committing to a singular meaning, once more returning us to the idea of open readings (Rosenberg, 2004, Kress, 2003, Lundby, 2008).

RESOURCE SYSTEMS AND SITUATED MEANINGS

The concept of a "resource system" helps organize the process of analysis by organizing certain kinds of meanings and/or categories of meaning (Baldry & Thibault, 2006, p. 18). In human services our discourses, language, locations, and tasks can be seen as resource systems helping us make meaning within the specific culture of our work. Resource systems are evident within Erahoneybee's story—for example, in her use of the assessment triage codes mentioned earlier.

Erahoneybee brings a formal professional knowledge to her story by using child welfare triage practices and standardized codes as a resource system to describe her experiences. These codes serve as a narrative of experience as produced through a highly technical and specialized language requiring the audience to hold specialized knowledge to glean the full scope of meaning.

The use of resource systems in a particular text is understood as the process of "resource integration." Resource integration includes the use of "particular modalities such as language, gestures, depiction, gaze and so on to serve particular functions in texts" (Baldry & Thibault, 2006, p. 18). Understanding comes about through consideration of both "use and function" as contributing to meaning (Baldry & Thibault, 2006, p. 18). In this way, particular tools generate particular meanings in context, as well as holding more generalized social meanings; thus, the way the tools are used shapes what they mean (Baldry & Thibault, 2006, p. 18). In Erahoneybee's story, child welfare triage codes create a link between their use and function in the field and their use and function in the story. These codes are not used as they are intended but still make meaning, a meaning that Erahoneybee has appropriated for her own purposes.

Baldry and Thibault (2010) point out that our participation in "community" allows us to learn about specific meanings and to develop "tacit knowledge" (Baines, 2004). This in turn allows us to identify specific meanings in specific cultural contexts and extrapolate other meanings from similar ideas or tools in different contexts. Meanings gleaned in this way are understood as elements of the "context of culture" present within the texts (Baldry & Thibault, 2006, p. 18).

While the "human services" may be represented as a singular community, those of us directly involved in the sector can also attest to the presence of much fragmentation and may better be described as a diverse set of communities cobbled together through links and overlaps (Baines, 2011; Payne,

2001). The existence of many subcommunities may mean "shared" meanings are often imprecise. For example, while the notion of "assessment" may be common in both child protection and developmental services work, we know the how, where, and when of assessment may not be shared across contexts. Erahoneybee brings this idea of shared and diffuse meanings to life in her story, as a variety of meanings can be made by a variety of audiences depending upon their knowledge of the child welfare system.

GENRE ANALYSIS

Genre is another element of analysis relevant to Erahoneybee's work. Baldry and Thibault (2006) describe genre as the organization of "particular thematics" within a text producing categories of social meaning (p. 34). For example, they argue that the simple notion of a "map" can be understood as a genre in the same way "Shakespearean tragedy" can be framed as a genre (Baldry & Thibault, 2006, p. 34). Genres are important, creating compact complex meanings by organizing themes into the resource systems. Genres allow for meanings to be transported from one situation to another, supporting audiences' understandings of how to approach the reading of a text (Baldry & Thibault, 2006; Kress, 2003). We can understand Erahoneybee's story simply as falling within the genre of "digital media story" or we could further specify the story as a "v-log" or "video diary" (Lange, 2009). We read and make meaning in part through activation of what we understand about these genres, so we might understand what Erahoneybee is doing as a kind of reflective practice (Baines, 2011), confessional practice (Lange, 2009) or testimonial (Lambert, 2008).

PHASE ANALYSIS

Baldry and Thibault (2006, p. 50) suggest that analyzing and considering the subdivisions present in texts are useful elements in analysis. In many cases texts can be easily divided into multiple phases. Phases are evident breaks resulting from the organization of content; a phase may be a section of a text that is "thematically homogeneous" or focuses on certain "participants" or certain "actions" or "other relevant circumstances" (Baldry & Thibault, 2006, p. 51). Phases can be nested inside of one another producing "meta-phases," "phases," and "subphases" (Baldry & Thibault, 2006, p. 51). For example, *Song About a Child Welfare Agency* presents two distinct phases: discussion of Erahoneybee's sore throat, and discussion of her child welfare internship. The first phase has no evident subphases, whereas the second phase can be further divided into three subphases: (a) narration, (b) song, and (c) reflection.

More formally, phases are defined as "a set of co-patterned semiotic selections that are co-deployed in a consistent way over a given stretch of text" (Baldry & Thibault, 2006, p. 47). Phases share the same kinds of resource systems, creating "an internal consistency which characterizes a given phase but which distinguishes that phase from another in the same text" (Baldry & Thibault, 2006, p. 47). Phases allow audiences to recognize clusters of information and to differentiate one set of aspects from another. Phases are made visible to the audience in part through "transition points" or the "boundaries between phases" (Baldry & Thibault, 2006, p. 47). Transitions "shift" viewers' attention from one phase to another demarking the point of departure, thus contrasting the various parts of the text and therefore supporting analysis (Baldry & Thibault, 2006, p. 47).

As previously mentioned *Song About a Child Welfare Agency* can be said to have two distinct phases. The first phase focuses on discussion of Erahoneybee's sore throat and swollen tonsils. The second phase centers her experiences of work in the child protective services sector and is mostly our focus here.

Phase One

The first phase of Erahoneybee's story presents the image of a young woman discussing her swollen tonsils and sore throat. What is most notable about this phase is the speed of playback, which is much faster than what we might understand as "real time." We join this fast-forward story in mid-sentence, a confusing experience. The voice of the sound track and visual images make Erahoneybee seem like a cartoon character rather than a real person. The verbal material is audible but her distorted "chipmunk" voice makes it hard to hear what she is saying. This speed makes it easy to gloss over what is said, yet the sound demands attention. Here we can understand "speed of playback" in this segment of the story as its own layer of meaning.

Phase Two

An abrupt edit marks the transition from the first to the second phase of this story. Change of topic and change of speed in the soundtrack further demark our entrance into the first subphase of this second phase of the story.

Subphase one: narration

Erahoneybee uses the first subsection of the second phase as an "introduction" narrating herself into the text and introducing the topic to her audience. She tells us she "works as an intern in a child protective services agency," which helps us make a relationship between who she is, her place in this story, and the title of the story.

Her choice of words tells us a lot; she states, "I work as an intern," and she does not say "I am an intern." Here narration understood as a discourse category in linguistic terms becomes a tool for understanding "subjectivity" within a "critical discourse" context (Baldry & Thibault, 2006; Davies, 2004; Kress, 2003). It signals her resistance to "becoming" a child protective services worker (Davies, 2004; Ringrose & Walkerdine, 2007; Smith, 2011).

This discussion activates considerations of professionalization as a context imbedded but largely unacknowledged within this text. Here intertextual knowledge becomes significant to the reading, indirectly determining whether and/or by whom these elements are read and understood.

Subphase Two: Song

After another sharp edit in the text, Erahoneybee launches into her song, using triage codes and jargon to bring to life work experience. Her words are both humorous and ironic. This idea, like many symbols present in Erahoneybee's story, suggests this story can be read as a political text. Erahoneybee's use of digital media storytelling is political as her text presents the genre of "virtual witness" (Ganasia, 2010). She allows us to witness her personal experiences opening up the door to a public audience and to deeper analysis by people like me who are members of the human service community at large (Ganasia, 2010).

Erahoneybee's use of the triage codes presents us with the practices of social control and surveillance as central to her daily practice (Baines, 2011; Mullaly, 2009; Smith, 2011). Erahoneybee tells us about what is happening in her workplace from a position of insider, using tools from "the inside." In this way she brings to life what Ganascia (2010) describes as *'sous'veillance.*

Erahoneybee's practice of "telling the tales" of work from the point of view of the intern challenges the traditional organization of power in which the view of the intern is usually invisible. The song makes what some might understand as *her* private/personal information public and in doing so may be understood to shift traditional power relations a shift facilitated by both the culture of social media and the capabilities of digital technologies (Baldry & Thibault, 2006, p. 491; Kress, 2003).

Erahoneybee makes this shift in part by making visible her own process of "sense making." Yet she adheres to the culture of "boundaries" common in this sector by doing so without ever uttering a word of criticism about the agency or disclosing confidential information about the work she is doing (Mandell, 2007). By allowing us to see what is happening *for her* and *to her* through her story she also inducts us. Our witnessing of her reflection makes it more difficult for us to deny that these realities are a part of human service work.

Subphase Three: Reflectivity

The third subphase of the second phase of this story presents Erahoneybee's practice of reflexivity. Here Erahoneybee demonstrates a "best practice" of human service work by engaging in reflection "on action" (Mandel, 2007). She looks back on what has happened at work and what she has been asked to do in her practice, performing for us her experience of the gap between the ideal and the real deal of child protection work.

This reflection is made more complex when she then reflects on her "reflection," questioning her own method of reflection, namely, the satirical song she has created. She performs her judgment of her own actions and feelings when she states: "I am not a bad person. You have to have a sense of humor when you do a job like this." Erahoneybee then looks sheepishly into the camera stating: "Okay I am a bad person," a statement that suggests she is uncomfortable with her own process.

Erahoneybee's willingness to engage in this self-reflection, while consistent with human service traditions, can also be understood in other ways. Notions of surveillance and 'sous'veillance previously discussed suggest reflection can be an internalized form of neoliberal regulation and control (Ganasia, 2010; Hutcheson, 1989; Ringrose & Walkerdine, 2005; Smith, 2011). Erahoneybee moves rapidly from resisting professional identity and normative power to adopting self-surveillance, bringing to life Foucault's notion of governmentality as a process of daily life (Davies, 2006; Ganasia, 2010; Smith, 2011). She leaves us with an unresolved dilemma, a dilemma that is a microcosm of the tensions we face in human service work more generally.

CONCLUSION

Baldry and Thibault's (2006) work supports analysis of digital media story telling practices as social media processes in human service. Multimodal analysis has been shown here in its capacity to support analysis of a single story text and to consider meaning made through the use of multiple forms and modes of communication. Here we can see how these multiple modes and convergence of these modes allows for a story of complementary tensions, disjunctures, ironies, and paradoxes to emerge: a story that contributes to an appreciation of the complexity of human service work.

Research focusing on individual texts like Erahoneybee's story allow for a complex reading of personal reflection. Her story provides us with access to a perspective from the field that is traditionally marginalized by organizational power structures. Her story allows audiences to see how digital stories may be read as political texts. Further, the text demonstrates reflection as simultaneously a practice both of interpellation and of resistance, illustrating the contradictory tensions faced by workers in the field. Moving beyond considerations of individual texts by establishing connections across multiple texts has the potential to facilitate a significant research agenda within the human service sector. Analysis of a larger corpus of these types of texts may support the development of more generalizable understandings of work in the field. Or perhaps they may support considerations of social media as a tool for supporting deeper connections among human service providers and clients by connecting experiences across roles and identities.

Digital media stories and digital media story research shows great potential as tools for knowledge generation and mobilization. There is great potential for individual experiences to be transmitted through social media, and to be used to establish long-desired connections between groups of workers and between workers and clients. Multimodal analysis presents many possibilities for contributing to these positive outcomes. This process of analysis allows for consideration of multiple kinds of meaning making activities through a number of different lens. The flexibility and openness of these texts suggests the potential of connections to occur using a variety of different modes of communication not necessarily possible with other more fixed research methods. The use of multimodal analysis as a tool for understanding digital media storytelling in the human services shows much promise.

REFERENCES

Baines, D. (2004). Loosing the 'eyes in the back of our heads' social service skills, lean caring and violence. *Journal of Sociology and Social Welfare, 31*(3), 31–50.

Baines, D. (2011). *Doing anti-oppressive practice: Building transformative politicized social work* (2nd ed.). Black Point, NS, Canada: Fernwood.

Baldry, A., & Thibault, P. (2006). Multimodal transcription and text analysis. Oakville, CT: Equinox.

Boler, M. (2008). The politics of making claims: Challenges of qualitative web-based research. In K. Gallagher (Ed.), *The methodological dilemma: Creative, critical and collaborative approaches to qualitative research* (pp. 11–33). Toronto, Canada: Routledge.

Brushwood Rose, C. (2009). The (im)possibilities of self representation: Exploring the limits of storytelling in the digital stories of women and girls. *Changing English, 16*(2), 211–220.

Davies, B. (2006). Subjectification: The relevance of Butler's analysis for education. *British Journal of Sociology of Education, 27*(4), 425–438.

Erahoneybee (creator). (2010, September 12). Song about a child welfare agency [Video]. Retrieved from http://www.youtube.com/watch?v=uA9PPndeZIA.

Ganasia, J. (2010). The generalized sousvaillance society. *Social Science Information, 49*(3), 489–507.

Hutcheson, L. (1989). *The politics of postmodernism*. London, UK: Routledge.

Kress, G. (2003). *Literacy in the new media age*. London, UK: Taylor & Francis e-Library.

Lambert, J. (2008). *Digital storytelling: Capturing lives, creating community*. Berkeley, CA: Life on the Water Inc.

Lange, P. (2009). Videos of affinity on YouTube. In P. Snickars & P. Vondereau (Eds.), *The YouTube reader* (pp. 78–88). Stockholm, Sweden: National Library of Sweden.

Lundby, K. (2008). Introduction: Digital storytelling, mediatised stories. In K. Lundby (Ed.), *Digital storytelling, mediatized stories: Self-representations in new media* (pp. 1–17). New York, NY: Peter Lang.

Mandel, D. (2007). Use of self: Contexts and dimension. In, *Revisiting the use of self: Questioning professional identities* (pp. 1–19). Toronto, Canada: Canadian Scholars Press Inc.

Niewolny, K., & Wilson, A. (2009). What happened to the promise? A critical (re) orientation of two sociocultural learning traditions. *Adult Education Quarterly*, *60*(1), 26–45.

Payne, M. (2001). Knowledge bases and knowledge biases in social work. *Journal of Social Work*, *1*(2), 133–146.

Ringrose, J., & Walkerdine, V. (2008). Regulating the abject: The TV make-over as site of neo-liberal reinvention toward bourgeois femininity. *Feminist Media Studies*, *8*(3), 227–246.

Rosenberg, S. (2004). An introduction to feminist poststructural theorizing. In N. Mandell (Ed.), *Feminist issues: Race, class and sexuality* (4th ed., pp. 35–57). Toronto, Canada: Pearson/Prentice Hall.

Rosenfeld Halverson, E., Bass, N., & Woods, D. (2012) The process of creation: A novel methodology for analyzing multimodal data. *The Qualitative Report*, *14*(21), 1–27.

Smith, K. (2011). *Activist social workers in neoliberal times: Who are we becoming now?* Doctoral dissertation, Ontario Institute for Studies in Education, University of Toronto.

Snickars, P., & Vondereau, P. (2009). Introduction. In P. Snickars & P. Vondereau (Eds.), *The YouTube reader* (pp. 9–20). Stockholm, Sweden: National Library of Sweden.

Thumim, N. (2008). 'It's good for them to know my story': Cultural mediation as tension. In K. Lundby (Ed.), *Digital storytelling, mediatized stories: Self representations in new media* (pp. 85–104). New York, NY: Peter Lang.

YouTube Essentials Guide. 2011. Retrieved from http://www.youtube.com/t/about_essentials4

Woods, D., & Dempster, P. (2011). Tales from the bleeding edge: The qualitative analysis of complex video data using transana. *Forum: Qualitative Research in the Social Sciences*, *12*(1), article 17. Retrieved from http://www.qualitative-research.net/index.php/fqs/article/view/1516/3120

Mark My Words: The Design of an Innovative Methodology to Detect and Analyze Interpersonal Health Conversations in Web and Social Media

MARTINE P. A. BOUMAN

Centre for Media & Health, Gouda, The Netherlands

CONSTANCE H. C. DROSSAERT, and MARCEL E. PIETERSE

University of Twente, Enschede, The Netherlands

Internet technology in which social media play a central role offers new opportunities for health communication. The Center for Media & Health (CMH) in the Netherlands in collaboration with the University of Twente developed a methodology called Mark My Words (MMW) to detect and monitor interpersonal conversations on social media. The MMW methodology is based on the concept of "markers" and on data analysis via text mining techniques. MMW is applied in an innovative web-based entertainment-education series called SndBites. This article describes the design of this new research methodology and shares the methodological advantages and challenges.

SOCIAL MEDIA AND THE NEED FOR INNOVATIVE RESEARCH METHODOLOGIES

Recent advances in Internet technologies, in particular the participative Internet known as social media, have transformed health-related communications

---

The research project Mark My Words, is made possible with a research grant of the Netherlands Organisation for Health Research and Development (ZonMw).

(De Nooijer et al. 2005; Crutzen, 2009; Van Deursen, 2010). More and more health organizations worldwide use web-based formats and digital entertainment media (e.g., virals, Internet drama series, videos and podcasts, serious games, and all kinds of transmedia and cross-media formats) in their communication strategies (Singhal, Wang, & Rogers, 2012). Recent examples are the Safe Sex campaign of SoaAids Netherlands and the Sound Effects hearing loss campaign of the Center for Media & Health (CMH) (Bouman, Van Tol, Rijnja, & De Regt, 2009).

These advances in Internet technology offer not only the possibility for innovative formats for health communication but also new ways of disseminating the health messages of such interventions. Social media's potential to reach large audiences is particularly important as the impact and effect of public health interventions depend to a large extent on their capability for diffusion. According to the five steps of the RE-AIM model, this capability comprises Reach, Effectiveness, Adoption, Implementation, and Maintenance (Glasgow, Vogt, and Boles, 1999; Glasgow, 2007). The ultimate aim of these interventions is to create social change by stimulating interpersonal conversations among peers around specific health issues.

In order to measure the potential impact of new digital and interactive health communication formats, however, we need more sophisticated and attuned research methodologies (Denzin & Lincoln, 2000; Kohler-Reismann, 2008; Gubrium & Holstein, 2009). In this article, we propose Mark My Words (MMW), a new methodology to address this gap in online research strategies. MMW aims to measure the potential impact of new digital and interactive (health communication) media. The MMW is currently being used to evaluate the impact of SndBites (an abbreviation of SoundBites), a web-based entertainment-education series, on teens and young adults ages 15–18 years in the Netherlands.

This article begins with background information on SndBites and its theoretical foundations. It continues with a discussion of monitoring and text mining strategies. On this basis, the MMW methodology is introduced, and its theoretical and practical implications are illustrated through concrete examples in the MMW study protocol design as it has been tailored for SndBites. The article closes with a discussion and critical reflection on the advantages and challenges of this new methodology.

SNDBITES: AN ONLINE ENTERTAINMENT-EDUCATION SERIES

Imagine the following scene:

> Backstage in a big discotheque, melting into the shadows cast by the stage light, Eltjo and Mariset are kissing. Eltjo: *"Damn, you're good."* Mariset, whispers: *"No, you are. You really turn me on ..."*. Eltjo kisses

> Mariset's neck, and Mariset presses her body closer to Eltjo. Eltjo takes her hand, and presses it to his chest. *"I'm crispy hot for you."* Mariset stretches her arm to get a better look at him, laughs curiously, then presses her body against his again. *"Crispy hot?"* she asks. "*Yes, crispy hot,*" he says. *"Come on, let's do it. Do you want to?"* Mariset nods. Eltjo fumbles at her bra, then: *"Oh, shit, I didn't bring a condom with me. Did you?"*

This dialogue is part of the drama script of SndBites, a Dutch web-based series launched in April 2012. The storyline is narrated from the perspectives of four main characters (see www.SndBites.nl).

SndBites was designed by the CMH and its partners[1] as an innovative digital entertainment platform to promote a healthy lifestyle among Dutch teens and young adults ages 15–18 years from middle and lower socioeconomic groups (see Figure 1). SndBites aims to inspire this target group to wear earplugs to prevent hearing loss, to practice safe sex, and to moderate alcohol consumption (Bouman, 2012). These health behaviors are all related to common leisure activities such as clubbing. Hence, the setting for SndBites is a (music) nightclub (see Box 1).

SndBites is a contemporary example of what is known as the entertainment-education (EE) communication strategy, which is defined as "the process of purposively designing and implementing a mediating communication form with the potential of entertaining and educating people, in order to enhance and facilitate different stages of prosocial (behaviour) change" (Bouman, 1999, p. 25). Entertainment platforms (such as Internet series, serious games, pop music, and television soaps) reach large sections of young audiences (Bouman, 2002). According to Montgomery (1990): "Popular art forms have a unique ability to engage viewers in ways that news and public affairs programs do

FIGURE 1 Screenshot www.SndBites.nl with Eltjo and Mariset. (Figure available in color online.)

*When **DJ Kozmoz** gets the chance to play a set at the SndBites dance night, he feels the pressure to stage a great performance. Desperate to control his nerves, he turns to every alcoholic drink he can get.*

*His best friend and roadie **Eltjo** lets him do it because he's absorbed by his new love interest Mariset. They have been seeing each other for a while now and are planning to have sex. They trust each other, and everything seems to be ready to give it a go tonight. Eltjo's former girlfriend Sjarda is the only one who stands between Eltjo and Mariset.*

***Sjarda** has been trying all night to get Eltjo's attention. Mariset thinks she still wants him and Eltjo is averting her as much as he can, but maybe it's not a bad idea to listen to what she has to say.*

*To make things worse there is **Tiejo**, a hyperactive newshunter, trying to score a shocking story. Collecting quotes, his eagerness seems to be rewarded when suddenly there's a conflict and the storylines of all four characters literally come together ... .*

BOX 1 Synopsis SndBites.

not. For young people, it serves as an 'electronic classroom,' in which lessons are taught each week through the actions of its characters" (p. 115).

SndBites places strong emphasis on interactivity, gamification, and interconnectivity. The interactivity in SndBites lies in the fact that the media user starts with the perspective of one character, and during the storyline, he/she can interactively switch to the perspective of another character. The gamification element is present by applying game-design thinking in the storyline of the series to make it more fun and engaging. SndBites audience members can unlock seven hidden codes (Easter eggs) around the three main issues (hearing loss prevention, safe sex, and moderate alcohol use) and have a chance to win tickets to a dance party for themselves and their six best friends. The goal of gamification is to motivate people and involve them in parts of the story through interactive processes. Gamification can be considered one of the most important trends in recent technology. The interconnectivity of SndBites is based on an integrated online communication strategy that incorporates several social media platforms: Hyves, Twitter, Facebook, and YouTube.

THEORETICAL FOUNDATION FOR THE DESIGN OF SNDBITES

The potential effects of SndBites primarily lie in interpersonal communication among peers. In order to stimulate interpersonal communication, the design of the SndBites series is based on the Elaboration Likelihood Model (ELM) (Petty & Cacioppo, 1986), Social Cognitive Theory (Bandura, 1994), and Agenda Setting Theory (McCombs & Shaw, 1972).

Petty and Cacioppo's (1986) ELM model suggests that people can follow two possible routes in the persuasion process: the *central route* and the *peripheral route*. Persuasion through the *central route* is achieved through the receiver's thoughtful examination of issue-relevant thinking (high elaboration likelihood). People will follow this route when they are able and motivated to engage in issue-relevant thinking. The peripheral route is relevant when thoughtful examination of issue relevant thinking is relatively low (low elaboration likelihood). In this route people employ simple decision rules or heuristic principles during information processing (Bouman, 1999). The CMH and its partners used in SndBites the peripheral route of persuasion to reach teens and young adults with low or no level of interest in health issues. The design team utilized emotional appeals and liking heuristics to attract attention to and increase audience involvement with the targeted health issues (hearing loss prevention, safe sex, and moderate alcohol). For example, one of the main characters of the series DJ Kozmoz is actually a well-known DJ with an international career in real life.

According to Social Cognitive Theory (Bandura, 1994), people learn not only in formal learning situations, such as in schools, but also vicariously, by observing the overt behavior of models. The models used in observational learning can be real-life people or characters in films and on television. In SndBites, social role models were selected with the specific goal of showing that a new behavior can be practiced feasibly in real life. For example, Tiejo, who plays a reporter in the series, exemplifies that earplugs can be used while clubbing, and Sjarda, one of the female characters, illustrates how it is possible to be an advocate in your social environment to protect others in case of a sexually transmitted infection. Furthermore, Agenda Setting Theory says that the media are not always successful at telling us what to think, but they are quite successful at telling us what to think *about* (McCombs & Shaw, 1972). Hence, agenda-setting is referred to as the power to "structure issues." In SndBites, agenda-setting has been embedded into social media in the form of trailers and YouTube clips. This way, SndBites can be on the social agenda of teens and young adults and inspire them to talk with friends about the serial's most intricate ideas and messages.

MARK MY WORDS: AN INNOVATIVE METHODOLOGY FOR WEB AND SOCIAL MEDIA RESEARCH

Mark My Words (MMW) is a promising methodology for researchers and practitioners to gain more insight on how social media can contribute to the dissemination and effect (on interpersonal communication) of web-based health communication interventions. In order to know whether this type of intervention creates change by stimulating online interpersonal conversations among peers around the campaign health issues, we have designed the research project MMW. MMW is designed to evaluate the reach and impact of web-based health communication interventions (in this case the SndBites series) by analyzing interpersonal conversations in social media.

MMW addresses the urgent need to bridge the gap between new media practices and traditional media research. Chou, Hunt, Beckjord, Moser, and Hesse (2009) state, "It is clear that the rapid development of new online media in health communication practice is not matched by an adequate and timely development of new research methodologies" (p. 1). Traditional evaluation designs in the field of health communication such as randomized controlled trials (RCTs) with pre–post control group designs are not suitable for analyzing and measuring the impact of interventions on social discourse in new media. This is for several reasons: (1) the Internet's open and free access makes it almost impossible to create (randomized) control groups; (2) online conversations and users' Internet behavior cannot be controlled or steered due to the autonomy of the open web; and (3) web-based information stays on the web (the "long tail") and does not have a clear endpoint. These new media characteristics make it difficult to use traditional pre–post control group designs.

Monitoring and Text Mining

Simple data such as number of visitors on a website, length of their stay, and geographical spread can be monitored using Google Analytics. One way to dive deeper and understand the nature of conversations is through text mining methods. Corley, Cook, Mikler, and Singh (2010) describe text mining as "the process of discovering information in large text collections and automatically identifying interesting patterns and relationships in textual data" (p. 600; see also Mihalcea, 2008). Text mining technologies use search engines that automatically collect conversations from social media according to specified search terms to explore relevant patterns within these conversations. These texts are then analyzed and interpreted. Until now, text mining has been used mostly by the marketing sector to measure branding impact and for reputation management; this is also known as opinion mining (Pang & Lee, 2008).

Recent studies in the field of health communication have used a combination of different text mining strategies. For example, Corley et al. (2010) used text mining to identify trends in online conversations in the United States about influenza on the web, to see whether web conversations correlated with real-world influenza-like illness patient report data. And Veldkamp, He, and De Vries (2010) collected 300 ego documents from Internet forums of people with posttraumatic stress syndrome (PTSS). They used text-mining techniques to develop a new Internet-based intake procedure (psychological measurement protocol).

These studies, however, have not been based on an entertainment-education and social media approach.

Hypothesis and Research Questions

The hypothesis and central idea behind the development of the MMW methodology is that the use of "markers" makes it possible to track the amount and type of interpersonal communication in web-based communication interventions and related social media use. Markers are distinctive and identifiable message elements incorporated into an EE intervention design (Singhal & Rogers, 2002). When markers are powerful (memorable to audiences) they can be a potential trigger for conversations. For example, in the EE radio soap series *Nasberry Street* about sexually responsible fatherhood in Jamaica, there was a skirt-chasing character called Scattershot. Scattershot became a common term in Jamaican discourse, as in "Oh, you Scattershot you," providing the opportunity to trace the direct and indirect effects of listening to the radio program (Singhal & Rogers, 1999). This principle of using markers is a central element in the design of the MMW methodology.

The MMW methodology will be used to detect (a) how and when online conversations around the markers of the SndBites web-based communication intervention started; (b) which and how many markers are identified in the conversations; and (c) what is the specific context in which these markers are used in the conversations (positive or negative valence, direct or indirect exposure, self-reported behavior, social cognitive determinants) and whether the conversations align with the aims of the web-based communication intervention and in the way the markers were intended.

The design of the MMW methodology has given way to two main research questions: (1) How can interpersonal conversations in web-based health communication interventions and related social media use be detected and monitored with the use of markers; and (2) what are the strengths and weaknesses of text mining and data mining as techniques used to analyze these online conversations?

Plan of Action

In order to answer the two main research questions, the following steps need to be taken: (1) design specific markers and integrate them into the SndBites storyline; (2) diffuse the series among the intended audience (middle and lower educated teens and young adults ages 15–18 years) via Internet and social media; (3) implement the use of a social media monitoring tool and define search strategies for data collection; and (4) analyze data using text mining techniques.

In the following sections the various research steps are described.

Design markers

The CMH is both executive producer of the SndBites series and principal investigator of the MMW research project. This makes it possible to combine these two projects and create markers for the storyline of SndBites. Designing specific markers around the specific health issues (hearing loss prevention, safe sex, and moderate alcohol use) for the series is a challenging process. The markers need to be specific enough to serve as a potential conversation topic, unique for the series, be attuned to the target group (youngsters aged 15–18 years from middle and lower socioeconomic groups), and fit organically into the storyline. Based on these criteria the following SndBites markers have been designed: *Double Dutch* (meaning "protected sex by using both birth control pill and condom"); *Crispy Hot* (meaning "sexually aroused"); *Go Out, Plug In* (meaning "enjoy clubbing and use ear plugs"); *Nocktails* and *Happy Drinks* (both meaning nonalcoholic cocktails). Aside from these specific health-related markers, the name of the series (SndBites) and the names of the characters in the series (DJ Kozmoz, Eltjo, Sjarda, Mariset, and Tiejo) serve as markers.

Social media communities

To attract the attention of teens and young adults and to generate traffic to the special interactive SndBites website the CMH has designed an integrated online communication strategy (see Figure 2). SndBites was launched in collaboration with the Dutch Social Media platform Hyves. Through various items on the Hyves platform, the target audience is encouraged to visit the SndBites website (www.SndBites.nl) and/or the SndBites-Hyves fan page (www.SndBites.Hyves.nl), where readers can get information about SndBites, watch the trailer(s), chat, and comment on SndBites.

The Netherlands has 595,000 inhabitants ages 15–18 years (out of a total Dutch population of 16.8 million) (NJI, 2011; CBS, 2011). Teen and young adult participation in social media sites has increased tremendously. Four out of five children aged 8–18 years (79%) have a profile on Hyves (the largest social media platform in the Netherlands), and almost half of this age group (49%) are also on Facebook (Pijpers, 2012).

The new Internet generation, called Netgeneration (Tapscott, 1998) or Digital Natives (Prensky, 2001), is, however, anything but a homogeneous group (Kutteroff & Behrens 2008; Lenhart, Purcell, Smith, & Zuckuhr, 2010; Van den Beemt, Akkerman, & Simonis, 2010; Van den Beemt et al., 2009). In the Netherlands, for example, teens and young adults from the age group 15–18 years with a high educational level are foremost active on Facebook and Twitter. They also use their smart and mobile phones (aside from their

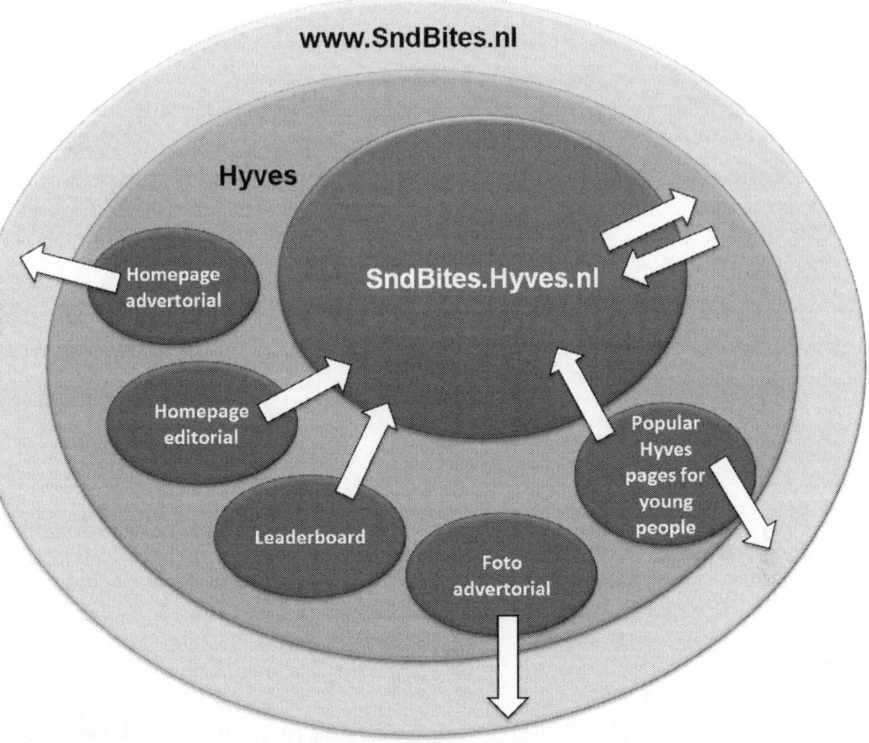

FIGURE 2 SndBites online communication strategy (Bouman 2012). (Figure available in color online.)

computers) more often to connect to social media platforms (Pijpers, 2012). Teens and young adults ages 15–18 years with a middle and lower education level tend to be very active on Hyves instead of on Facebook and Twitter (Pijpers, 2012). Since SndBites targets teens and young adults with a middle and lower educational level, the series was launched on Hyves.

Social Media Monitoring Tool and Search Strategies

To find markers in social media conversations, a social media monitoring tool needs to be in place and search strategies need to be defined. The functionalities of various social media monitoring tools differ. Some search systems are more elaborate and extensive than others.

Finchline, a social media monitoring tool developed by Howard's Home, was chosen for this MMW research project. Finchline is capable of searching large numbers of websites for a specific topic and monitors all the well-known channels such as Twitter, Facebook, YouTube, and Hyves, but also monitors tens of thousands of blogs, forums, review websites, and knowledge sites. Within these websites and types of social media, the program searches every two hours for new mentions of the topic within status updates, reviews, comments, uploads, and so on. Twitter is monitored separately due to the enormous amount of content that is generated. Tweets are monitored every couple of minutes for a mention of a topic. For each topic the researchers can specify whether they want to search social media, news media, and/or Twitter. As soon as a topic has been introduced, Finchline begins the data collection and processing. A topic can consist of one or multiple words using Boolean logic.

After an initial Finchline training program, the MMW researchers have introduced more than 20 different search strings (e.g., SndBites OR SoundBites; Snd AND Bites; Tiejo; Eltjo). Based on the markers that are interwoven in the storylines of the SndBites series, the search engine system selects and retrieves the online conversations. This can be done directly or even months after the start of the series, as long as the keywords and markers are known from the start. Mark My Words data will be selected during a period of 16 weeks.

Text Mining

Text mining is a method for the automatic classification of large volumes of documents (Weiss, Indurkhya, Zhanga, & Damerau, 2005). Himmel, Reincke and Michelmann (2009, p. 2) state that "it usually consists of finite steps, such as parsing a text into separate words, finding terms and reducing them to their basics ('truncation') followed by analytical procedures such as clustering and classification to derive patterns [...], and finally evaluation and interpretation of the output." Depending on the amount of online conversations about SndBites in social media, MMW data will be analyzed using text mining techniques. First we define the corpus (a collection of online conversations) and create a data analysis framework. A text mining software is selected and adapted in order to recognize the specific markers used in SndBites and to classify the content of the discussions (e.g., positive or negative) that teens and young adults have in online conversations.

To answer the questions in MMW—(a) how and when do online conversations around the markers of the Internet series start, and (b) which and how many markers are identified in the conversations—goes far beyond merely counting how frequently markers are found in the online conversations. These questions are about recognition of the markers in the conversations. For this, it is less important how many conversations are collected because all of the conversations will be analyzed. To answer question (c) —what is the specific context in which these markers are used in the conversations (positive or negative; direct or indirect exposure; self-reported behavior, social cognitive determinants) and are the conversations in line with the aims of the Internet series and with the way the markers were intended,—text mining techniques are helpful. Enough conversations will be needed (around 300–1,000) to train the text mining program on dichotomy decisions and to conduct a more refined categorization (e.g., using five categories: very negative, negative, neutral, positive, very positive) with a description of strengths and weaknesses. It is difficult to indicate how many online conversations we will be able to collect because we do not know how many teens and young adults will spontaneously begin communicating in social media platforms about the SndBites series. If the number of retrieved online conversations is not high, other data analysis methods (e.g., manual or via MAXQAD) will be more appropriate and cost-effective, such as applied in earlier research, for example, by Van Uden-Kraan et al. (2008), who analyzed online conversations of patients in self-help groups.

REFLECTIONS AND DISCUSSION

In this article we have argued why there is an urgent need to bridge the gap between new media practices and traditional media research, especially to gain more insights regarding the way social media can contribute to the dissemination and effect of web-based health communication interventions. We have presented an innovative methodology called Mark My Words that may compensate for the limitations of traditional designs (such as randomized controlled trials) and that may enable researchers to capture the particular mechanisms involved in web-based and social media interventions. This alternative methodology, including data-analytical techniques, is worked out in a study protocol for a new web-based entertainment-education series in the Netherlands called SndBites.

The central idea behind Mark My Words is to use markers in order to detect the number and type of interpersonal communication in web-based communication interventions and social media. One could discuss whether the use of (predefined) markers is necessary, for text mining techniques can also be applied on web-based interventions around specific topics (such as safe sex practices) without using markers. The use of special markers (such as in the SndBites intervention) has an added value due to the fact that finding causal inferences on intervention effects in social media is possible. If, for example, online conversations around safe sex practices use unique predefined markers, such as *Crispy Hot*, there is a strong likelihood that such use can be attributed to the specific (in this case SndBites) intervention.

There are several advantages of using text mining methodologies such as those embedded in MMW to conduct research on web and social media-based interventions: (1) They are considerably less expensive and less time-consuming compared to existing methodologies (i.e., cohort studies, interviewing); (2) data are available at any time, and results can be assessed almost without delay; (3) data is collected nonintrusively, thus avoiding bias due to nonresponse rates or social desirability; (4) data can be collected retrospectively without the bias of social desirability or memory and interpretation bias that comes with this, as Internet data remain accessible over time; and (5) longitudinal research is feasible and relatively easy as new samples can repeatedly be taken without much effort.

It is important to note that collecting and analyzing Internet data comes with a set of ethical challenges. MMW deals with spontaneous and unstructured conversations of teens and young adults on the web and in social media. A major challenge is the blurring of the public and private sphere (Eysenbach & Till, 2001; Rizk, 2005). In this MMW research project, only open, publicly accessible Internet forums and online social communities are used for data collection. Furthermore, there is the issue of anonymity. Data are tied to online user names. The research participants are generally unknown and can construct alternative identities. Spontaneity and openness prevent researchers from taking every necessary precaution since in this dynamic environment it is impossible to predict what every precaution will be. Nonetheless, because data can be collected nonintrusively and retrospectively, there is a certain flexibility of time and space in averting undesirable ethical issues situations.

Because this methodology is new, in addition to the ethical challenges just noted, MMW's continuous improvement is fueled by method-related questions that arise in practice. Online conversations and the Internet behavior of teens and young adults cannot be controlled or steered due to the autonomy of users of the open web. This is an open-field experiment with its own risks. So for example, when not enough data are collected (spontaneous online conversations), what does this mean? Does it mean that the SndBites series is not attractive and entertaining enough to watch? Or do teens and young adults watch and appreciate it but not start spontaneous online conversations? In the case that teens and young adults enlist themselves as members of the SndBites Hyves group but they do not respond to polls or blogs posted within the SndBites Hyves community, does that mean they are not interested? Van den Beemt et al. (2009) differentiate the Dutch Netgeneration into four user types: Traditionalists, Gamers, Networkers, and Active Creators (p. 9). The majority of Dutch teens and young adults belong to the group of Traditionalists (40%) and Networkers (42%) (Van den Beemt et al., 2009, p. 13). The Traditionalists mainly consume social media content in terms of browsing, surfing, and searching for information. The Networkers preliminarily focus on the interchange of information on social media platforms and are busier with their own profiles on social media, instead of actively posting, exchanging and commenting on others' content. We know that teens and young adults in the 15–18 years old group with a lower educational level tend to be overrepresented in the Traditionalists user group; they tend to have a more passive attitude and are not very actively creating content (Van den Beemt et al., 2009; Pijpers 2012). Therefore, we do not know, at this time, whether it is realistic to expect them to post comments and start conversations.

The MMW methodology operates under the complexity of the Internet and social interactions. In its initial stages, it shows potential to go deeper than other tools. And its focus on "markers" makes it a unique and promising methodology to monitor effects of web-based health communication interventions.

NOTE

1. SndBites is a project of the Center for Media & Health, designed in collaboration with Trimbos-institute (alocohol issue) and Soa Aids Netherlands (STD issue) and creative producer De Filmwinkel and Interactive Design Bureau IDVision in the Netherlands.

REFERENCES

Bandura, A. (1994). The social cognitive theory of mass communication. In J. Bryant & D. Zillmann (Eds.), *Media effects: advances in theory and research* (pp. 61–90). Hillsdale, NJ: Lawrence Erlbaum Associates.

Bouman, M. P. A. (1999). *The turtle and the peacock; Collaboration for prosocial change: The entertainment-education strategy on television*. Published thesis, University of Wageningen, Wageningen, The Netherlands.

Bouman, M. P. A. (2002). Turtles and peacocks: Collaboration in entertainment-education television. *Communication Theory, 12*(2), 225–244.

Bouman, M. P. A. (2012). *SndBites; Eindrapportage ZonMw*. Gouda, The Netherlands: Centrum Media & Gezondheid.

Bouman, M. P. A., Van Tol, C. P. M., Rijnja, G. W., & De Regt, W. (Eds.). (2009). *Gebundelde Inspiratie: Leefstijlcampagnes in de schijnwerpers*. Den Haag, The Netherlands: ZonMw.

Centraal Bureau voor de Statistiek. (2011). *Bevolking, kerncijfers*. Den Haag, The Netherlands: Author.

Chou, W. S., Hunt, Y. M., Beckjord, E. B., Moser, R. P., & Hesse, B. W. (2009). Social media use in the United States, Implications for health communication. *Journal of Medical Internet Research, 11*(4), e48.

Corley, C. D., Cook, D. J., Mikler, A. R., & Singh, K. P. (2010). Text and structural data mining in influenza mentions on the web and in social media. *International Journal of Environmental Research and Public Health, 7*, 596–615. doi:10.3390/ijerph7020596

Crutzen, R. (2009). *Hard to get, hard to keep. Dissemination of and exposure to Internet-delivered health behaviour change interventions aimed at adolescents*. PhD dissertation, Maastricht University, Maastricht, The Netherlands.

De Nooijer, J., Oenema, A., Kloek, G., Brug, H., De Vries, H., & De Vries, N. (2005). *Bevordering van gezond gedrag via internet: nu en in de toekomst*. Research report. Maastricht, The Netherlands: University of Maastricht and Erasmus Medical Center.

Denzin, N. K., & Lincoln, Y. (Eds.). (2000). *Handbook of qualitative research* (2nd ed.). London, UK: Sage.

Eysenbach, G., & Till, J. E. (2001). Ethical issues in qualitative research on internet-communities. *British Medical Journal, 323*, 1103–1105.

Glasgow, R. E. (2007). eHealth evaluation and dissemination research. *American Journal of Preventive Medicine*, 32, S119–S126.

Glasgow, R. E., Vogt, T. M., & Boles, S. M. (1999). Evaluating the public health impact of health promotion interventions: The RE-AIM framework. *American Journal of Public Health, 89*, 1322–1327.

Gubrium, J. F., & Holstein, J. A. (2009). *Analyzing narrative reality*. Los Angeles, CA: Sage.

Himmel, W., Reincke, U., & Michelmann, H. W. (2009). Text mining and mining and natural language processing approaches for automatic categorization of lay requests to web-based expert forums. *Journal of Medical Internet Research, 3*(e25), 1–13.

Kohler-Reissman, C. (2008). *Narrative methods for the human sciences*. Los Angeles, CA: Sage.

Kutteroff, A., & Behrens, P. (2008). *JIM 2008: Jugend, Information, (Multi-) Media, Basisstudie zum Medienumgang 12-bis 19-jähriger in Deutschland*. Retrieved from http://www.mpfs.de

Lenhart, A., Purcell, K., Smith, A., & Zickuhr, K. (2010). *Social media & mobile Internet use among teens and young adults*. Pew Research Center, Washington DC. Retrieved from http://pewinternet.org/Reports/2012/Social-Media-and-Young-Adults.aspx

McCombs, M., & Shaw, D. L. (1972). The agenda-setting function of the mass media. *Public Opinion Quarterly, 36*, 176–185.

Mihalcea, R. (2008). The text mining handbook: Advanced approaches to analyzing unstructured data. Ronen Feldman and James Sanger (Bar-Ilan University and ABS Ventures) Cambridge, England: Cambridge University Press, 2007, xii+410. *Comput. Linguist., 34*, 125–127.

Montgomery, K. C. (1990). Promoting health through entertainment television. In C. K. Atkin & L. Wallack (Eds.), *Mass communication and public health. Complexities and conflicts* (pp. 114–128). Newbury Park, CA: Sage.

Nederlands Jeugd Instituut. (2011). *Feiten en Cijfers Jeugd en Opvoeding*. Utrecht, The Netherlands: Author.

Pang, B., & Lee, L. (2008). Opinion mining and sentiment analysis. *Foundations and Trends in Information Retrieval, 2*(1–2), 1–135.

Petty, R. E., & Cacioppo, J. T. (1986). The elaboration likelihood model of persuasion. In L. Berkowitz (Ed.), *Advances in experimental social psychology* (Vol. 19, pp. 123–205). San Diego, CA: Academic Press.

Pijpers, R. (2012). *Kinderen op Hyves, Facebook en Twitter: nieuwe cijfers*. Retrieved from http://www. Frankwatching.com/archive/2012/03/29

Prensky, M. (2001, October). *Digital natives, digital immigrants*. On the horizon, No. 5 MCB University Press.

Rizk, N. (2005). Ethics in electronic qualitative research. *NDU Spirit* [Notre Dame University, Louaïze], *33*, 86–89.

Singhal, A., & Rogers, E. M. (1999). *Entertainment-education. A communication strategy for social change*. Mahwah, NJ: Lawrence Erlbaum Associates.

Singhal, A., & Rogers, E. M. (2002). A theoretical agenda for entertainment-education. *Communication Theory, 12*(2), 117–135.

Singhal, A., Wang, H., & Rogers, E. M. (2012). The rising tide of entertainment-education in communication campaigns. In R. E. Rice & C. K. Atkin (Eds.), *2012 Public communication campaigns* (4th ed., pp. 323–335). Beverley Hills, CA: Sage.

Tapscott, D. (1998). *Growing up digital: The rise of the net generation.* New York, NY: McGraw-Hill.

Van den Beemt, A., Akkerman, S., & Simons, R.-J. (2009). *Jongeren en interactieve media. Diversiteit in het gebruik van interactieve media onder jongeren.* Zoetermeer, The Netherlands: Stichting Kennisnet.

Van den Beemt, A., Akkerman, S., & Simons, R.-J. (2010). Considering young people's motives for interactive media use. *Educational Research Review, 6*, 55–66.

Van Deursen, A. J. A. M. (2010). *Internet skills, vital aspects in an information society.* PhD dissertation, University of Twente, Gouda, The Netherlands.

Van Uden-Kraan, C. F., Drossaert, C. H. C., Taal, E., Lebrun, C. E. I., Drossaers-Bakker, K. W., Smit, W. M., … van de Laar, M. A. F. J. (2008). Coping with somatic illnesses in online support groups: Do the feared disadvantages actually occur? *Computers in Human Behavior, 24*, 309–324. Retrieved from http://dx.doi.org/10.1016/j.chb.2007.01.014

Veldkamp, B. P., He, Q., & de Vries, T. (2010). *Verkorting en verbetering intaketrajecten bij personen met post-traumatisch stress syndroom.* Research report. Zeist, The Netherlands: SSS.

Weiss, S. M., Indurkhya, N., Zhang, T., & Damerau, F. J. (2005). *Text mining: Predictive methods for analyzing unstructured information.* New York, NY: Springer.

Index

Page numbers in **bold** type refer to figures
Page numbers in *italic* type refer to tables